Ethics and Personality

Ethics and Personality

ESSAYS IN MORAL PSYCHOLOGY

EDITED BY JOHN DEIGH

The University of Chicago Press

Chicago and London

The essays in this volume originally appeared in various issues of *Ethics*. Acknowledgment of the original publication date may be found on the first page of each essay.

The University of Chicago Press, Chicago 60637

The University of Chicago Press, Ltd., London

Printed in the United States of America.
ISBN 0·226·14127-6 (cl.)
ISBN 0·226·14128-4 (pa.)

97 96 95 94 93 92 5 4 3 2 1

Library of Congress Cataloging-in-Publication Data

Ethics and personality : essays on moral psychology / edited by John
   Deigh.
      p.   cm.
   Includes bibliographical references and index.
   ISBN 0-226-14127-6 : $36.95.—ISBN 0-226-14128-4 (pbk.) : $15.95
   1. Ethics.   2. Personality.   I. Deigh, John.
BJ1012.E888   1992
170'.1'9—dc20   92-3114
                                                                      CIP

The paper used in this publication meets the minimum requirements of American National Standard for Information Science—Permanence of Paper for Printed Library Materials, ANSI Z39.48-1984. ∞

CONTENTS

Introduction

John Deigh

Ethics is the study of moral values and moral principles. We pursue it out of an interest in discovering what a good life consists in, what things are truly valuable, and what it takes to be a decent person. An examination of these questions inevitably becomes an examination of ourselves: what are we like, what makes us tick, and what happens when we go haywire? We start with questions about good and evil, right and wrong, and they lead us to questions about the human soul, about its powers and capacities and the forces and disturbances to which it is subject. We make uncertain progress in answering the former as long as we remain in the dark about the latter. A deeper understanding of the good life, the truly valuable, and the requirements of decency depends on our knowing something about the soul's complexities. Ethics is inseparably tied to psychology.

This understanding of the discipline goes back to antiquity. Aristotle, who took ethics to be a branch of politics and for whom questions of human happiness and human virtue defined the field, expressed it as well as anyone when he wrote, "By human virtue we mean not that of the body but that of the soul; and happiness also we call an activity of soul. But if this is so, clearly the student of politics must know somehow the facts about soul, as the man who is to heal the eyes must know about the whole body also; and all the more since politics is more prized and better than medicine. . . . The student of politics, then, must study the soul, and must study it with these objects in view."[1] In saying this Aristotle simply put into words ideas about the study of moral values and moral principles that Plato before him had followed. These ideas are plainly at work, for instance, in *The Republic*'s famous tripartite division of the soul and its application to questions about the nature of justice and whether being just is compatible with achieving happiness. For Plato, fundamental questions of ethics turned on the most basic matters of human psychology.

The moderns too followed these ideas. Thomas Hobbes, arguably the first great moral philosopher of the modern period, built his system on psychological premises, most importantly his thesis that all human action springs from motives of self-preservation and self-interest. The thesis excited strenuous objections, and much seventeenth- and eigh-

---

1. Aristotle, *Nichomachean Ethics* (trans. Ross), 1102a13–23.

1

teenth-century English moral philosophy is devoted to its refutation, to showing that not every spring of human action is egoistic, and to finding other foundations than self-interest for ethics. These developments culminated in the works of Joseph Butler and David Hume, works that are paradigms of Aristotle's dicta.

Hume's work, in particular, significantly changed the landscape of moral philosophy. While Hume rejected Hobbes's egoistic thesis, he accepted its underlying premiss that reason on its own could not initiate action. What is more, he elevated this premiss to a central doctrine in his account of human agency and used it to great effect in pressing a series of skeptical attacks on rationalist ethics. "Reason is and ought only to be the slave of the passions," Hume notoriously declared at the end of a brilliant and controversial argument for taking reason in its practical sphere to be nothing more than the determination of means to the ends supplied by our desires and emotions.[2] And having thus reduced reason's practical import, he then traced various moral phenomena back to other elements in human psychology: our capacity for love, our bent toward sympathy for those who are like us, and our disposition to delight in what gives us pleasure and appears useful to our endeavors. Since Hume, many of the principal issues to which the relation of ethics to psychology gives rise have centered on the extent of reason's role in moral judgment, moral feeling, and moral motivation and the possibility of explaining these phenomena as products of psychological processes that work independently of reason. After two hundred years, these issues still burn.

Opposition to Hume was and continues to be fierce. Its most powerful statement occurs in the works of Hume's younger contemporary, Immanuel Kant. Kant's ethics has the reputation of being supremely formal, yet it includes a substantial and compelling account of human motivation. Indeed, this account is essential to his conception of morality as a system of laws for a community of free and rational beings. Echoing the ancients, Kant distinguished between the rational and the irrational parts of the soul, reason and desire. The former is the source of our moral nature. Conscience is a form of practical reason, and its prods and compunctions are due to the operations of such reason. The latter is the source of our sensuous nature. Appetite and passion reflect our sensitivity to pleasure and pain, our attraction to the former and aversion to the latter. And, in keeping with the views of the ancients, Kant further held that we realize true freedom, what he called autonomy, when the rational part of the soul governs the irrational, when reason masters desire. The opposition to Hume could not be more striking.

2. David Hume, *A Treatise of Human Nature*, bk. 2, pt. 3, sec. 3.

Both Hume and Kant, like their predecessors in modern philosophy, focused on what they took to be universal or nearly universal features of human psychology, and their ethical theories reflected this focus. Some of their most influential successors, by contrast, came to emphasize a view of human beings as individuals each with a distinctive identity or the potential for developing one. The importance of this view was reflected in the prominence that concerns about individuality, its special value and the freedom necessary for its flourishing, came to have in the ethical and political studies of the last one hundred fifty years. Thinkers as widely divergent in their philosophical thought as John Stuart Mill, Friedrich Nietzsche, and Jean-Paul Sartre gave these concerns a central place in their ethical writings, and each in his own way deepened and resolved them through an understanding of the sources in human psychology of our individuality and the powers or processes by which we realize and maintain it.

These developments, from Plato to Sartre, outline a rich tradition in moral philosophy, a tradition of studying human psychology for the light it sheds on questions of ethics. The tradition has had a resurgence in recent years, and the essays collected in this volume exemplify this renewed interest in its concerns and contributions. The primary subject of these essays is human emotion and motivation. Within it they cover a variety of topics, from the rudiments of our sociality and the emotional capacities that specially identify us as moral beings to the disorders of the depraved and the gifts of the saintly. In some of the essays one can readily see the marks of the historical influences canvassed above and of comparable influences deriving from other great figures in the history of Western philosophy. In others these influences operate more subtly. All, nevertheless, belong to the ongoing tapestry of thought that constitutes the field of moral psychology.

* * *

The first three essays, Annette Baier's "Trust and Antitrust," Barbara Herman's "Agency, Attachment, and Difference," and Stephen Darwall's "Two Kinds of Respect," are excellent examples of contemporary work rooted in the ethics of Hume and Kant. Baier develops an account of social relations and the importance of trust in founding them that captures themes from Hume. Herman and Darwall take up questions at the heart of Kant's moral psychology and work out answers that illuminate its strengths and resources. In addition, the opposition between Hume and Kant can be glimpsed in the essays of Baier and Herman. It appears in the form of a dispute over the extent to which we should let egalitarian ideals affect our understanding of human fellowship. Thus, Hume's naturalism, which represents the unequal distribution of affection and sympathy among friends, family, acquaintances, and strangers as necessarily shaping our moral practices and customs, is pitted against Kant's rationalism, which sees all human beings as fundamentally joined together in an ideally democratic republic of reason and accordingly prescribes the regulation of our moral practices and customs by this ideal.

Specifically, Baier, in the spirit of Hume's enterprise, brings our attention to the various moral equations between people that the different forms of trust that cement their relations can create, and against this background she observes how tunneled the vision of human fellowship is that we get from an ethics like Kant's. Herman, speaking for Kant, as it were, addresses this objection to his ethics and shows how it can be deflected. While the Kantian commitment always to treat others and oneself with equal respect means seeing one's connection to others as fundamentally that of coequal membership in a democratic republic of reason, it does not mean that one must devalue one's personal relations or ignore the greater significance they have in one's life. Belief that it does, Herman argues, rests on Hume-sponsored assumptions about how the different things that matter to us affect our deliberations. These assumptions, she points out, are foreign to Kant's thought, and once they are abandoned the belief loses its attraction.

Whatever the outcome of this dispute, egalitarian forms of fellowship will remain the moral ideal for the conduct of *public* life. The followers of Hume no less than the followers of Kant would generally if not unanimously accept this point. They too regard equality in human affairs as the appropriate ideal for the social relations that the public institutions of our society define. Correspondingly, respect for one's fellows is seen as the principal moral attitude to bear in this public domain, for the ideal of equality, to be realized, requires an entrenched culture of mutual respect. Such an attitude in one's dealings with others was regarded by Kant as essential to moral conduct, and many contemporary philosophers who share Kant's conception of morality as a public institution have seconded this view. Yet what Kant and these other philosophers have meant when they have called for universal respect for man is often not clear, and a further puzzle arises when we notice that, while this call assumes that each of us is owed respect as a human being, sometimes we think respect is not something to which a person is automatically entitled but rather something that he must earn. Clarifying the confusion surrounding philosophical discussions of respect is the aim of Darwall's essay, and he pursues it by fashioning and deploying a distinction between two kinds of respect. The results both illuminate the place of respect in Kant's ethics and enlarge our understanding of the different ways in which philosophers have appealed to a notion of respect in charting the elements of ethical theory.

The fourth and fifth essays, Lynne McFall's "Integrity" and James Childress's "Appeals to Conscience," exemplify the influence in ethics of the concerns about individuality that have emerged in the last one hundred fifty years. McFall, in her study of integrity, speaks to one such concern. Integrity, one could say, is the virtue most prized by the advocates of individuality. It is the trait one needs to preserve a distinctive identity and to achieve the sincerity of purpose and authenticity in action that these thinkers locate at the core of a truly human or moral life. Applying her analysis, McFall reasons that, because integrity entails commitments that one cannot abandon without betraying oneself and thus surrendering one's identity and because these commitments may consist in personal loyalties rather than impersonal values, integrity turns out to be a virtue whose exercise can require the violation of impartial principles of right and wrong. This is not a happy result for philosophers who understand morality as a system of such principles. It leads McFall to conclude that this traditional understanding of morality imposes burdens we should not have to bear. Kant, of course, is one philosopher who has such a traditional understanding, and McFall's argument, construed then as an objection to Kant, invites comparison with the Humean objection Herman addresses in her essay. A nice test for Herman's reply to the latter, then, is whether it can handle as well the concern about individuality that McFall's conclusion represents.

Childress, with his account of the role of conscience in maintaining a person's integrity, continues the discussion of the issues raised in McFall's essay. Conscience, as Childress understands it, fulfills this role by imposing sanctions on its possessor for acts of self-betrayal. The appeals to conscience that people under social pressure or legal injunctions to violate its dictates commonly make, that such violation would forever rob them of peace of mind, that they could never again live with themselves or forgive themselves, strongly testify, he points out, to the severity and so effectiveness of these sanctions. And it is clear that the conflicts these appeals imply can arise in just as well as corrupt societies, that the conflict, which McFall underscores, between preserving one's integrity and complying with impartial principles of right and wrong can be dramatically portrayed in the kind of conflict with which Childress is concerned. McFall's interest lies in the problem such conflicts pose for ethical theory. Childress's, by contrast, lies in questions about the public policies a society that affirms the value of individuality should adopt for handling them. His essay ends with some salutary suggestions on these questions.

Childress's account of how conscience serves to maintain its possessor's integrity focuses on the painful feelings it inflicts when its counsel is ignored. These are its sanctions, and the chief ones, according to Childress, are guilt and shame. The two essays that follow, Herbert Morris's "The Decline of Guilt" and my essay "Shame and Self-Esteem:

A Critique," examine in greater detail the nature of these feelings and the moral conceptions they presuppose. Morris uses the notion of legal guilt as a springboard for a series of connected reflections on the significance of guilt to our understanding of ourselves as free and responsible beings joined together with others in a fellowship we deeply value. We could not, he argues, retain this understanding of ourselves if we changed the institutions and practices in our society that define this fellowship, particularly the criminal law, in ways that eliminated their concern with guilt and innocence or, what comes to the same thing, if we altered our emotional capacities in ways that made us immune to feelings of guilt. Against Freud's famous view that our sense of guilt is a source of inescapable unhappiness, a steep price we must pay to live in a civilized society, Morris maintains that our sense of guilt is essential to our humanity, something whose disappearance in civilized society, were this possible, would be a tragedy. Thus, he concludes, the intellectual and social forces presently working to diminish the importance of guilt in the operations of our institutions and to weaken our sense of guilt in the regulation of our conduct should not be regarded as vehicles of progress but rather as moving us toward increasingly dehumanized modes of existence.

Morris's thesis that the sense of guilt is essential to our humanity is, we should note, controversial. Many twentieth-century thinkers have held, to the contrary, that the sense of guilt is the product of cultural practices characteristic of some but not all human societies. Others, influenced by Freud, have held that it necessarily develops in the process of civilization but, like religion, eventually diminishes in its significance as human beings acquire increasingly intelligent views of themselves and their world. By contrast, the thesis that shame is an essentially and universally human emotion has rarely if ever been seriously questioned. The liability to feel shame is at one with a capacity for self-reflection and a sense of one's own worth or dignity, and these traits are often cited as characteristics that distinguish human beings from other animals. The question, then, that arises in philosophical discussions of shame concerns the nature of the self-reflection and sense of our own worth that make us liable to experiences of this emotion.

In my essay, I critically examine one influential answer to this question. According to this answer, in experiencing shame we discover either that we lack the excellences we need to achieve the ends to which our lives are devoted or that those ends are shallow or shoddy, that they represent false values. Shame, in this view, is a shock to our self-esteem, a blow to a positive estimation we make of ourselves as having worthy pretensions and the talents and gifts necessary to succeed in them. This answer, I argue, despite its attractions, leaves out aspects of our identity crucial to experiences of shame and to the sense of worth these experiences imply. My argument, in other words, is that the sense of worth implicit in self-esteem, as this attitude is understood on the view I criticize, is not the sense of worth at work in shame, and thus we must understand the emotion differently. Comparison here with the distinction between two kinds of self-respect that Darwall draws in the last section of his essay may help to test the argument. The question to ask is which kind, if either, constitutes our liability to shame.

Revenge too is a universal feature of human life, though not one that any but the most cynical among us would propose as a sign of our humanity. Jon Elster, in his essay "Norms of Revenge," begins by remarking on its universality and then turns to a discussion of alternative explanations. The best hope for finding a satisfactory one, he thinks, lies in attempts to explain norms regulating the taking of revenge that are prominent in many premodern societies, societies that lack a strong, centralized government. Such explanations, were they successful, would show that seeking revenge was for individuals either a rational action or one that, albeit irrational from the perspective of the individual, was rational from the perspective of the society or the relevant genetic lineage. Elster, however, upon surveying various explanations of this sort that social scientists have offered, finds none satisfactory. He then proposes in conclusion an alternative idea: a strong, nonrational, psychological factor, "a deep-rooted urge to show oneself to be superior to others," powers revenge.[3] He identifies this factor with a sense of honor or self-esteem, and again one question to ask, in light of Darwall's and my essays, is what concept of self-esteem best fits Elster's idea.

Like Elster, M. W. Barnes, in the essay that follows Elster's, proposes a psychological factor to explain a common feature of human life. The feature in question is vulgarity, and Barnes's essay, entitled "Vulgarity," offers an account of what it is to be a vulgar person and why this category of person has the significance it has in our lives. Drawing on differences between vulgarity and immorality, Barnes suggests that our concern with the former indicates a special human sensitivity to an order of values larger than morality and a desire to strive for excellence that explains our substantial aversion to being vulgar despite the rather trivial character of some vulgarities. Through this suggestion, Barnes reaches back to the ideas of the ancient Greeks, who characteristically took goodness to be an object of peception and took its perception to be, owing to a desire to seek the good that is fundamental in human motivation, a stimulus to virtuous action. Barnes's essay, more than any other in the collection, reflects doctrines of moral psychology common to Plato and Aristotle.

3. P. 176 of this volume.

The last four essays represent the extremes of depravity and generosity in the human spirit. S. I. Benn's "Wickedness" and Jeffrie Murphy's "Moral Death: A Kantian Essay on Psychopathy" examine the former. Benn begins his study by defining a wicked person as someone who has organized his life according to a plan or plans that are largely evil. He then distinguishes different types of wicked people by the character of these plans. Most of these types, Benn notes, present no philosophical problems. Rather, the issues they raise concern the degree of condemnation such people deserve. The last type, however, what Benn calls malignant wickedness, because the kind of plan that defines it implies an interest in doing evil for its own sake, does raise deep problems in moral psychology and moral philosophy. How is it humanly possible to desire evil for its own sake? Is the idea even intelligible? The primary philosophical grounds for answering these questions negatively are found in the Platonic and Aristotelian doctrines that Barnes's essay reflects. Benn takes the opposing view. He argues the case for the idea's intelligibility and for its being humanly possible to have such intrinsically evil desires. He concludes with a scheme for understanding how a person could be so malignantly wicked.

Another personality type that Benn considers, the psychopath, is the subject of Murphy's essay. Murphy treats this subject within the framework of Kant's ethics. His thesis is that psychopaths lack moral standing, which is to say that they neither have any rights that they can assert against others nor any duties that others or society in general can demand they perform. He bases this thesis on the incapacity of psychopaths to experience moral feelings and to be subject to moral motives, which is what defines their type of personality. Because of these deficits, Murphy argues, psychopaths cannot enter into relations of mutual trust and cooperation, and it is on the basis of these relations that individuals are accorded rights and reciprocal duties. On this view, in other words, they are disqualified from being persons. Hence, while morality forbids treating psychopaths cruelly or abusively just as it forbids the torture or abuse of animals, Murphy observes, it does not hold that they are owed any justice.

Murphy's thesis goes strikingly against received opinion and accepted practice, and he acknowledges in the final section of his essay that the dangers of putting it into practice may be too great to allow doing so. A view opposed to his thesis and more in line with received opinion is articulated by Benn in his brief discussion of the subject. He takes psychopaths to be persons and thus to possess some basic rights. His reason is that, although psychopaths can be likened to wild animals, they are nonetheless minimally rational and capable of choosing their own actions. The opposition between his view and Murphy's nicely defines the issues of what qualifies human beings as persons and what is the basis for attributing rights to them.

At the other extreme from psychopathy and malignant wickedness are states of magnanimity, such as forgiveness and gratitude. These are the subjects of the volume's closing essays, Norvin Richards's "Forgiveness" and Fred Berger's "Gratitude." Richards's target, in his discussion of forgiveness, is the orthodox Christian view that to forgive those who have insulted or injured one is always a mark of moral goodness. To the contrary, Richards argues, sometimes one does nothing wrong in refusing to forgive someone who has insulted or injured one, and sometimes it is itself wrong to forgive such a person. An insult or injury, if serious enough, Richards maintains, calls for anger at the offender, and the reasons that in some circumstances justify and even mandate forgiving an offender may not in other circumstances outweigh the importance of sustaining that anger and so refusing to forgive. To those drawn to the Christian ideal of universal love, Richards's argument poses the challenge of whether that ideal is consistent with the anger he thinks a serious insult or injury calls for and, if not, whether one must therefore forsake the ideal. These are the themes of Butler's celebrated sermons on resentment and forgiveness,[4] and Richards's essay continues the investigations of those sermons.

Berger, in his discussion of gratitude, analyzes first the moral requirements to show gratitude toward a benefactor and then the feelings and attitudes that constitute the emotion. This two-step analysis reveals that the requirements to show gratitude are essentially requirements to convey these feelings and attitudes in response to the feelings and attitudes that one's benefactor conveyed by his beneficent action. Thus, as Berger explains, demonstrations of gratitude play a dynamic role in the development and maintenance of relations of mutual respect and fellow feeling among people, in preserving closeness in personal relations and solidarity in the relations among the members of a larger community. Berger offers this result and the study that produced it as an object lesson for moral philosophers. Proper feeling and attitude have an important place in our moral lives, and no program of research in ethics that excludes their study can yield an adequate understanding of morality. Berger's hope in explicating the subtle ways in which the requirements of gratitude foster friendship and social cohesion is to spur others to examine the place of feelings and attitudes in morality.

* * *

Berger ended his essay with the following paragraph.

I shall close by pointing out that, if the present analysis is correct, a number of similar topics bear serious philosophical

---

4. Joseph Butler, *Fifteen Sermons preached at the Rolls Chapel*, sermons 8, 9.

treatment, as there are large patterns of our moral relations which involve elements of the kinds I have isolated in gratitude. Among such related topics are: friendship, trust, loyalty, fidelity, pity, charity, disgust, resentment, hatred, etc. These and other such notions are importantly involved in the morality of our interpersonal relationships, and some of them can be more important for us to understand in our daily lives than, say, the logic of promising or even the principles of justice.[5]

At the time, seventeen years ago, Anglo-American philosophers were just beginning to revive the tradition of approaching questions in ethics through studies in human psychology. In previous decades interest in the tradition had waned. Berger saw the impoverishment of ethics that resulted from this trend, and he urged a new agenda that would place matters of moral psychology among the discipline's main concerns. The essays collected in this volume confirm the fertility of this agenda. They demonstrate the vitality of this great tradition in moral philosophy.

5. P. 256 of this volume.

Trust and Antitrust*

Annette Baier

TRUST AND ITS VARIETIES

"*Whatever* matters to human beings, trust is the atmosphere in which it thrives." [SISSELA BOK][1]

Whether or not everything which matters to us is the sort of thing that can thrive or languish (I may care most about my stamp collection) or even whether all the possibly thriving things we care about need trust in order to thrive (does my rubber tree?), there surely is something basically right about Bok's claim. Given that I cannot myself guard my stamp collection at all times, nor take my rubber tree with me on my travels, the custody of these things that matter to me must often be transferred to others, presumably to others I trust. Without trust, what matters to me would be unsafe, unless like the Stoic I attach myself only to what can thrive, or be safe from harm, *however* others act. The starry heavens above and the moral law within had better be about the only things that matter to me, if there is no one I can trust in any way. Even my own Stoic virtue will surely thrive better if it evokes some trust from others, inspires some trustworthiness in them, or is approved and imitated by them.

To Bok's statement, however, we should add another, that not all the things that thrive when there is trust between people, and which matter, are things that should be encouraged to thrive. Exploitation and

---

* I owe the second half of my title to the salutary reaction of Alexander Nehamas to an earlier and more sanguine version of this paper, read at Chapel Hill Colloquium in October 1984. I also owe many important points which I have tried to incorporate in this revised version to John Cooper, who commented helpfully on the paper on that occasion, to numerous constructive critics at later presentations of versions of it at CUNY Graduate Center, Brooklyn College, Columbia University, the University of Pennsylvania, and to readers for this journal. I received such a flood of helpful and enthusiastic advice that it became clear that, although few philosophers have written directly on this topic, very many have been thinking about it. It is only by ruthlessly putting finis to my potentially endless revisions and researches into hitherto unfamiliar legal, sociological, psychological, and economic literature that any paper emerged from my responses to these gratifying and generous responses.

1. Sissela Bok, *Lying* (New York: Pantheon Books, 1978), p. 31n. Bok is one of the few philosophers to have addressed the ethics of trust fairly directly. The title of the chapter from which this quotation comes is "Truthfulness, Deceit and Trust."

This essay originally appeared in *Ethics*, vol. 96, no. 2, January 1986.

conspiracy, as much as justice and fellowship, thrive better in an atmosphere of trust. There are immoral as well as moral trust relationships, and trust-busting can be a morally proper goal. If we are to tell when morality requires the preservation of trust, when it requires the destruction of trust, we obviously need to distinguish different forms of trust, and to look for some morally relevant features they may possess. In this paper I make a start on this large task.

It is a start, not a continuation, because there has been a strange silence on the topic in the tradition of moral philosophy with which I am familiar. Psychologists and sociologists have discussed it, lawyers have worked out the requirements of equity on legal trusts, political philosophers have discussed trust in governments, and there has been some discussion of trust when philosophers address the assurance problem in Prisoner's Dilemma contexts. But we, or at least I, search in vain for any general account of the morality of trust relationships. The question, Whom should I trust in what way, and why? has not been the central question in moral philosophy as we know it. Yet if I am right in claiming that morality, as anything more than a law within, itself requires trust in order to thrive, and that immorality too thrives on some forms of trust, it seems pretty obvious that we ought, as moral philosophers, to look into the question of what forms of trust are needed for the thriving of the version of morality we endorse, and into the morality of that and other forms of trust. A minimal condition of adequacy for any version of the true morality, if truth has anything to do with reality, is that it not have to condemn the conditions needed for its own thriving. Yet we will be in no position to apply that test to the trust in which morality thrives until we have worked out, at least in a provisional way, how to judge trust relationships from a moral point of view.

Moral philosophers have always been interested in cooperation between people, and so it is surprising that they have not said more than they have about trust. It seems fairly obvious that any form of cooperative activity, including the division of labor, requires the cooperators to trust one another to do their bit, or at the very least to trust the overseer with his whip to do his bit, where coercion is relied on. One would expect contractarians to investigate the forms of trust and distrust parties to a contract exhibit. Utilitarians too should be concerned with the contribution to the general happiness of various climates of trust, so be concerned to understand the nature, roots, and varieties of trust. One might also have expected those with a moral theory of the virtues to have looked at trustworthiness, or at willingness to give trust. But when we turn to the great moral philosophers, in our tradition, what we find can scarcely be said to be even a sketch of a moral theory of trust. At most we get a few hints of directions in which we might go.

Plato in the *Republic* presumably expects the majority of citizens to trust the philosopher kings to rule wisely and expects that elite to trust their underlings not to poison their wine, nor set fire to their libraries, but neither proper trust nor proper trustworthiness are among the virtues he dwells on as necessary in the cooperating parties in his good society. His version of justice and of the "friendship" supposed to exist between ruler and ruled seems to *imply* such virtues of trust, but he does not himself draw out the implications. In the *Laws* he mentions distrust as an evil produced by association with seafaring traders, but it is only a mention.[2] The same sort of claim can also be made about Aristotle—his virtuous person, like Plato's, must place his trust in that hypothetical wise person who will teach him just how much anger and pride and fear to feel with what reasons, when, and toward which objects. Such a wise man presumably also knows just how much trust in whom, on what matters, and how much trustworthiness, should be cultivated, as well as who should show trust toward whom, but such crucial wisdom and such central virtues are not discussed by Aristotle, as far as I am aware. (He does, in the *Politics,* condemn tyrants for sowing seeds of distrust, and his discussion of friendship might be cited as one place where he implicitly recognizes the importance of trust; could someone one distrusted be a second self to one? But that is implicit only, and in any case would cover only trust between friends.) Nor do later moral philosophers do much better on this count.[3]

There are some forms of trust to which the great philosophers *have* given explicit attention. Saint Thomas Aquinas, and other Christian moralists, have extolled the virtue of faith and, more relevantly, of hope, and so have said something about trust in God. And in the modern period some of the great moral and political philosophers, in particular John Locke, looked at trust in governments and officials, and some have shown what might be called an obsessive trust in contracts and contractors, even if not, after Hobbes's good example here, an equal obsession with the grounds for such trust. It is selective attention then, rather than total inattention, which is the philosophical phenomenon on which I wish to remark, tentatively to explain, and try to terminate or at least to interrupt.

Trust, the phenomenon we are so familiar with that we scarcely notice its presence and its variety, is shown by us and responded to by

2. Plato, *Laws* 4.705a. I owe this reference to John Cooper, who found my charge that Plato and Aristotle had neglected the topic of trust ungenerous, given how much they fairly clearly took for granted about its value and importance. (But taking for granted is a form of neglect.)

3. Besides Bok and Locke, whom I refer to, those who have said something about it include N. Hartmann, *Ethik* (Berlin: W. de Gruyter, 1962), pp. 468 ff.; Virginia Held, *Rights and Goods* (New York and London: Free Press, 1984), esp. chap. 5, "The Grounds for Social Trust"; D. O. Thomas, "The Duty to Trust," *Aristotelian Society Proceedings* (1970), pp. 89–101. It is invoked in passing by Aurel Kolnai in "Forgiveness," in *Ethics, Value and Reality,* ed. Bernard Williams and David Wiggins (Indianapolis: Macmillan Co., 1978): "Trust in the world, unless it is vitiated by hairbrained optimism and dangerous irresponsibility, may be looked upon not to be sure as the very starting point and very basis but perhaps as the epitome and culmination of morality" (p. 223); and by John R. S. Wilson in "In One Another's Power," *Ethics* 88 (1978): 303.

us not only with intimates but with strangers, and even with declared enemies. We trust our enemies not to fire at us when we lay down our arms and put out a white flag. In Britain burglars and police used to trust each other not to carry deadly weapons. We often trust total strangers, such as those from whom we ask directions in foreign cities, to direct rather than misdirect us, or to tell us so if they do not know what we want to know; and we think we should do the same for those who ask the same help from us. Of course we are often disappointed, rebuffed, let down, or betrayed when we exhibit such trust in others, and we are often exploited when we show the wanted trustworthiness. We do in fact, wisely or stupidly, virtuously or viciously, show trust in a great variety of forms, and manifest a great variety of versions of trustworthiness, both with intimates and with strangers. We trust those we encounter in lonely library stacks to be searching for books, not victims. We sometimes let ourselves fall asleep on trains or planes, trusting neighboring strangers not to take advantage of our defenselessness. We put our bodily safety into the hands of pilots, drivers, doctors, with scarcely any sense of reck-lessness. We used not to suspect that the food we buy might be deliberately poisoned, and we used to trust our children to day-care centers.

We may still have no choice but to buy food and to leave our children in day-care centers, but now we do it with suspicion and anxiety. Trust is always an invitation not only to confidence tricksters but also to terrorists, who discern its most easily destroyed and socially vital forms. Criminals, not moral philosophers, have been the experts at discerning different forms of trust. Most of us notice a given form of trust most easily after its sudden demise or severe injury. We inhabit a climate of trust as we inhabit an atmosphere and notice it as we notice air, only when it becomes scarce or polluted.

We may have no choice but to continue to rely on the local shop for food, even after some of the food on its shelves has been found to have been poisoned with intent. We can still rely where we no longer trust. What is the difference between trusting others and merely relying on them? It seems to be reliance on their good will toward one, as distinct from their dependable habits, or only on their dependably exhibited fear, anger, or other motives compatible with ill will toward one, or on motives not directed on one at all. We may rely on our fellows' fear of the newly appointed security guards in shops to deter them from injecting poison into the food on the shelves, once we have ceased to trust them. We may rely on the shopkeeper's concern for his profits to motivate him to take effective precautions against poisoners and also trust him to *want* his customers not to be harmed by his products, at least as long as this want can be satisfied without frustrating his wish to increase his profits. Trust is often mixed with other species of reliance on persons. Trust which is reliance on another's good will, perhaps minimal good will, contrasts with the forms of reliance on others' reactions and attitudes which are shown by the comedian, the advertiser, the blackmailer, the kidnapper-extortioner, and the terrorist, who all depend on particular attitudes and reactions of others for the success of their actions. We all depend on one another's psychology in countless ways, but this is not yet to trust them. The trusting can be betrayed, or at least let down, and not just disappointed. Kant's neighbors who counted on his regular habits as a clock for their own less automatically regular ones might be disappointed with him if he slept in one day, but not let down by him, let alone had their trust betrayed. When I trust another, I depend on her good will toward me. I need not either acknowledge this reliance nor believe that she has either invited or acknowledged such trust since there is such a thing as unconscious trust, as unwanted trust, as forced receipt of trust, and as trust which the trusted is unaware of. (Plausible conditions for proper trust will be that it survives consciousness, by both parties, and that the trusted has had some opportunity to signify acceptance or rejection, to warn the trusting if their trust is unacceptable.)

Where one depends on another's good will, one is necessarily vulnerable to the limits of that good will. One leaves others an opportunity to harm one when one trusts, and also shows one's confidence that they will not take it. Reasonable trust will require good grounds for such confidence in another's good will, or at least the absence of good grounds for expecting their ill will or indifference. Trust then, on this first approximation, is accepted vulnerability to another's possible but not expected ill will (or lack of good will) toward one.

What we now need to do, to get any sense of the variety of forms of trust, is to look both at varieties of vulnerability and at varieties of grounds for not expecting others to take advantage of it. One way to do the former, which I shall take, is to look at the variety of sorts of goods or things one values or cares about, which can be left or put within the striking power of others, and the variety of ways we can let or leave others "close" enough to what we value to be able to harm it. Then we can look at various reasons we might have for wanting or accepting such closeness of those with power to harm us, and for confidence that they will not use this power. In this way we can hope to explicate the vague terms "good will" and "ill will." If it be asked why the initial emphasis is put on the trusting's vulnerability, on the risks rather than the benefits of trust, part of the answer has already been given—namely, that we come to realize what trust involves retrospectively and posthumously, once our vulnerability is brought home to us by actual wounds. The other part of the answer is that even when one does become aware of trust and intentionally continues a particular case of it, one need not intend to achieve any particular benefit from it—one need not trust a person in order to receive some gain, even when in fact one does gain. Trusting, as an intentional mental phenomenon, need not be purposive. But intentional trusting does require awareness of one's confidence that the trusted will not harm one, although they could harm one. It is not a Hobbesian obsession with strike force which dictates the form of analysis

I have sketched but, rather, the natural order of consciousness and self-consciousness of trust, which progresses from initially unself-conscious trust to awareness of risk along with confidence that it is a good risk, on to some realization of why we are taking this particular risk, and eventually to some evaluation of what we may generally gain and what we may lose from the willingness to take such risks. The ultimate point of what we are doing when we trust may be the last thing we come to realize.

The next thing to attend to is why we typically do leave things that we value close enough to others for them to harm them. The answer, simply, is that we need their help in creating, and then in not merely guarding but looking after the things we most value, so we have no choice but to allow some others to be in a position to harm them. The one in the best position to harm something is its creator or its nurse-cum-caretaker. Since the things we typically do value include such things as we cannot singlehandedly either create or sustain (our own life, health, reputation, our offspring and their well-being, as well as intrinsically shared goods such as conversation, its written equivalent, theater and other forms of play, chamber music, market exchange, political life, and so on) we must allow many other people to get into positions where they can, if they choose, injure what we care about, since those are the same positions that they must be in in order to help us take care of what we care about. The simple Socratic truth that no person is self-sufficient gets elaborated, once we add the equally Socratic truth that the human soul's activity is *caring* for things into the richer truth that no one is able by herself to look after everything she wants to have looked after, nor even alone to look after her own "private" goods, such as health and bodily safety. If we try to distinguish different forms of trust by the different valued goods we confidently allow another to have some control over, we are following Locke in analyzing trusting on the model of *en-trusting*. Thus, there will be an answer not just to the question, Whom do you trust? but to the question, *What* do you trust to them?—what good is it that they are in a position to take from you, or to injure? Accepting such an analysis, taking trust to be a three-place predicate (A trusts B with valued thing C) will involve some distortion and regimentation of some cases, where we may have to strain to discern any definite candidate for C, but I think it will prove more of a help than a hindrance.

One way in which trusted persons can fail to act as they were trusted to is by taking on the care of more than they were entrusted with—the babysitter who decides that the nursery would be improved if painted purple and sets to work to transform it, will have acted, as a babysitter, in an untrustworthy way, however great his good will. When we are trusted, we are relied upon to realize *what* it is for whose care we have some discretionary responsibility, and normal people can pick up the cues that indicate the limits of what is entrusted. For example, if I confide my troubles to a friend, I trust her to listen, more or less sympathetically, and to preserve confidentiality, but usually not, or not without consulting me, to take steps to remove the source of my worry. That could be interfering impertinence, not trustworthiness as a confidante. She will, nevertheless, within the restricted scope of what is trusted to her (knowledge of my affairs, not their management) have some discretion both as to how to receive the confidence and, unless I swear her to absolute secrecy, as to when to share it. The relativization of trust to particular things cared about by the truster goes along with the discretion the trusted usually has in judging just what should be done to "look after" the particular good entrusted to her care. This discretionary power will of course be limited by the limits of what is entrusted and usually by some other constraints.

It is plausible to construe all cases of being trusted not merely as cases of being trusted by someone with access to what matters to the truster, but as some control over that, expected to be used to take care of it, and involving some discretionary powers in so doing?[4] Can we further elaborate the analysis of a relationship of trust as one where A has entrusted B with some of the care of C and where B has some discretionary powers in caring for C? Admittedly there are many cases of trust where "caring for C" seems much more than A expects of B even when there is no problem in finding a fairly restricted value for C. Suppose I look quickly around me before proceeding into the dark street or library stacks where my business takes me, judge the few people I discern there to be nondangerous, and so go ahead. We can say that my bodily safety, and perhaps my pocketbook, are the goods I am allowing these people to be in a position to threaten. I trust them, it seems, merely to leave me alone. But this is not quite right, for should a piece of falling masonry or toppling books threaten to fall on my head, and one of these persons leap into action and shove me out of this danger, I would regard that as rather more than less than I had trusted these strangers to do— a case for gratitude, not for an assault charge, despite the sudden, unceremonious, possibly painful or even injurious nature of my close encounter with my rescuer. So *what* do I trust strangers in such circumstances to do? Certainly not anything whatever as long as it is done with good will, nor even anything whatever for my bodily safety and security of property as long as it is done with good will. Suppose someone I have judged nondangerous as I proceed into the stacks should seize me from behind, frightening but not harming me, and claim with apparent sincerity that she did it for my own good, so that I would learn a lesson and be

4. A reader for *Ethics* suggested that, when one trusts one's child to mail an important letter for one at the mailbox on the corner, no discretionary powers are given, although one is trusting him with the safe, speedy transfer of the letter to the box. But life is full of surprises—in Washington on Inauguration day mailboxes were sealed closed as a security precaution, and in some parts of Manhattan mailboxes are regularly sealed after dark. One trusts the child to do the sensible thing if such an unforeseen problem should arise— to bring the letter back, not leave it on the ledge of the sealed mailbox or go too far afield to find another.

more cautious in the future. I would not respond with gratitude but demand what business my long-term security of life was of hers, that she felt free to subject me to such unpleasant educational measures. In terms of my analysis, what I trusted her with was my peace and safety here and now, with "looking after" that, not with my long-term safety. We need some fairly positive and discretion-allowing term, such as "look after" or "show concern for," to let in the range of behavior which would not disappoint the library user's trust in fellow users. We also need some specification of what good was in question to see why the intrusive, presumptuous, and paternalistic moves disappoint rather than meet the trust one has in such circumstances. "Look after" and "take care of" will have to be given a very weak sense in some cases of trust; it will be better to do this than to try to construe cases where more positive care is expected of the trusted as cases of trusting them to leave alone, or merely safeguard, some valued thing. Trusting strangers to leave us alone should be construed as trusting them with the "care" of our valued autonomy. When one trusts one's child to one's separated spouse, it is all aspects of the child's good as a developing person which are entrusted to the other parent's care. Trusting him or her with our children can hardly be construed as trusting them not to "interfere" with the child's satisfactory development. The most important things we entrust to others are things which take more than noninterference in order to thrive.

The more extensive the discretionary powers of the trusted, the less clear-cut will be the answer to the question of when trust is disappointed. The truster, who always needs good judgment to know whom to trust and how much discretion to give, will also have some scope for discretion in judging what should count as failing to meet trust, either through incompetence, negligence, or ill will. In any case of a questionable exercise of discretion there will be room both for forgiveness of unfortunate outcomes and for tact in treatment of the question of whether there is anything to forgive. One thing that can destroy a trust relationship fairly quickly is the combination of a rigoristic unforgiving attitude on the part of the truster and a touchy sensitivity to any criticism on the part of the trusted. If a trust relationship is to continue, some tact and willingness to forgive on the part of the truster and some willingness on the part of the trusted both to be forgiven and to forgive unfair criticisms, seem essential.[5] The need for this will be greater the more discretion the trusted has.

5. This point I take from the fascinating sociological analysis of trust given by Niklas Luhmann (*Trust and Power* [Chichester, N.Y., 1979]) which I discovered while revising this paper. In many ways my analysis agrees with his, inasfar as I understand the implications of his account of it as "reduction of complexity," in particular of complex future contingencies. He makes much of the difference between absence of trust and distrust, and distinguishes trust from what it presupposes, a mere "familiarity," or taking for granted. I have blurred these distinctions. He treats personal trust as a risky investment and looks at mechanisms for initiating and maintaining trust. Tact is said to play an important role in both. It enables

If part of what the truster entrusts to the trusted are discretionary powers, then the truster risks abuse of those and the successful disguise of such abuse. The special vulnerability which trust involves is vulnerability to not yet noticed harm, or to disguised ill will. What one forgives or tactfully averts one's eyes from may be not well-meant but ill-judged or incompetent attempts to care for what is entrusted but, rather, ill-meant and cleverly disguised abuses of discretionary power. To understand the moral risks of trust, it is important to see the special sort of vulnerability it introduces. Yet the discretionary element which introduces this special danger is essential to that which trust at its best makes possible. To elaborate Hume: "'Tis impossible to separate the chance of good from the risk of ill."[6]

It is fairly easy, once we look, to see how this special vulnerability is involved in many ordinary forms of trust. We trust the mailman to deliver and not tamper with the mail, and to some extent we trust his discretion in interpreting what "tampering" covers. Normally we do not expect him to read our mail but to deliver it unread, even when the message is open, on a postcard. But on occasion it may be proper, or at least not wrong, for him to read it. I have had friendly mailmen (in Greek villages and in small Austrian towns) who tell me what my mail announces as they hand it over: "Your relatives have recovered and can travel now, and are soon arriving!" Such interest in one's affairs is not part of the normal idea of the role of mailman and could provide opportunity for blackmail, but in virtue of that very interest they could give much more knowledgeable and intelligent service—in the above case by knowing our plans they knew when and where we had moved and delivered to the new address without instructions. What do we trust our mailmen to do or not to do? To use their discretion in getting our mail to us, to take enough interest in us and in the nature of our mail, (compatibly with their total responsibility) to make intelligent decisions about what to do with it when such decisions have to be made. Similarly with our surgeons and plumbers—*just* what they should do to put right what is wrong is something we must leave to them. Should they act incompetently, negligently, or deliberately against our interests, they may conceal these features of their activities from us by pretense that whatever happened occurred as a result of an honest and well-meaning exercise of the discretion

---

trust-offering overtures to be rejected without hostility ensuing, and it enables those who make false moves in their attempts to maintain trust to recover their position without too much loss of face. "A social climate . . . institutionalizes tact and knows enough escape routes for self presentation in difficult situations" (p. 84). It is important, I think, to see that tact is a virtue which needs to be added to delicacy of discrimination in recognizing *what* one is trusted with, good judgment as to whom to trust with what, and a willingness to admit and forgive fault, as all functional virtues needed in those who would sustain trust.

6. See David Hume, *Treatise*, ed. L. A. Selby-Bigge and P. H. Nidditch (Oxford: Clarendon Press, 1978), p. 497.

given to them. This way they may retain our trust and so have opportunity to harm us yet further. In trusting them, we trust them to use their discretionary powers competently and nonmaliciously, and the latter includes not misleading us about how they have used them.

Trust, on the analysis I have proposed, is letting other persons (natural or artificial, such as firms, nations, etc.) take care of something the truster cares about, where such "caring for" involves some exercise of discretionary powers. But not all the variables involved in trust are yet in view. One which the entrusting model obscures rather than highlights is the degree of explicitness. To entrust is intentionally and usually formally to hand over the care of something to someone, but trusting is rarely begun by making up one's mind to trust, and often it has no definite initiation of any sort but grows up slowly and imperceptibly. What I have tried to take from the notion of entrusting is not its voluntarist and formalist character but rather the possible specificity and restrictedness of *what* is entrusted, along with the discretion the trustee has in looking after that thing. Trust can come with no beginnings, with gradual as well as sudden beginnings, and with various degrees of self-consciousness, voluntariness, and expressness. My earlier discussion of the delicacy and tact needed by the truster in judging the performance of the trusted applied only to cases where the truster not merely realizes that she trusts but has some conscious control over the continuation of the trust relationship. The discussion of abuses of discretionary power applied only to cases where the trusted realizes that she is trusted and trusted with discretionary powers. But trust relationships need not be so express, and some important forms of them cannot be verbally acknowledged by the persons involved. Trust between infant and parent is such a case, and it is one which also reminds us of another crucial variable in trust relations to which so far I have only indirectly alluded. This is the relative power of the truster and the trusted, and the relative costs to each of a breakdown of their trust relationship. In emphasizing the toleration of vulnerability by the truster I have made attitudes to relative power and powerlessness the essence of trust and distrust; I have not yet looked at the varieties of trust we discern when we vary the power of the truster in relation to the power of the trusted, both while the trust endures and in its absence. Trust alters power positions, and both the position one is in without a given form of trust and the position one has within a relation of trust need to be considered before one can judge whether that form of trust is sensible and morally decent. Infant trust reminds us not just of inarticulate and uncritical or blind trust, but of trust by those who are maximally vulnerable, whether or not they give trust.

TRUST AND RELATIVE POWER

I have been apparently preoccupied up till now with dimensions of trust which show up most clearly in trust between articulate adults, in a position to judge one another's performance, and having some control over their degree of vulnerability to others. This approach typifies a myopia which, once noticed, explains the "regrettably sparse" attempts to understand trust as a phenomenon of moral importance.[7] For the more we ignore dependency relations between those grossly unequal in power and ignore what cannot be spelled out in an explicit acknowledgment, the more readily will we assume that everything that needs to be understood about trust and trustworthiness can be grasped by looking at the morality of contract. For it takes an adult to be able to make a contract, and it takes something like Hegel's civil society of near equals to find a use for contracts. But one has to strain the contractarian model very considerably to see infant-parent relations as essentially contractual, both because of the nonexpressness of the infant's attitude and because of the infant's utter powerlessness. It takes inattention to cooperation between unequals, and between those without a common language, to keep one a contented contractarian. To do more, I must both show how infant trust, and other variations along the relative power dimension, can be covered and also indicate just where trust in contracts fits into the picture we then get.

Infant trust is like one form of non-contract-based trust to which some attention has been given in our philosophical tradition, namely, trust in God. Trust in God is total, in that whatever one cares about, it will not thrive if God wills that it not thrive. A young child too is totally dependent on the good will of the parent, totally incapable of looking after anything he cares about without parental help or against parental will. Such total dependence does not, in itself, necessarily elicit trust— some theists curse God, display futile distrust or despair rather than trust. Infants too can make suspicious, futile, self-protective moves against the powerful adults in their world or retreat into autism. But surviving infants will usually have shown some trust, enough to accept offered nourishment, enough not to attempt to prevent such close approach. The ultra-Hobbist child who fears or rejects the mother's breast, as if fearing poison from that source, can be taken as displaying innate distrust, and such newborns must be the exception in a surviving species. Hobbes tells us that, in the state of nature, "seeing the infant is in the power of the Mother, and is therefore obliged to obey her, so she may either nourish or expose it; if she nourish it, it oweth its life to the Mother and is therefore obliged to obey her rather than any other" (*Leviathan*, chap. 20). Even he, born a twin to fear, is apparently willing to take mother's

7. Luhmann, p. 8, n. 1. It is interesting to note that, unlike Luhmann and myself, Bernard Barber begins his sociological treatment of trust in *The Logic and Limits of Trust* (New Brunswick, N.J.: Rutgers University Press, 1983) not by remarking on the neglect of the topic but rather, by saying, "Today nearly everyone seems to be talking about 'trust' " (p. 1). He lists "moral philosophers" along with "presidential candidates, political columnists, pollsters, social critics and the man in the street" as among those talking so much about it but cites only two moral philosophers, Bok and Rawls (who by his own account is *not* always talking about it). Between Luhmann's work on trust, first published in Germany in 1973, and Barber's, sociologists had ten years to get the talk about trust going, but it has scarcely spread yet to most of the moral philosophers I have encountered.

milk on trust. Some degree of innate, if selective, trust seems a necessary element in any surviving creature whose first nourishment (if it is not exposed) comes from another, and this innate but fragile trust could serve as the explanation both of the possibility of other forms of trust and of their fragility.

Infant trust that normally does not need to be won but is there unless and until it is destroyed is important for an understanding of the possibility of trust. Trust is much easier to maintain than it is to get started and is never hard to destroy. Unless some form of it were innate, and unless that form could pave the way for new forms, it would appear a miracle that trust ever occurs. The postponement of the onset of distrust is a lot more explicable than hypothetical Hobbesian conversions from total distrust to limited trust. The persistent human adult tendency to profess trust in a creator-God can also be seen as an infantile residue of this crucial innate readiness of infants to initially impute goodwill to the powerful persons on whom they depend. So we should perhaps welcome, or at least tolerate, religious trust, if we value any form of trust. Nevertheless the theological literature on trust in God is of very limited help to us if we want to understand trust in human persons, even that trust in parents of which it can be seen as a nostalgic fantasy-memory. For the child soon learns that the parent is not, like God, invulnerable, nor even, like some versions of God, subject to offense or insult but not injury. Infant trust, although extreme in the discrepancy of power between the truster and the trusted, is to some extent a matter of mutual trust and mutual if unequal vulnerability. The parents' enormous power to harm the child and disappoint the child's trust is the power of ones also vulnerable to the child's at first insignificant but ever-increasing power, including power as one trusted by the parent. So not very much can be milked from the theological literature on the virtues of trust, faith, and hope in God and returned to the human context, even to the case of infant and parent. Indeed we might cite the theological contamination of the concept of trust as part of the explanation for the general avoidance of the topic in modern moral philosophy. If trust is seen as a variant of the suspect virtue of faith in the competence of the powers that be, then readiness to trust will be seen not just as a virtue of the weak but itself as a moral weakness, better replaced by vigilance and self-assertion, by self-reliance or by cautious, minimal, and carefully monitored trust. The psychology of adolescents, not infants, then gets glorified as the moral ideal. Such a reaction against a religious version of the ethics of trust is as healthy, understandable, and, it is hoped, as passing a phenomenon as is adolescent self-assertive individualism in the life of a normal person.

The goods which a trustworthy parent takes care of for as long as the child is unable to take care of them alone, or continues to welcome the parent's help in caring for them, are such things as nutrition, shelter, clothing, health, education, privacy, and loving attachment to others. Why, once the child becomes at all self-conscious about trusting parents to look after such goods for her, should she have confidence that parents are dependable custodians of such goods? Presumably because many of them are also goods to the parent, through their being goods to the child, especially if the parent loves the child. They will be common goods, so that for the trusted to harm them would be self-harm as well as harm to the child. The best reason for confidence in another's good care of what one cares about is that it is a common good, and the best reason for thinking that one's own good is also a common good is being loved. This may not, usually will not, ensure agreement on what best should be done to take care of that good, but it rules out suspicion of ill will. However, even when a child does not feel as loved by a parent as she would like, or as she thinks her siblings or friends are, she may still have complete confidence that at least many of the goods she cares about can be entrusted to her parents' care. She can have plenty of evidence that, for reasons such as pride, desire to perpetuate their name, or whatever, they do care as she herself does about her health, her success, and her ties with them. She can have good reason to be confident of the continued trustworthiness of her parents in many regards, from what she knows of their own concerns.

As the child approaches adulthood, and as the parents draw nearer to the likely dependency of old age, the trust may approximate much more closely to mutual trust and mutual vulnerability between equals, and they may then make explicit or even formal agreements about what is to be done in return for what. But no such contractual or quasi-contractual agreement can convert the young child's trust and the parents' trustworthiness retrospectively into part of a contractual mutual exchange. At most it can transform what was a continuing relation of mutual trust into a contractual obligation to render some sort of service to one's parents. The previous parental care could become a moral *reason* for making a contract with parents, but not what one received as 'consideration' in such a contract. At best that could be a virtual 'consideration,' perhaps symbolized by the parents' formal cancelling of any until then outstanding 'debt' of gratitude, in return for the rights the contract gives them. But normally whatever grateful return one makes to another is not made in exchange for a 'receipt' which is proof against any outstanding 'debt.' Only those determined to see every proper moral transaction as an exchange will construe every gift as made in exchange for an IOU, and every return gift as made in exchange for a receipt. Only such trade fetishists will have any reason to try to construe the appropriate adult response to earlier parental care as part of a virtual contract, or as proper content for an actual contract. As Hume says, contract should not replace "the more generous and noble intercourse of friendship and good offices," which he construes as a matter of spontaneous service responded to by "return in the same manner."[8] We can resist this reduction of the more

8. Hume, p. 521.

noble responses of gratitude to the fulfilling of contractual obligations if we focus our moral attention on other sorts of trust than trust in contracts. Looking at infant trust helps one do that. Not only has the child no concept of virtual contract when she trusts, but the parent's duty to the child seems in no way dependent on the expectation that the child will make a later return. The child or the parent may die before the reversal of dependency arrives. Furthermore, parent's knowledge either that the child, or that he himself, or both, will die within say ten years, in itself (and disability apart) makes no difference to the parent's responsibility while he lives, as that is usually understood. Parental and filial responsibility does not rest on deals, actual or virtual, between parent and child.

TRUST AND VOLUNTARY ABILITIES

The child trusts as long as she is encouraged to trust and until the trust is unmistakably betrayed. It takes childhood innocence to be able to trust simply because of encouragement to trust. "Trust me!" is for most of us an invitation which we cannot accept at will—either we do already trust the one who says it, in which case it serves at best as reassurance,[9] or it is properly responded to with, "Why should and how can I, until I have cause to?"[10] The child, of course, cannot trust at will any more than experienced adults can—encouragement is a condition of not lapsing into distrust, rather than of a move from distrust to trust. One constraint on an account of trust which postulates infant trust as its essential seed is that it not make essential to trusting the use of concepts or abilities which a child cannot be reasonably believed to possess. Acts of will of any sort are not plausibly attributed to infants; it would be unreasonable to suppose that they can do at will what adults cannot, namely, obey the instruction to trust, whether it comes from others or is a self-instruction.

To suppose that infants emerge from the womb already equipped with some ur-confidence in what supports them, so that no choice is needed to continue with that attitude, until something happens to shake or destroy such confidence, is plausible enough. My account of trust has been designed to allow for unconscious trust, for conscious but unchosen trust, as well as for conscious trust the truster has chosen to endorse and cultivate. Whereas it strains the concept of agreement to speak of unconscious agreements and unchosen agreements, and overstrains the

---

9. My thoughts about the role of the words "Trust me!" are influenced by an unpublished paper on promising by T. M. Scanlon. Indeed Scanlon's talk on this topic to the University of Pittsburgh philosophy department in April 1984 was what, along with Hume's few remarks about it, started me thinking about trust in and out of voluntary exchanges.

10. Luhmann says, "It is not possible to demand the trust of others; trust can only be offered and accepted" (p. 43). I am here claiming something stronger, namely, that one cannot offer it or accept it by an act of will; that one cannot demand it of oneself or others until some trust-securing social artifice invents something like promise that *can* be offered and accepted at will.

concept of contract to speak of unconscious or unchosen contracts, there is no strain whatever in the concept of automatic and unconscious trust, and of unchosen but mutual trust. Trust between infant and parent, at its best, exhibits such primitive and basic trust. Once it is present, the story of how trust becomes self-conscious, controlled, monitored, critical, pretended, and eventually either cautious and distrustful of itself, or discriminatory and reflexive, so that we come to trust ourselves as trusters, is relatively easy to tell. What will need explanation will be the ceasings to trust, the transfers of trust, the restriction or enlargements in the fields of what is trusted, when, and to whom, rather than any abrupt switches from distrust to trust. Even if such occurrences do ever occur (when one suddenly falls in love or lust with a stranger or former enemy, or has a religious conversion), they take more than the mere invitation "Trust me."

In his famous account of what a promise (and a contract) involves, Hume strongly implies that it is an artificially contrived and secured case of mutual trust. The penalty to which a promisor subjects himself in promising, he says, is that of "never being trusted again in case of failure."[11] The problem which the artifice of promise solves is a generally disadvantageous "want of mutual confidence and security."[12] It is plausible to construe the offer whose acceptance counts as acceptance of a contract or a promise as at least implicitly including an invitation to trust. Part of what makes promises the special thing they are, and the philosophically intriguing thing they are, is that we *can* at will accept *this* sort of invitation to trust, whereas in general we cannot trust at will. Promises are puzzling because they seem to have the power, by verbal magic, to initiate real voluntary short-term trusting. They not merely create obligations apparently at the will of the obligated, but they create trust at the will of the truster. They present a very fascinating case of trust and trustworthiness, but one which, because of those very intriguing features, is ill suited to the role of paradigm. Yet in as far as modern moral philosophers have attended at all to the morality of trust, it is trust in parties to an agreement that they have concentrated on, and it is into this very special and artificial mold that they have tried to force other cases of trust, when they notice them at all.

Trust of any particular form is made more likely, in adults, if there is a climate of trust of that sort. Awareness of what is customary, as well as past experience of one's own, affects one's ability to trust. We take it for granted that people will perform their role-related duties and trust any individual worker to look after whatever her job requires her to. The very existence of that job, as a standard occupation, creates a climate of some trust in those with that job. Social artifices such as property, which allocate rights and duties as a standard job does, more generally also

11. Hume, p. 522.
12. Ibid., p. 521.

create a climate of trust, a presumption of a sort of trustworthiness. On the Humean account of promises and contracts which I find more or less correct,[13] their establishment as a customary procedure also reverses a presumption concerning trustworthiness, but only in limited conditions. Among these is a special voluntary act by the promisor, giving it to be understood that what he offers is a promise, and another voluntary act by the promisee, acceptance of that promise. Promises are "a bond or security,"[14] and "the sanction of the interested commerce of mankind."[15] To understand them is to see what sort of sanction is involved, what sort of security they provide, and the social preconditions of each. Then one understands how the presumption about the trustworthiness of self-interested strangers can be reversed, and how the ability to trust them (for a limited time, on a limited matter) can become a voluntary ability. To adapt Hume's words, "Hence I learn to count on a service from another, although he bears me no real kindness."[16] Promises are a most ingenious social invention, and trust in those who have given us promises is a complex and sophisticated moral achievement. Once the social conditions are right for it, once the requisite climate of trust in promisors is there, it is easy to take it for a simpler matter than it is and to ignore its background conditions. They include not merely the variable social conventions and punitive customs Hume emphasizes, but the prior existence of less artificial and less voluntary forms of trust, such as trust in friends and family, and enough trust in fellows to engage with them in agreed exchanges of a more or less simultaneous nature, exchanges such as barter or handshakes, which do not require one to rely on strangers over a period of time, as exchange of promises typically does.

Those who take advantage of this sophisticated social device will be, mainly, adults who are not intimate with one another, and who see one another more or less as equal in power to secure the enforcement of the rules of the contracting game (to extract damages for broken contracts, to set in motion the accepted penalty for fraudulent promises, and so on). As Nietzsche emphasized, the right to make promises and the power to have one's promises accepted are not possessed by everyone in relation to everyone else. Not only can the right be forfeited, but it is all along an elite right, possessed only by those with a certain social status. Slaves, young children, the ill, and the mentally incompetent do not fully possess it. For those who do possess it, whose offer or acceptance of a promise has moral force, the extent to which use of it regulates their relations with others varies with their other social powers. Women whose property, work, and sexual services became their husbands' on marriage did not

---

13. I have discussed and defended Hume's account in "Promises, Promises, Promises," in my *Postures of the Mind: Essays on Mind and Morals* (Minneapolis: University of Minnesota Press, 1985).

14. Hume, p. 541.

15. Ibid., p. 522.

16. Ibid., p. 521.

have much left to promise, and what was left could usually be taken from them without their consent and without the formality of exchange of promises. Their right to promise anything of significance was contracted into the right to make one vow of fixed and non-negotiable content, the marriage vow, and even that was often made under duress. The important relationships and trust relationships which structured women's lives for most of the known history of our species, relations to spouse, children, fellow workers, were not entered into by free choice, or by freely giving or receiving promises. They were, typically, relationships of which the more important were ones of intimacy, relationships to superiors or inferiors in power, relationships not in any strong sense freely chosen nor to chosen others. Like the infant, they found themselves faced with others to trust or distrust, found themselves trusted or not trusted by these given others. Their freely given and seriously taken promises were restricted in their content to trivialities. Contract is a device for traders, entrepreneurs, and capitalists, not for children, servants, indentured wives, and slaves. They were the traded, not the traders, and any participation they had in the promising game was mere play. It is appropriate, then, that Nietzsche, the moral philosopher who glorifies promise more even than contemporary contractarians, was also the one who advised his fellow male exchangers or givers of promises thus, "He must conceive of woman as a possession, as a property that can be locked, as something predestined for service and achieving her perfection in that."[17] Nietzsche faces squarely what Hume half faced, and what most moral philosophers have avoided facing, that the liberal morality which takes voluntary agreement as the paradigm source of moral obligation must either exclude the women they expect to continue in their traditional role from the class of moral subjects, or admit internal contradiction in their moral beliefs. Nor does the contradiction vanish once women have equal legal rights with men, as long as they are still expected to take responsibility for any child they conceive voluntarily or nonvoluntarily, either to abort or to bear and either care for or arrange for others to care for. Since a liberal morality both *must* let this responsibility rest with women, and yet cannot conceive of it as self-assumed, then the centrality of voluntary agreement to the liberal and contractarian morality must be challenged once women are treated as full moral fellows. Voluntary agreement, and trust in others to keep their agreements, must be moved from the center to the moral periphery, once servants, ex-slaves, and women are taken seriously as moral subjects and agents.

THE MALE FIXATION ON CONTRACT

The great moral theorists in our tradition not only are all men, they are mostly men who had minimal adult dealings with (and so were then

17. Nietzsche, *Beyond Good and Evil*, pt. 7, §238, trans. Walter Kaufmann, *Basic Writings of Nietzsche* (New York, 1968), p. 357.

minimally influenced by) women. With a few significant exceptions (Hume, Hegel, J. S. Mill, Sidgwick, maybe Bradley) they are a collection of gays, clerics, misogynists, and puritan bachelors. It should not surprise us, then, that particularly in the modern period they managed to relegate to the mental background the web of trust tying most moral agents to one another, and to focus their philosophical attention so single-mindedly on cool, distanced relations between more or less free and equal adult strangers, say, the members of an all male club, with membership rules and rules for dealing with rule breakers and where the form of cooperation was restricted to ensuring that each member could read his *Times* in peace and have no one step on his gouty toes. Explicitly assumed or recognized obligations toward others with the same obligations and the same power to see justice done to rule breakers then are seen as the moral norm.

Relations between equals and nonintimates will *be* the moral norm for adult males whose dealings with others are mainly business or restrained social dealings with similarly placed males. But for lovers, husbands, fathers, the ill, the very young, and the elderly, other relationships with their moral potential and perils will loom larger. For Hume, who had several strong-willed and manipulative women to cooperate or contend with in his adult life, for Mill, who had Harriet Taylor on his hands, for Hegel, whose domestic life was of normal complication, the rights and duties of equals to equals in a civil society which recognized only a male electorate could only be *part* of the moral story. They could not ignore the virtues and vices of family relationships, male-female relationships, master-slave, and employer-employee relationships as easily as could Hobbes, Butler, Bentham, or Kant. Nor could they as easily adopt the usual compensatory strategies of the moral philosophers who confine their attention to the rights and duties of free and equal adults to one another—the strategy of claiming, if pressed, that these rights are the *core* of all moral relationships and maybe also claiming that any other relationships, engendering additional or different rights and duties, come about only by an exercise of one of the core rights, the right to promise. Philosophers who remember what it was like to be a dependent child, or know what it is like to be a parent, or to have a dependent parent, an old or handicapped relative, friend, or neighbor will find it implausible to treat such relations as simply cases of comembership in a kingdom of ends, in the given temporary conditions of one-sided dependence.

To the extent that these claims are correct (and I am aware that they need more defense than I have given them here)[18] it becomes fairly easy to see one likely explanation of the neglect in Western moral philosophy of the full range of sorts of trust. Both before the rise of a society which needed contract as a commercial device, and after it, women were counted

18. I defend them a little more in "What Do Women Want in a Moral Theory?" *Nous* 19 (March 1985): 53–64.

on to serve their men, to raise their children to fill the roles they were expected to fill and not deceive their men about the paternity of these children. What men counted on one another for, in work and war, presupposed this background domestic trust, trust in women not merely not to poison their men (Nietzsche derides them for learning less than they might have in the kitchen), but to turn out sons who could trust and be trusted in traditional men's roles and daughters who would reduplicate their own capacities for trust and trustworthiness. Since the women's role did not include the writing of moral treatises, any thoughts they had about trust, based on their experience of it, did not get into our tradition (or did Diotima teach Socrates something about trust as well as love?). And the more powerful men, including those who did write the moral treatises, were in the morally awkward position of being, collectively, oppressors of women, exploiters of women's capacity for trustworthiness in unequal, nonvoluntary, and non-contract-based relationships. Understandably, they did not focus their attention on forms of trust and demands for trustworthiness which it takes a Nietzsche to recognize without shame. Humankind can bear only so much reality.

The recent research of Carol Gilligan has shown us how intelligent and reflective twentieth-century women see morality, and how different their picture of it is from that of men, particularly the men who eagerly assent to the claims of currently orthodox contractarian-Kantian moral theories.[19] Women cannot now, any more than they could when oppressed, ignore that part of morality and those forms of trust which cannot easily be forced into the liberal and particularly the contractarian mold. Men may but women cannot see morality as essentially a matter of keeping to the minimal moral traffic rules, designed to restrict close encounters between autonomous persons to self-chosen ones. Such a conception presupposes both an equality of power and a natural separateness from others, which is alien to women's experience of life and morality. For those most of whose daily dealings are with the less powerful or the more powerful, a moral code designed for those equal in power will be at best nonfunctional, at worst an offensive pretense of equality as a substitute for its actuality. But equality is not even a desirable ideal in all relationships—children not only are not but should not be equal in power to adults, and we need a morality to guide us in our dealings with those who either cannot or should not achieve equality of power (animals, the ill, the dying, children while still young) with those with whom they have unavoidable and often intimate relationships.

Modern moral philosophy has concentrated on the morality of fairly cool relationships between those who are deemed to be roughly equal in power to determine the rules and to instigate sanctions against rule breakers. It is not surprising, then, that the main form of trust that any

---

19. Carol Gilligan, *In a Different Voice* (Cambridge, Mass.: Harvard University Press, 1982).

attention has been given to is trust in governments, and in parties to voluntary agreements to do what they have agreed to do. As much as possible is absorbed into the latter category, so that we suppose that paying for what one takes from a shop, doing what one is employed to do, returning what one has borrowed, supporting one's spouse, are all cases of being faithful to binding voluntary agreements, to contracts of some sort. (For Hume, none of these would count as duties arising from contract or promise.) Yet if I think of the trust I show, say, in the plumber who comes from the municipal drainage authority when I report that my drains are clogged, it is not plausibly seen as trust that he will fulfill his contractual obligations to me or to his employer. When I trust him to do whatever is necessary and safe to clear my drains, I take his expertise and his lack of ill will for granted. Should he plant explosives to satisfy some unsuspected private or social grudge against me, what I might try to sue him for (if I escaped alive) would not be damages for breach of contract. His wrong, if wrong it were, is not breach of contract, and the trust he would have disappointed would not have been that particular form of trust.

Contract enables us to make explicit just what we count on another person to do, in return for what, and should they not do just that, what damages can be extracted from them. The beauty of promise and contract is its explicitness.[20] But we can only make explicit provisions for such contingencies as we imagine arising. Until I become a victim of a terrorist plumber I am unlikely, even if I should insist on a contract before giving plumbers access to my drains, to extract a solemn agreement that they not blow me up. Nor am I likely to specify the alternative means they *may* use to clear my drains, since if I knew enough to compile such a list I would myself have to be a competent plumber. Any such detailed instructions must come from their plumbing superiors; I know nothing or little about it when I confidently welcome the plumber into the bowels of my basement. I trust him to do a nonsubversive plumbing job, as he counts on me to do a nonsubversive teaching job, should he send his son to my course in the history of ethics. Neither of us relies on a contract with the other, and neither of us need know of any contract (or much about its contents) the other may have with a third coordinating party.

It does not, then, seem at all plausible, once we think about actual moral relations in all their sad or splendid variety, to model all of them

20. Norbert Hornstein has drawn my attention to an unpublished paper by economist Peter Murrell, "Commitment and Cooperation: A Theory of Contract Applied to Franchising." Murrell emphasizes the nonstandard nature of franchise contracts, in that they typically are vague about what is expected of the franchisee. The consequent infrequency of contract termination by the franchisor is linked by him to the long duration of the contracts and to the advantage, to the more powerful proprietor of the trademark, of keeping the trust of the less powerful scattered franchisees and maintaining quality control by means other than punitive contract terminations. This, I persuade myself, is a case where the exception proves the rule, where the nonstandardness of such inexplicit and trusting contracts points up to the explicitness and minimal trustingness of standard contracts.

on one rather special one, the relation between promisor to promisee. We count on all sorts of people for all sorts of vital things, without any contracts, explicit or implicit, with them or with any third coordinating party. For these cases of trust in people to do their job conscientiously and not to take the opportunity to do us harm once we put things we value into their hands are different from trust in people to keep their promises in part because of the very indefiniteness of what we are counting on them to do or not to do. The subtlety and point of promising is to declare precisely *what* we count on another to do, and as the case of Shylock and Bassanio shows, that very definiteness is a limitation as well as a functional excellence of an explicit agreement.

Another functional excellence of contracts, which is closely connected with the expressness that makes breach easily established and damages or penalty decidable with a show of reasonable justice, is the *security* they offer the trusting party. They make it possible not merely for us to trust at will but to trust with minimal vulnerability. They are a device for trusting others enough for mutually profitable future-involving exchanges, without taking the risks trusters usually do take. They are designed for cooperation between mutually suspicious risk-averse strangers, and the vulnerability they involve is at the other extreme from that incurred by trusting infants. Contracts distribute and redistribute risk so as to minimize it for both parties, but trusting those more powerful persons who purport to love one increases one's risks while increasing the good one can hope to secure. Trust in fellow contracters is a limit case of trust, in which fewer risks are taken, for the sake of lesser goods.

Promises do, nevertheless, involve some real trust in the other party's good will and proper use of discretionary powers. Hume said that "to perform promises is requisite to beget trust and confidence in the common offices of life."[21] But performing promises is not the only performance requisite for that. Shylock did not welsh on an agreement, but he was nevertheless not a trustworthy party to an agreement. For to insist on the letter of an agreement, ignoring the vague but generally understood unwritten background conditions and exceptions, is to fail to show that discretion and goodwill which a trustworthy person has. To be someone to be trusted with a promise, as well as to be trusted as a promisor, one must be able to use discretion not as to when the promise has been kept but, rather, as to when to insist that the promise be kept, or to instigate penalty for breach of promise, when to keep and when not to keep one's promise. I would feel morally let down if someone who had promised to help me move house arrived announcing, "I had to leave my mother, suddenly taken ill, to look after herself in order to be here, but I couldn't break my promise to you." From such persons I would accept no further promises, since they would have shown themselves untrustworthy in the always crucial respect of judgment and willingness to use their discretionary

21. Hume, p. 544.

powers. Promises *are* morally interesting, and one's performance as party to a promise is a good indicator of one's moral character, but not for the reasons contractarians suppose.

The domination of contemporary moral philosophy by the so-called Prisoner's Dilemma problem displays most clearly this obsession with moral relations between minimally trusting, minimally trustworthy adults who are equally powerful. Just as the only trust Hobbist man shows is trust in promises, provided there is assurance of punishment for promise breakers, so is this the only sort of trust nontheological modern moral philosophers have given much attention at all to, as if once we have weaned ourselves from the degenerate form of absolute and unreciprocated trust in God, all our capacity for trust is to be channelled into the equally degenerate form of formal voluntary and reciprocated trust restricted to equals. But we collectively cannot bring off such a limitation of trust to minimal and secured trust, and we can deceive ourselves that we do only if we avert our philosophical gaze from the ordinary forms of trust I have been pointing to. It was not really that, after Hobbes, people *did* barricade their bodies as well as their possessions against all others before daring to sleep. Some continued to doze off on stagecoaches, to go abroad unarmed, to give credit in business deals, to count on others turning up on time for appointments, to trust parents, children, friends, and lovers not to rob or assault them when welcomed into intimacy with them. And the usual array of vicious forms of such trust, trustworthiness, and demands for them, continued to flourish. Slaves continued to be trusted to cook for slaveowners; women, with or without marriage vows, continued to be trusted with the property of their men, trusted not to deceive them about the paternity of their children, and trusted to bring up their sons as patriarchs, their daughters as suitable wives or mistresses for patriarchs. Life went on, but the moral philosophers, or at least those we regard as the great ones, chose to attend only to a few of the moral relations normal life exhibited. Once Filmer was disposed of, they concentrated primarily *not* on any of the relations between those of unequal power—parent to child, husband to wife, adult to aged parent, slaveowner to slave, official to citizen, employer to employee—but on relations between roughly equal parties or between people in those respects in which they could be seen as equals.

Such relationships of mutual respect are, of course, of great moral importance. Hobbes, Locke, Rousseau, Hume, Kant, Sidgwick, Rawls, all have helped us to see more clearly how we stand in relation to anonymous others, like ourselves in need, in power, and in capacity. One need not minimize the importance of such work in moral philosophy in order to question its completeness. But a complete moral philosophy would tell us how and why we should act and feel toward others in relationships of shifting and varying power asymmetry and shifting and varying intimacy. It seems to me that we philosophers have left that task largely to priests and revolutionaries, the self-proclaimed experts on the proper attitude of the powerless to the powerful. But these relationships of inequality—some of them, such as parent-child, of unavoidable inequality—make up much of our lives, and they, as much as our relations to our equals, determine the state of moral health or corruption in which we are content to live. I think it is high time we look at the morality and immorality of relations between the powerful and the less powerful, especially at those in which there is trust between them.

A MORAL TEST FOR TRUST

The few discussions of trust that I have found in the literature of moral philosophy assume that trust is a good and that disappointing known trust is always prima facie wrong, meeting it always prima facie right. But what is a trust-tied community without justice but a group of mutual blackmailers and exploiters? When the trust relationship itself is corrupt and perpetuates brutality, tyranny, or injustice, trusting may be silly self-exposure, and disappointing and betraying trust, including encouraged trust, may be not merely morally permissible but morally praiseworthy. Women, proletarians, and ex-slaves cannot ignore the virtues of watchful distrust, and of judicious untrustworthiness. Only if we had reason to believe that most familiar types of trust relationship were morally sound would breaking trust be any more prima facie wrong than breaking silence. I now turn to the question of when a given form of trust is morally decent, so properly preserved by trustfulness and trustworthiness, and when it fails in moral decency. What I say about this will be sketchy and oversimplified. I shall take as the form of trust to test for moral decency the trust which one spouse has in the other, in particular as concerns their children's care.

Earlier in discussing infant trust I said that the child has reason to trust the parents when both child and parents care about the same good—the child's happiness, although the child may not see eye to eye with those trusted parents about how that is best taken care of. When one parent, say the old-style father, entrusts the main care of his young child's needs to the old-style mother, there, too, there can be agreement on the good they both want cared for but disagreement about how best it is cared for. The lord and master who entrusts such care to his good wife, the mother, and so gives her discretionary power in making moment-by-moment decisions about what is to be done, will have done so sensibly if these disagreements are not major ones, or if he has reason to think that she knows better than he does about such matters. He should defer to her judgment, as the child is encouraged to do to the parents', and as I do to my plumber's. He sensibly trusts if he has reason to think that the discretionary powers given, even when used in ways he does not fully understand or approve of, are still used to care for the goods he wants cared for. He would be foolish to trust if he had evidence that she had other ends in view in her treatment of the child, or had a radically different version of what, say, the child's healthy development and proper relation to his father consisted in. Once he suspects that she, the trusted nurse of his sons and daughters, is deliberately rearing the daughters to be patriarch-toppling Amazons, the sons to be subverters of the father's values, he will sensibly withdraw his trust and dispatch his children to suitably chosen female relatives or boarding schools. What would properly undermine his trust would be beliefs he came to hold about the formerly trusted person's motives and purposes in her care of what was entrusted to her. The disturbing and trust-undermining suspicion is not necessarily that she doesn't care about the children's good, or cares only about her own—it is the suspicion that what she cares about conflicts with rather than harmonizes with what he cares about and that she is willing to sacrifice his concerns to what she sees as the children's and her own. Trusting is rational, then, in the absence of any reason to suspect in the trusted strong and operative motives which conflict with the demands of trustworthiness as the truster sees them.

But trusting can continue to be rational, even when there are such unwelcome suspicions, as long as the truster is confident that in the conflict of motives within the trusted the subversive motives will lose to the conformist motives. Should the wife face economic hardship and loss of her children if she fails to meet the husband's trust, or incurs too much of his suspicion, then she will sensibly continue as the dutiful wife, until her power position alters—sensibly, that is, given what she cares about. The husband in a position to be sure that the costs to the wife of discovered untrustworthiness are a sufficient deterrent will sensibly continue in trusting her while increasing his vigilance. Nor is he relying only on her fear, since, by hypothesis, her motives are conflicting and so she is not without some good will and some sympathy for his goals. Should he conclude that *only* fear of sanctions keeps her at her wifely duties, then the situation will have deteriorated from trust to mere reliance on his threat advantage. In such a case he will, if he has any sense, shrink the scope of her discretionary powers to virtually zero, since it is under cover of those that she could not merely thwart his purposes for his children but work to change the power relations in her own favor. As long as he gives her any discretion in looking after what is entrusted to her, he must trust her, and not rely solely on her fear of threatened penalties for disappointing his expectations.

The trusted wife (who usually, of course, also trusts her husband with many things that matter to her) is sensible to try to keep his trust, as long as she judges that the goods which would be endangered should she fail to meet his trust matter more to her than those she could best look after only by breaking or abusing trust. The goods for the sake of whose thriving she sensibly remains trustworthy might include the loving relation between them, their mutual trust for its own sake, as well as their agreed version of their children's good; or it might be some vestiges of these plus her own economic support or even physical safety, which are vulnerable to his punitive rage should she be found guilty of breach of trust. She will sensibly continue to meet trust, even when the goods with whose case she is trusted are no longer clearly common goods, as long as she cares a lot about anything his punitive wrath can and is likely to harm.

Sensible trust could persist, then, in conditions where truster and trusted suspect each other of willingness to harm the other if they could get away with it, the one by breach of trust, the other by vengeful response to that. The stability of the relationship will depend on the trusted's skill in cover-up activities, or on the truster's evident threat advantage, or a combination of these. Should the untrustworthy trusted person not merely have skill in concealment of her breaches of trust but skill in directing them toward increasing her own power and increasing her ability to evade or protect herself against the truster's attempted vengeance, then that will destabilize the relation, as also would frequent recourse by the truster to punitive measures against the trusted.

Where the truster relies on his threat advantage to keep the trust relation going, or where the trusted relies on concealment, something is morally rotten in the trust relationship. The truster who in part relies on his whip or his control of the purse is sensible but not necessarily within his moral rights in continuing to expect trustworthiness; and the trusted who sensibly relies on concealment to escape the penalty for untrustworthiness, may or may not be within her moral rights. I tentatively propose a test for the moral decency of a trust relationship, namely, that its continuation need not rely on successful threats held over the trusted, or on her successful cover-up of breaches of trust. We could develop and generalize this test into a version of an expressibility test, if we note that knowledge of what the other party is relying on for the continuance of the trust relationship would, in the above cases of concealment and of threat advantage, itself destabilize the relation. Knowledge of the other's reliance on concealment does so fairly automatically, and knowledge of the other's partial reliance on one's fear of his revenge would tend, in a person of normal pride and self-assertiveness, to prompt her to look for ways of exploiting her discretionary powers so as to minimize her vulnerability to that threat. More generally, to the extent that what the truster relies on for the continuance of the trust relation is something which, once realized by the truster, is likely to lead to (increased) abuse of trust, and eventually to destabilization and destruction of that relation, the trust is morally corrupt. Should the wife come to realize that the husband relies on her fear of his revenge, or on her stupidity in not realizing her exploitation, or on her servile devotion to him, to keep her more or less trustworthy, that knowledge should be enough to begin to cure these weaknesses and to motivate untrustworthiness. Similarly, should the truster come to realize that the trusted relies on her skill at covering up or on her ability to charm him into forgiveness for breaches of trust, that is, relies on *his* blindness or gullibility, that realization will help cure that blindness and gullibility. A trust relationship is morally bad to the extent that either party relies on qualities in the other which would be weakened by the knowledge that the other relies on them. Where each relies on the other's love, or concern for some common good, or professional pride in competent discharge of responsibility, knowledge of what the other is relying on in one need not undermine but will more likely strengthen those relied-on features. They survive exposure as what others rely on in one, in a way that some forms of stupidity, fear, blindness, ignorance, and gullibility normally do not. There are other mental states whose sensitivity to exposure as relied on by others seems more variable: good nature, detachment, inattention, generosity, forgivingness, sexual bondage to the other party to the trust may not be weakened by knowledge that others count on their presence in one to sustain some wanted relationship, especially if they are found equally in both parties. But the knowledge that others are counting on one's nonreciprocated generosity or good nature or forgiveness can have the power of the negative, can destroy trust.

I assume that in some forms of trust the healthy and desired state will be mere self-maintenance, while in others it will be change and growth. Alteration of the trust relationship need not take the form of destruction of the old form and its replacement by a new form, but of continuous growth, of slight shifts in scope of discretionary powers, additions or alterations in scope of goods entrusted, and so on. Of course some excitement-addicted persons may cultivate a form of trust in part for the opportunity it provides for dramatic disruption. Trust is the atmosphere necessary for exhilarating disruptions of trust, and satisfyingly spectacular transfers of trust, as well as for other goods we value. For persons with such tastes, immoral forms of trust may be preferable to what, according to my test, are moral forms of trust.

It should be noted that my proposed test of the moral decency of trust is quite noncommittal as to what cases of reliance on another's psychology will be acceptable to the other. I have assumed that most people in most trust situations will not be content to have others rely on their fear, their ignorance, and their spinelessness. In some cases, however, such as trusting police to play their role effectively, and trusting one's fellows to refrain from open crime, some element of fear must play a role, and it is its absence not its presence which would destabilize trust in such contexts. In others, such as trust in national intelligence and security officers to look after national security, some ignorance in the trusting is proper, and awareness that such persons may be relying on one's not knowing what they know will not destabilize any trust one has in them to do what they are entrusted to do. What will be offensive forms of reliance on one's psychological state will vary from context to context, depending on the nature of the goods entrusted and on other relationships between the trusting and the trusted. Variations in individual psychology will also make a difference. Some are much more tolerant than others of having their good nature or preoccupation taken advantage of—not merely in that they take longer to recognize that they are victims of this, but they are less stirred to anger or resentment by the awareness that they are being deceived, blackmailed, or exploited in a given trust relation. I have used the phrase "tend to destroy" in the test for moral decency in the assumption that there is a normal psychology to be discerned and that it does include a strong enough element of Platonic *thumos*. Should that be false, then all sorts of horrendous forms of trust may pass my test. I do not, in any case, claim that it is the only test, merely an appropriate one. It is a test which amounts to a check on the will and good will of the truster and trusted, a look to see how good their will to one another is, knowing what they do about each other's psychology.

It may be objected that the expressibility test I have proposed amounts to a reversion, on my part, to the contractarian attitude which I have deplored.[22] Have I not finally admitted that we must treat trust relationships as hypothetical contracts, with all the terms fully spelled out in order to determine their moral status? The short answer is that contractualists do not have a monopoly on expressibility tests. In any case, I have applied it at a place no contractualist would, and *not* applied it where he does. Where he assumes self-interest as a motive and makes explicit what goods or services each self-interested party is to receive from the other, I have left it open what motives the trusting and trusted have for maintaining the relation, requiring only that these motives, insofar as they rely on responses from the other, survive the other's knowledge of that reliance, and I have not required that relied-on services be made explicit. What the contractualist makes explicit is a voluntary mutual commitment, and what services each is committed to provide. I have claimed that such explicitness is not only rare in trust relationships, but that many of them must begin inexplicitly and nonvoluntarily and would not do the moral and social work they do if they covered only what contract does — services that could be pretty exactly spelled out. My moral test does not require that these nonexplicit elements in trust should be made explicit but, rather, that something else survive being made explicit, one's reliance on facts about others' psychological states relevant to their willingness to continue serving or being served, states such as love, fear, ignorance, sense of powerlessness, good nature, inattention, which one can use for one's secret purposes. It is not part of contracts or social contracts to specify what assumptions each party needs to make about the other in respect of such psychological factors. Perhaps constraints regarding duress and fraud can be linked with the general offensiveness of having others rely on one's ignorance, fear, or sense of powerlessness, especially when these are contrived by the one who relies on them; but contracts themselves do not make express what it is in the state of mind of the other that each party relies on to get what he wants from the deal. What I have proposed as a general moral test of trust is indeed a generalization of one aspect

---

22. Objections of this sort were raised by a reader for *Ethics*.

of the contractarian morality, namely, of the assumptions implicit in the restrictions of valid contracts to those not involving fraud or duress. Whereas contracts make explicit the services (or service equivalent) exchanged, trust, when made express, amounts to a sort of exchange of responses to the motives and state of mind of the other, responses, in the form of confident reliance. Contractualists and other exchange fetishists can see this as a spiritual exchange, if it pleases them to do so, but it is not voluntary in the way contracts are, nor does it presuppose any equality of need or of power in the parties to this "exchange." The relation of my account of the morality of trust to standard contractarian morality seems to me as close as it should be, and at roughly the right places, if, as I have claimed, trust in fellow contracters is a limit case of trust.

Nevertheless, there are two aspects of my test which worry me, which may indicate it is not sufficiently liberated from contractarian prejudices. One difficulty is that it ignores the *network* of trust, and treats only two-party trust relationships. This is unrealistic, since any person's attitude to another in a given trust relationship is constrained by all the other trust and distrust relationships in which she is involved. Although I have alluded to such society-wide phenomena as climates of trust affecting the possibilities for individual trust relationships, my test is not well designed for application to the whole network but has to be applied piecemeal. That is a defect, showing the same individualist limitations which I find in contractarianism. The second thing that worries me is that the test seems barely applicable to brief trusting encounters, such as those with fellow library frequenters. As the contractarian takes as his moral paradigm a relationship which has some but not a very complex temporal depth, assimilating simultaneous exchange to the delayed delivery which makes a contract useful, and treats lifelong mutual trust as iterated mutual delayed deliveries, so I have shown a bias toward the medium-length trust relationship, thereby failing to say or imply anything very helpful either about brief encounters or about cross-generational trust. Probably these two faults are connected. If one got a test for the whole network of trust, with all the dependencies between the intimate and the more impersonal forms properly noted, and had the right temporal dimensions in that, then both the morality of brief trusting encounters and the morality of trust between generations who do not encounter each other would fall into place.

Since I have thus oversimplified the problem of morally evaluating trust relationships by confining my attention to relationships one by one, my account of trusting as acceptance of having as it were entrusted and my consequent expansion of trusting from a two-place into a three-place predicate will seem forced and wrong. For there are some people whom one would not trust with anything, and that is not because one has considered each good one might entrust to that one and rejected that possibility. We want then to say that unless we first trust them we will not trust them *with anything*. I think that there is some truth in this, which my account has not captured. For some kinds of enemy (perhaps class enemies?) one will not trust even with one's bodily safety as one raises a white flag, but one will find it 'safer' to fight to the death. With some sorts of enemies, a contract may be too intimate a relation. If the network of relationships is systematically unjust or systematically coercive, then it may be that one's status within that network will make it unwise of one to entrust anything to those persons whose interests, given their status, are systematically opposed to one's own. In most such corrupt systems there will be limited opportunity for such beleaguered persons to "rescue" their goods from the power of their enemies—they usually will have no choice but to leave them exposed and so to act as if they trusted, although they feel proper distrust. In such conditions it may take fortitude to display distrust and heroism to disappoint the trust of the powerful. Courageous (if unwise) untrustworthiness and stoic withdrawal of trust may then be morally laudable. But since it usually will take such heroic disruptions of inherited trust relationships for persons to distance themselves from those the system makes their enemies, my test will at least be usable to justify such disruptions. In an earlier version of this paper I said that the ghost of plain trust and plain distrust haunted my account of goods-relativized or 'fancy' trust. I think that I now see that ghost for what it is and see why it ought to continue to haunt. Still, such total oppositions of interest are rare, and one satisfactory thing about my account is that it enables us to see how we can salvage some respects in which we may trust even those whose interests are to some extent opposed to our own.

Meanwhile, my account of what it is to trust, and my partial account of when it is immoral to expect or meet trust, will have to be treated as merely a beginning (or, for some, a resumption, since there doubtless are other attempts at this topic which have escaped my notice). Trust, I have claimed, is reliance on others' competence and willingness to look after, rather than harm, things one cares about which are entrusted to their care. The moral test of such trust relationships which I have proposed is that they be able to survive awareness by each party to the relationship of *what* the other relies on in the first to ensure their continued trustworthiness or trustingness. This test elevates to a special place one form of trust, namely, trusting others with knowledge of what it is about them which enables one to trust them as one does, or expect them to be trustworthy. The test could be restated this way: trust is morally decent only if, in addition to whatever else is entrusted, knowledge of each party's reasons for confident reliance on the other to continue the relationship could in principle also be entrusted—since such mutual knowledge would be itself a good, not a threat to other goods. To the extent that mutual reliance can be accompanied by mutual knowledge of the conditions for that reliance, trust is above suspicion, and trustworthiness a nonsuspect virtue. "Rara temporum felicitas . . . quae sentias dicere licet."[23]

This paper has an antiphonal title and a final counterpoint may not be out of order. Although I think this test is an appropriate moral test, it is another matter to decide whether and when it should be applied to actual cases of trust. Clearly in some cases, such as infant trust and parental trustworthiness, which could in principle pass it, it cannot actually be applied by both parties to the relationship. That need not unduly worry us. But in other cases it may well be that the attempt to apply it will ensure its failing the test. Trust is a fragile plant, which may not endure inspection of its roots, even when they were, before the inspection, quite healthy. So, although some forms of trust would survive a suddenly achieved mutual awareness of them, they may not survive the gradual and possibly painful process by which such awareness actually comes about. It may then be the better part of wisdom, even when we have an acceptable test for trust, not to use it except where some distrust already exists, better to take nonsuspect trust on trust. Luhmann says that "it is a characteristic mark of civilizing trust that it incorporates an element of reflexivity."[24] But to trust one's trust and one's distrust enough to refrain from applying moral tests until prompted by some distrust is to take a very risky bet on the justice, if not the "civilization," of the system of trust one inhabits. We may have to trade off civilization for justice, unless we can trust not only our trust but, even more vitally, our distrust.

---

23. Hume placed on the title page of his *A Treatise of Human Nature* these words of Tacitus: "Rara Temporum felicitas, ubi sentire, quae velis, and quae sentias, dicere licet."
24. Luhmann, p. 69.

Agency, Attachment, and Difference*

Barbara Herman

It is for no trivial reason that Kant's ethics is the standard model of an impartial ethical system. Persons have moral standing in virtue of their rationality, and the morally dictated regard we are to have for one another reflects this deep sameness: we are never to fail to treat one another as agents with autonomous rational wills. This yields impartial treatment of persons and impartial judgment across cases. Although these features of Kant's ethics have traditionally been a source of its appeal, in many recent discussions just this sort of impartiality has come to stand for a kind of vice—mostly a vice of theory.[1] To the extent, however, that persons embody the values of impartiality, it is sometimes thought to be in them, if not quite a vice, then a lack or limit or defect of moral sensibility.[2]

In this article I want to examine a cluster of criticisms of Kantian ethics associated with its impartiality. They arise from concern for the moral standing of relationships of attachment between persons and extend to claims for the nonrational nature of the moral agent and the moral relevance of difference. Each strand of criticism has the form: because of its commitment to impartiality (or one of the grounds of impartiality—e.g., rationality), Kantian ethics fails to make room for X, where X is something no acceptable moral theory can ignore. Without making a general argument in praise of impartiality, I want to look to see whether its Kantian instantiation really fails to accommodate things no moral theory can afford to omit.

* My thanks to the participants of the 1990 Hollins Institute for Ethics and Public Policy for their thoughtful responses to this paper, and to Miles Morgan, Amélie Rorty, Sally Sedgwick, and Carol Voeller for valuable suggestions and criticisms of the penultimate draft.

1. The vanguard of this complaint is to be found in the work of Bernard Williams (esp. in "Morality and the Emotions," in his *Problems of the Self* [Cambridge: Cambridge University Press, 1973], pp. 223–29, and "Persons, Character and Morality," in his *Moral Luck* [Cambridge: Cambridge University Press, 1981]); Michael Stocker (esp. "The Schizophrenia of Modern Ethical Theories," *Journal of Philosophy* 73 [1976]: 453–56); and Lawrence Blum (*Friendship, Altruism and Morality* [London: Routledge & Kegan Paul, 1980]).

2. Criticisms of the so-called justice perspective find fault this way. See Carol Gilligan, *In a Different Voice* (Cambridge, Mass.: Harvard University Press, 1982) and her later introductory essay to *Women and Moral Theory*, ed. E. Kittay and D. Meyers (Totowa, N.J.: Rowman & Littlefield, 1987).

This essay originally appeared in *Ethics*, vol. 101, no. 4, July 1991.

Relationships of attachment pose a serious problem for Kantian ethics if attachment is a source of distinctive moral claims that impartiality disallows or if the features of persons that support and express attachment are devalued by its conception of moral agency. While friends of Kantian ethics have described ways to accommodate the concerns that motivate the criticism, *what* has to be accommodated has to a large extent been accepted in the critics' terms. It is among my purposes here to initiate a more independent examination of the value of partiality.

It is important to say at the outset that I do not intend this article in the spirit of endless defense of a favorite system. The cluster of criticisms are worth attention because they do point to important matters that have been omitted or ignored by Kantian theorists (though whether by Kant himself is another matter). Moral theories should not be static. As we discover (or uncover) things a theory as formulated did not know about or attend to, we have occasion to further elaborate or develop the theory in the light of what we now know. Sometimes a theory can absorb new things; sometimes not. Whichever, we do best if we make the effort and see what happens to the theory under strain. Its success may suggest we have misunderstood the theory all along. Its failure can only instruct if we are scrupulous in finding the source of the fact. The fact that a theory as traditionally understood omits something should be the beginning, not the end, of inquiry.

I

Impartiality per se is the requirement that like cases be treated alike. As a requirement on justification, it is not trivial. Differential treatment or judgment requires the demonstration of relevant difference. But as a substantive moral requirement, impartiality by itself demands little. Do we violate impartiality when we favor friends over strangers in the distribution of some good? Does impartiality show that if pregnancy is accorded the status of a disability, employment law will not be impartial between men and women? Because there is nothing in the idea of impartiality to indicate when or in what terms cases are alike, it can seem that impartiality is an empty (or uninstructive) moral value. It is then hard to see what all the fuss could be about.

There is an interesting asymmetry here. For if impartiality is empty, partiality (in its different manifestations) is the stuff our lives are said to be about: *my* life, *my* loves, *my* ideals. To the extent then that impartiality defines the moral perspective, partiality creates tension with and within morality. When I attend specially to the needs of my children and friends because I am partial to them, either I have acted as I ought not (morality requires that I count their needs no more than others'), or I have done what I ought to do, because there are obligations to one's children and friends, but I have done it the wrong way: my actions were expressions of my partiality, not of my moral understanding and commitment. Partiality is then either a sign or an occasion of moral failure, or a value that morality cannot acknowledge in a direct way. Those unhappy with this will say: impartial ethics does not allow room (or the right sort of room) for the relationships and structures of attachment that constitute good or normal human lives. It devalues the affective life—the life constituted by feeling, intimacy, connection. And if affect-grounded connection creates partiality of attachment, then impartial ethics pushes us away from such attachments.

I want to think more about this claim and about the nature of what makes it disturbing. In particular, I want to investigate the argument that takes a positive moral attitude toward feelings to be the basis for asserting the disvalue of impartiality as a moral norm for relationships. What I want to show is that much of the conflict between concerns of partiality and impartial ethics is caused by a misunderstanding of the requirements of both.

Let us first survey the kind of room Kantian ethics provides for actions motivated by care and concern for the other—what I will call "motives of connection." As we see where reasonable grounds for complaint remain, we will have the issues that need attention. In an earlier article I argued that Kantian ethics does not block the satisfaction of certain obligations from motives of connection as they are available and/or appropriate, so long as the agent's volition (her maxim) is regulated by the motive of duty functioning as a secondary motive or limiting condition.[3] That is to say: in acting from a motive of connection I must also recognize that I am in circumstances in which action is morally required, be willing and able to act even if connection wavers, and act only on the condition that the particular action I am moved to take is permissible. But permitting action from motives of connection does not fully resolve the problem. Even though there is nothing wrong with acting from a motive of connection in circumstances of obligation, the Kantian is likely to insist that action so motivated has no moral worth. The Kantian position is that the value moral worth signals is action done from a motive that tracks morality (the motive of duty): only then is there a maxim of action with moral content. A dutiful action done from a motive of connection has a maxim with a different content. The critic of Kantian ethics objects to the fact that no moral value is assigned to maxims or motives of connection. Toleration is not enough.

There are counter-moves the Kantian may make at this point. One may note that in most cases the actions at issue are ones required by "imperfect duties." What one is required to do is adopt morally required ends from the motive of duty. That leaves open how (from what motive) one acts for that end. An agent may act for a morally required end from motives of connections. Indeed, a helping action guided by connection may be more successful than one done from the moral motive working alone. The agent's complete maxim then includes not only the motive

3. Barbara Herman, "Integrity and Impartiality," *Monist* 66 (1983): 234–40.

of connection but also the underlying moral commitment to the required end (from the motive of duty).[4] The complete maxim has moral content. If this treatment secures moral worth to the agent acting from motives of connection, it still fails to accord moral value to these motives, except indirectly. The motives of connection are placed among those which can lend support to a morally required end, but the moral value of connection remains in question.

One might try to argue that since there is an indirect duty to maintain one's happiness (to secure stability for moral character),[5] and since attachments are necessary to human happiness, then the motives of connection have moral value as they are means to happiness.[6] But this will not really satisfy those who find the issue in the need to justify the motives of connection in the first place. Nor should it. In this way of arguing the value of connection or attachment is dependent on its role in supporting the "mental health" of the moral agent.[7]

Perhaps we should have asked first: Why should it matter that maxims of connection do not have *moral* value? Why can't we say: morality is one kind of value, connection another? Not everything that matters to us must have moral value. A reason for caring about this might turn on the relative value weight of connection, especially if one thought that regulative priority implied value priority. That is, if morality (impartial morality) trumps connection, the value of connection is diminished. But, of course, even assigning moral value to motives of connection would not resolve the priority issue unless we thought that the moral value of connection was at least sometimes greater than the value associated with the motive of duty. And this the Kantian cannot accept.

There is an additional worry. Given the association in Kantian ethics between morality and rationality on the one hand, and connection with affect and feeling on the other, the assignment of (at best) subordinate value to the motives of connection supports the idea that our affective nature is not essential to our moral agency (or at least the idea that our moral agency would remain intact in the absence of the grounds of connection). We will return to this concern later.

---

4. An agent's "complete" maxim is the fully elaborated subjective principle of volition, including not only the motive and end of the action to be taken but also the regulative conditions the agent accepts in acting. In the case imagined, the complete maxim reflects the agent's commitment to the morally required end of helping and her belief that the best means of acting in the circumstances is in a way that is expressive of connection.

5. Kant, *Groundwork of the Metaphysics of Morals,* trans. H. J. Paton (New York: Harper & Row, 1964), p. 67.

6. Henning Jensen offers an interesting variant of this, arguing that a perfect duty to maintain the rights of humanity in ourselves entitles us to act from motives of connection from the motive of duty (see his "Kant and Moral Integrity," *Philosophical Studies* 57 [1989]: 193–205).

7. We should at least mark that there is a question about why something that is slotted as of instrumental value does not bear the value of its end. This may have to do with a tendency to believe that instruments are fungible. It does not seem to be a necessary truth about value.

Does regulative priority translate into value priority? I think not. When we require that belief and argument meet standards of theoretical rationality, we are hardly committed to the thought that we thereby care more about rationality than we care about the substance of our inquiry. Regulative rules may serve what we value. We think that caring about theoretical rationality is part of caring about our other projects because rationality has instrumental value.[8] But of course sometimes it does not—as when we may recognize that false belief will facilitate some important activity. However we diagnose the tension in such cases, the very fact that there is tension would seem to undermine any automatic translation from regulative to value priority.

If theoretical rationality draws authority from its relation to conditions of success in action and belief, perhaps the problem with impartial morality is that it does not serve our purposes. So it cannot just be part of caring about what we care about. An instrumental claim is made on behalf of morality by some contract theorists.[9] But it is hard to see how such a claim could be supported in Kantian ethics, given its rejection of heteronomous (subjective, interest-based) foundations and its commitment to there being substantive moral questions about ends. Morality can be seen as the expression of a highest order rational interest (as it is in Rawls), but that does not join the question of the relations between morality and interests per se, and motives of connection in particular.

One might argue that just as theoretical rationality and prudential practical rationality have their authority based in the fact that we are interest- and truth-pursuers, so morality has its authority based in some equi-primordial fact—say, of our sociality. We need not take the Humean circumstances of justice to be the full terms that define (or set) the moral agenda for success as a human being among others (of our kind, language, culture).[10] Along these lines, morality would be necessary (and in that sense instrumental) given the complex of requirements needed to support acceptable (or suitable) conditions of sociality. There is much to find attractive in this way of proceeding. And if sociality involved connection (as partiality) in an essential way, it would certainly ease the tension between morality and connection. But it is not clear what sociality (in this role) involves. And it is not in any case a form of argument that is readily available to the Kantian.

Where does this leave us? I want to accept that it is reasonable to expect a moral theory to give (noninstrumental) expression to the role that sociality and the partiality of connection play in a human life. To show that and how Kantian ethics does this, we must re-start the discussion

8. In a Humean mood one might conjecture that what we take theoretical rationality to be is that manner of thinking that promotes our ends: the method of thinking that works.

9. David Gauthier's *Morals by Agreement* (Oxford: Oxford University Press, 1986) offers an extremely sophisticated version of such an argument.

10. A recent example of such an account can be found in Stuart Hampshire, *Innocence and Experience* (Cambridge, Mass.: Harvard University Press, 1989).

taking instruction from the fact that the affective life is not (in general) independent of various norms of rationality. This creates space for the claim that connection itself could be partially dependent on or a function of moral value.

II

We begin then with acknowledgment that intimacy and connection are necessary not just to a happy human life but to the form of life that we call human. (This is to be understood in the sense that deprivation of the possibility of intimacy and connection threatens a person's humanity. Thus the peculiar violence of solitary confinement.)[11] And: the relationships between parents and children, between friends, lovers, neighbors, are essentially partial. It is because someone is *my* neighbor, lover, or child that I have reasons for action of a certain sort. Having these relationships is to have these reasons. They are reasons of considerable strength and/ or priority, and they are reasons such that acting on them (and not on other reasons that can produce the same outcomes) is important to maintaining the relationships that generate them. The importance of these reasons derives from connections of feeling, familiarity, love, etc.

If my child is among those who are at risk, I do not act for my child as a moral agent but as a mother. That is to say, even when morality permits mothers to act for their children first among others (and it will not always do this), I do not act for my child because morality permits it, but because I am his mother. To be a parent is to be a person constituted by a set of motives and reasons for action. This is a matter of personal identity. The strength of these reasons, their priority, and the fact that acting on them gives expression to constitutive commitments, all add to the sense that moral reasons—reasons that do not arise directly from the natural affective connection between parent and child—are out of place here.[12]

There have been different philosophical responses to these facts.[13] Some suppose they show the limits of morality as regulative of our concerns.[14] Not only are moral reasons not ubiquitous, they must stand aside when they conflict with personal commitments that are constitutive of selves. Others do not find in the facts reason to question the authority of morality but rather the claim of impartial morality to be the paradigm

11. That someone might choose a solitary life or live well without intimate connection to others no more undermines this fact about human beings than the possibility of extreme physical stoicism or a high pain threshold undermines the fact that physical assault interferes with successful human activity.

12. Thus Freud identifies an antisocial rather than a presocial role for the family in the "origins of society." But then as he sees it, there is a primal antagonism between the partiality of family and the sociality of "fraternal" bonds (see his *Civilization and Its Discontents* [New York: Norton, 1962], chap. 3).

13. I view them as facts about feelings we take to be reasons.

14. Bernard Williams's influential notion of constitutive "ground projects" provides the most direct version of this view (see "Persons, Character and Morality").

of moral concern. So, it may be claimed, just these sorts of reasons, with their grounding in feeling and connection, provide the model for a "morality of care" or, as some have argued, for the distinctive moral perspective of women.[15] With either response, any claim for the priority of impartial morality is rejected as a de-valuing of constitutive human concerns.

Such arguments against impartial morality are based on the feeling that our commitments and relationships of connection are (sometimes) of greater and/or deeper importance than those of impartial morality. But because it feels this way is reason to take such feelings seriously, not reason to give their claims automatic authority. For example: Part of what growing up as a parent involves is the recognition of the place and point of such feelings. I think it is generally true that one feels like hurting anyone who causes one's child undeserved pain, but that is not sufficient reason to do it. That someone close to you may suffer terribly in failing to get what he or she wants is not reason to make it happen when that is inappropriate. Sometimes it is the welfare of the loved one that is jeopardized by what one would do out of feeling. So the feeling needs to mature (or we who have the feeling need to mature); we need to be able to ask whether a particular expression of love is good for the one loved. And we sometimes need to let changes in those we love change our feelings (or what will count as expression of those feelings).

Since accepting limits set by autonomy, maturation, and change do not necessarily interfere with the way our supporting actions give expression to our connection with others, why should we be so easily disposed to accept that morality will interfere? We mistake the nature of feelings and their role in constituting our character to think that they are "original existences" whose modification cannot or should not be tolerated.

Let us look a little closer at the moral dimension of a relationship of connection. In addition to involving a deep bond of connection, parent-to-child is a relationship of *trust* between unequals: an essential kind of moral relationship that Annette Baier has argued cannot be expressed in impartial morality.[16] Trust, as Baier describes it, is a noncontractual moral relationship between persons where there is vulnerability on the one hand and an implied reliance on goodwill and caring on the other (explicit or not, conscious or not). Because it is centered on cool, voluntary relationships between equals, Baier contends that moral theories such as Kant's cannot provide guidance in these regions. Yet, as we must agree, "a complete moral philosophy would tell us how and why we should act and feel toward others in relationships of shifting and varying power asymmetry and shifting and varying intimacy."[17]

15. In addition to Gilligan and some of the essays in the Kittay and Meyers vol., see also N. Noddings, *Caring: A Feminine Approach to Ethics and Moral Education* (Berkeley: University of California Press, 1984).

16. Annette Baier, "Trust and Antitrust," *Ethics* 96 (1986): 231–60. (Reprinted here, pp. 11–40.)

17. Baier (p. 32 in this volume).

If there is tension between trust and the morality of impartiality, there is no secure alliance between trust and partiality.[18] From the fact that my child trusts that my concern for him will lead me to guard and preserve his well-being as I can, it does not follow that I violate his trust if I refrain from doing some things that will benefit him (because they are wrong or unfair) or if I act for someone else first, as when I tend to the younger child hurt in the playground, or expend finite resources on a needier sibling. What my son has reason to trust is that I am committed to his well-being: that among the things that matter to me most and that will determine how I act is that he do well and flourish. But, as I must often remind him (and myself), his interests are not the only ones I care about (there are not only my friends, my spouse, my students, and myself, but sometimes complete strangers or causes that claim my attention and resources), and further, he will do fine, indeed he will often do better, if he relies on me less, and if my life is increasingly separate from his.[19] Because I care about him, he can trust that I will count his well-being as among the basic facts that determine what I do, not as special reasons at work when I have to choose between his and someone's equal or greater claim, but as a set of changing needs that will partially (only) determine the shape of my life.

How we understand the role of impartial morality here depends upon how we represent its place in deliberation. I want to suggest that failure to recognize two quite different models of practical concern and deliberation leads to serious distortion of the problem thought to be posed by impartial morality to concerns of trust and connection. I will call them, for reasons that should become clear, the "plural interest" and the "deliberative field" models.

According to the first or plural interest model, where there is connection, there are those I care about, and the effect of my caring is to give their interests greater deliberative weight: for me. They matter more. And they matter more to me because I care about them. When I need to balance or weigh interests—should I do some good for my son or his friend—my son counts more. Of course I have a variety of interests and concerns, and they have different weights (as I care about them and as they matter directly and/or instrumentally). The interests of my child weigh more than the next career step which weighs more than my enjoyment of movies, and morality (if it has regulative priority) weighs more than all of the above. Deliberation involves further weighing and balancing. Inter-interest comparisons of various sorts will be necessary. The descriptions of interests will often need to be more qualified and

18. This, of course, is just an extension of Baier's point, reinforcing the claim that a moral theory must have the means to talk about connection, inequality, power, etc. (ibid.). A moral theory that cannot get it right about these relationships cannot generate the appropriate regulative norms.

19. Of course I would not have said this when he was six months old. But that is just the point.

situationally explicit: a minor desire of my child won't count against going to a film I've waited years to see, etc. There will be tension between looking to get the most interests satisfied and getting the most important interests satisfied. Over all these differently weighted interests looms the requirements of impartial morality in which I am not only supposed to have an interest, but an interest sufficient to support its supremely regulative role.[20]

On the plural interest model, when morality contends with attachments it forces one against the grain, attacking the immediacy of connection. It would be natural to feel hostile to or alienated from the requirements of morality if they in this way denied a deeply felt claim of partiality. I do not mean to suggest that one would necessarily feel alienated whenever one acts for morality in a context in which connection draws you in a different direction. There are many times, especially with children, when the fact that a choice must be made impartially provides the occasion for useful moral lessons. In such circumstances, acting impartially expresses trustworthiness. The problem arises when it looks like "over here" is what I most care about, what I want to happen (and cannot not want to happen), but "over there" is what impartial morality demands. There is then deep conflict and tension. And when impartial morality wins, it is not only at the expense of what I most care about, it provides no deliberative space even to acknowledge my concerns. The fact that I care about my son is in no way to affect the deliberative outcome.

If this is the way I see it, I can learn to take these losses, even to believe that they are necessary. They are the price you pay for . . . , and then some account of the role of morality that presumably justifies such losses by pointing to greater gains elsewhere. What other kind of justification of morality could work, given the imposition of losses? And if I am unmoved by the greater gains to be had elsewhere (often gains to be had by those other than myself or those I care about)—not because I am selfish, but because of who I am (a person who cares about . . .), then my life will not seem to be valued from the moral point of view. I will act either morally badly or against myself. Clearly, so long as we stick with the plural interest model, we will have difficulty negotiating the terrain between impartial morality and attachment.

Among the elements of a full moral theory we should find an account of how one is to integrate the requirements of morality into one's life. One could be someone whose interest in morality was an interest (if a very strong or strongest interest) among others. But such a connection to morality is not in itself morally neutral; it will follow from the substantive

20. It is not, of course, a necessary feature of the plural interest model that impartial morality have this role. I present it in this form because some such version of the plural interest model is commonly introduced in preparation for criticism of the implausibility of the demands of impartial morality. Although I am primarily concerned with the limited ability of this model to represent the claims of morality, the causes of its failure in this area suggest more general inadequacies.

nature of moral requirements. There is no unique atheoretic model of a morally serious or committed moral agent. Depending on how this feature of a moral theory is elaborated, there will be more than one answer to the question of the effects of moral requirements on the motives of connection. Since on the first, or plural interest model, commitment to morality is at the expense of other commitments, especially attachments, there will be reason to favor a different model if it is better able to integrate these elements in a morally good life.

On the second model, deliberation addresses a field only partially shaped by those commitments, concerns, and relationships that determine my conception of the good. They stand there as myself—as interests that I need no further (or instrumental) reason to care about. It is not that I care about my son and therefore when interests are to be weighed his weigh more. Rather, because I care about my son—because of the way I care about my son—his interests (his good) are part of my good: *the* good as I see it. But just as I know in advance that I cannot do whatever will promote my own well-being, so I know in advance and as part of my caring that I may not be able to promote his good when determining the effective practical weight of interests by how much I care about them is inappropriate.

According to this deliberative field model, the practical self does not have as its major task negotiating a settlement among independent competing claims. Insofar as one has interests and commitments, one is a (human) self. But a human life is not the resultant of a "bundle" of competing interests (among which is an interest in morality). One's interest are present on a deliberative field that contains everything that gives one reasons. Thus, in addition to interests and attachments, there are also grounds of obligation, principles of prudential rationality, and, depending on the individual, a more or less complex conception of the Good. Not everything that may seek a place on my deliberative field is good for me to have there: bad habits, destructive relationships, incompatible goals and projects. And if there is a real question about what enters (or remains on) the deliberative field—this is often a question about ends—the conditions for accepting desires or interests as ends may (and often will) shape the result.

An agent with a deliberative field partly constructed by moral principles recognizes from the outset, in the adoption of ends, that pursuit of important goals may unforeseeably lead one to means that are morally inappropriate (not permissible). The commitment to pursue an end is always conditional (this is so whether the ends are ends of interest or necessary ends). In this way ends are absorbed into a moral structure as they enter the deliberative field.

This resetting of ends in the deliberative field is not unique to moral requirements. Something analogous occurs because of potential practical conflict between different nonmoral goals. Wanting both to have a career of a certain sort and a family, I can pursue both and hope for the best, or I can give one end priority (absolute or weighted) over the other, or I can make action on one conditional on noninterference with the other. With other ends—say, teaching and writing—I have additional possibilities, including the revision of each of these ends to include aspects of the other (I value my teaching as an integral part of the process that leads me to successful writing, or vice versa). These need not be once and for all decisions: my sense of the relative importance of ends may change, the likelihood of conflict may diminish, still other relevant interests may come on the scene. But having set ends in a complex deliberative framework, my sense of loss on abandoning one is different than it would be if I thought of myself simply as acting for diverse and separate goals having to give up or limit or frustrate one for the sake of another. Acting from a deliberative framework, I am in a better position to accept the outcome. This is not a matter of resignation so much as acknowledgment. Absent such a framework, the decision will seem more contingent— more a matter of bad luck—and the outcome arbitrary.[21]

To make sense of the deliberative field model (and so, I believe, of Kantian ethics),[22] we must resist the tendency to think of the Good—an agent's conception of what is good—as a composite cluster of objects of desire, perhaps structured by priority principles and other success-oriented practical devices which are external to the ends we have in virtue of the desires we have. This leaves the desire-object relation too much intact, and the agent passive with respect to her bundle of desires. Desires do not give reasons for action: they may explain why such and such is a reason for action, or even why something can be an effective reason for action, but the desire itself is not a reason. One can take the fact of a desire to be a reason, but that just is to hold that desire, or this desire, is good.[23] Nor is it enough to replace desire with "end that it is rational or good to have." That still suggests discrete sets of interests and ends. What is missing—what you are supposed to learn as a maturing agent— is the integration and transformation of the ends in light of one another, of one's practical situation, and of one's conception of place and impor-

---

21. I do not mean to imply that desire must be understood to have its practical effect only in one of these two ways—in the deliberative field or as an intensity-weighted reason. There are accounts of desire that build reasons into them. In the tradition of Kant criticism, however, the simpler Humean model of desire has been thought to suffice in showing the weaknesses of the Kantian account of practical activity. The deliberative field model is intended both to describe more accurately Kantian practical deliberation and activity and to show certain limits of the simple Humean model.

22. Although I do not argue for it here, plainly I see this model as Kant's. Textual and other support for this can be found in my "Obligation and Performance," in *Identity, Character and Morality*, ed. A. Rorty and O. Flanagan (Cambridge, Mass.: MIT Press, 1990).

23. I have borrowed this way of putting things from Philippa Foot (manuscript, 1988), who sees confusion about this occurring because so often it is reasonable to satisfy desires. If we imagine a very different sort of creature who had desires that were not in general good (for it) to satisfy, it is not clear how we would then regard "desires."

tance understood through the regulative principles—aesthetic, moral, prudential—one accepts. One has, or tries to have, a good life.

We will be inclined to view deliberation differently as we take ourselves to be either active or passive with respect to our desires. If we take the paradigmatic deliberative situation to be either means-end calculation or the resolution of conflict between ends, it will look as though our starting point is the pursuit of discrete goods (the objects of desires or interests) whose compatibility is a matter of luck. Now sometimes this is just the way things are. Circumstances can sharpen conflict, as they can make deliberation look like a search for the least costly compromise. But focusing on these cases reinforces a sense of our passivity as agents: what Kant meant, I believe, by a heteronomy of the will.

Our sense of things is different if we look instead at the ways we are or can be active with respect to our desires. We have desires we do not want to act on; we have desires we act on but do not value; we come to discover that some of what we want is caused by needs that would be better met some other way (as when an underlying insecurity leads to placing excessive demands on others). Refusing desires of the last two types is importantly not like restraining one's desire for sweets: a kind of desire we like to think we can turn our back on at will (or fail at controlling because of "weakness of will"—a kind of muscular insufficiency). Activity involves more than effective second-order wants.

When, for example, I hear my mother's parental anxieties in my voice as I criticize my son, I cannot resolve the problem I discover just by abandoning some end or disowning some desire, however much distress I feel about what I am doing. Part of what I discover in these moments is who I am—or who I am as a parent. I listen and find out what I desire. But then it is not enough to say that I do not want to act on these desires, and also not enough to say that I do not want to have them. I want them not to have a place in the complex of desires and thoughts that constitute myself as a parent. This may be no easy thing, for the very desires I would disavow may hold together things I like about myself as a parent.

Someone who is otherwise a good friend cannot come through when there is illness involved: he simply cannot see what there is to do. Suppose that he comes to believe that he acts inadequately in these circumstances. What can he do? He wants to act as a good friend. He has the relevant ends. The problem is that illness makes him panic. Perhaps as a child he was made to feel responsible for a sick parent. Now, confronted with illness in others, he feels inadequate; he withdraws in the face of what he feels will be certain failure.

When we discover that with our children or our friends we are acting in ways that do not match our values or ideals, the practical task involves special difficulties, in the sense that we must come to see why we would do what we do not seem to want to do (this is importantly *not* weakness of will). Success at this task may still leave us trying to figure out what to do with (or what we are able to do with) what we find. This is a function of what we might think of as the enmeshedness or even geology of desire.

Encountering (or more often stumbling against) such a complex, we may be enlightened or transformed, or moved to therapy, or despair. Affective disorders alert us to inertial features of character. We cannot just choose to care (about some things), and we cannot just prize out an unwanted desire by identifying and rejecting its object. So also we come to see that you cannot just add ends: not only because there may be conflict in realizing ends but also because the adoption of ends (some ends) resonates in the deliberative field. For the good friend to lose his panic in the face of illness, he may have to revise his relations with his mother (now and in the past).

The point here is not to argue for therapy or discuss the relative merits of deep versus shallow psychological change, but to let the difficulty of these matters direct us to a different picture (or set of pictures) about the Good as the complex object, not of desire, but of practical agency.

If the attempt to abandon ends may draw us into more complexity than expected, we should not suppose that adopting an end is any simple matter either. Ends are not adopted in isolation from one another. It is not just that their joint pursuit may not be possible. Adopting an end is (or can be) wanting some interest to be effective in my life. This may alter other ends I already have and affect what ends I may come to have. Wanting friendship to play a greater role in my life does not just mean creating more time for friends (and so less for the pursuit of other ends). It may make me see in my present attachment to other ends a lack of concern for others. Or vice versa: coming to take my work more seriously may reveal a will to distraction in my absorption with others. (When everything works for the best, this kind of insight need not lead to a conflict with friendship: it can make me a better friend.)

Because of the complexity of relations among ends, it can be difficult to predict the outcome of deliberation—for another agent, but equally, sometimes, for ourselves. We may not know in advance what impact circumstances will have on ends. When situations are new or complex, what an agent wants can depend on her response to the situations she finds herself in and on the way she makes use of whatever knowledge and sensitivity she can bring to bear. Some deliberative outcomes will reshape ends, others can lead her to see the world in a different way. Deliberation itself will then reshape or reconfigure the deliberative field.

Deliberation structured by *substantive* regulative principles involves still more. If, for example, in all of my relationships I am to treat people as ends, then as this conception has deliberative priority, what is possible for me in relationships will be different. My ends of friendship and intimacy will not be what they would have been otherwise. It is not that I must replace motives of connection with moral motives; I will have *different* motives of connection. Perhaps I will be more sensitive to problems of exclusion or of fairness. Perhaps I will be less tempted to interfere "for the best." It does not follow from the interpenetration of motives of connection with moral concerns that these will be the changes: what the changes are will depend on what I discover about the structure and tendencies of my relationships.

This transformational process does not go only one way. Commitment to treat others as ends (or in accordance with the dictates of some moral conception or ideal) does not by itself guide deliberation. As I come to understand more of what is involved in friendship and intimacy, so I also come to see more of what the moral requirement amounts to. Without knowledge of how intimacy engages vulnerabilities, I cannot see that or how certain behaviors which could be acceptable among strangers are impermissibly manipulative among intimates (and vice versa). Where power and/or inequality mix with intimacy, questions of exploitation and abuse are raised. Such questions are not part of the concept of treating persons as ends. They are what we discover treating persons as ends amounts to, given what human relationships tend to be like, or what particular relationships involve. Absent such knowledge, moral judgment is not possible.[24]

Let us briefly retrace our steps. I wanted to argue that the sense of conflict and loss that we think follows from the regulation of relationships and attachments by impartial moral principles might instead be a function of the way we understood the connection between ends and deliberative principles. The discussion of the difference between activity and passivity with respect to our desires and ends was aimed, on the one hand, to defeat a picture of an autarchy of ends slotted into a legalistic or merely formal deliberative framework and, on the other hand, to replace that picture with the idea of the Good as a constructed object of practical agency.[25] Locating attachments in a deliberative field we uncover a mutual practical dependence between formal moral principle (as it applies to us) and the structure of attachment.

Some resistance to this move may come from a presumed tension between moral and personal reasons that follows from a split in the practical between the moral and the natural. There is the thought that personal attachments—and especially what is good in them—are in some special way natural or spontaneous or pure. So one might worry that moral transformation might involve loss of this natural good. This concern is to be met with the reminder that "natural" relationships are, among other things, the locales of abuse, infantilization, exploitation, and other sins of intimacy. Intimacy may be a natural need, or arise from natural motives, but the relationships among adults usually are, when healthy, complex and much mediated descendants of spontaneous or natural attachments.

24. This more general conclusion of this sort is argued for in my "The Practice of Moral Judgment," *Journal of Philosophy* 82 (1985): 414–36.
25. See John Rawls, "Themes in Kant's Moral Philosophy," in *Kant's Transcendental Deductions,* ed. E. Förster (Stanford, Calif.: Stanford University Press, 1989), pp. 90–95.

When there is moral criticism of a relationship, we should not think that morality aims to replace the structure of attachment. Love for another may be necessary to effectively change a relationship whose premises or practices are morally faulty. Morality alone can do no more than indicate the fault and give reason not to accept terms of relationship in which the fault is embodied; it cannot by itself direct the parties to a satisfactory resolution *within* the framework of intimacy.

As our conception of the Good becomes increasingly complex (involving morality but also work and children and the various kinds of intimacy), our understanding of our activities and attachments should reflect that complexity. This is not a loss of innocence that we have reason to reject (or rationally regret).

If the deliberative field were empty[26] until the agent brought to it— from outside, as it were—her interests, projects, and commitments, looking to use its principles to maximize satisfaction while attending to the demands of morality, one could safely predict frustration of one for the sake of satisfaction of the other. If the deliberative field is not empty at the outset, things look different. The alternative, or Kantian, model suggests that we think of an agent's deliberative field as containing representations of her interests, projects, and commitments that have been "normalized" to varying degrees to the principles of practical agency, both moral and nonmoral. Kantian deliberation requires the prior processing of the material it takes up. Maxims and ends we know to be impermissible, if attractive, are represented as such; tasks we would take up as means toward desired goals are not represented as independently valuable (unless they also are); and so on. The normalization of the material of interest and desire to the principles of practical agency minimizes the degree to which deliberation and choice must involve sorting and weighing things of incommensurable or conflicting value.

Desires and interests are normalized to beliefs and values as well. Take a nonmoral example. Suppose it is normal (given certain patterns of upbringing, socialization, etc.) that, faced with certain kinds of situations, people have sharply competitive reactions. For one sort of person, these reactions may be taken as the direct and natural response to a challenge, and so give reason to act competitively. Someone else may have a view about the etiology of such reactions in herself (anxiety, status-hunger, aggression) that leads her to conclude that they should not be taken at face value: in and of themselves they are not reason-giving. If one describes the effects of such psychological facts as introducing a deliberative problem when circumstances provoke the reaction in question, the second person is misdescribed in an important way. Suppose that in addition to recognizing the origins of the competitive impulse in herself the second person believes that the kinds of action it generates are by and large counterproductive

---

26. Using metaphors this way will eventually—if not immediately—be misleading. But since all talk about deliberation is metaphoric (formalized versions no less so), the limits and presuppositions of the different pictures are worth exploration.

(or just contrary to what she holds is good). She need not be faced with a choice each time the reaction occurs, for she does not regard the reaction as making a claim or having automatic reason-giving status. One might say that the impulse to competition enters her deliberative field already discounted, if it enters at all.

Discounted impulses need not be entirely "counted out." The agent in the second case may believe that letting a competitive response regulate action can sometimes be useful. But even when it is, the impulse to competition is normalized in the agent's deliberative field to the discounted value. (That is, it is indulged for a special purpose; acting on it is not, in the usual way, an expression of competitiveness.) One could, I suppose, think that such impulses are held in check and then in special circumstances set free. But it seems truer to the pattern of increased and practically effective self-knowledge that the desires themselves be modified, or at least under principled constraint in the way they are given access to the deliberative field. It is not just the pressure they exert that gains them entry.[27]

The advantage gained from taking natural motives to be normalized to the principles of practical agency is that it eliminates the deliberative quandary of having always to choose between natural motives and moral motives (or even motives of prudence). Without this, the tension between natural and moral concerns seems unavoidable: a tension which will recur within the domain of the moral between virtues and moral requirements insofar as the virtues rely on natural motives (like compassion). If the natural motive of compassion has as its object the well-being of another, normalized compassion—concern for another framed by a practical awareness of the place of compassion in the moral life (suppose this is right)—would not shift the object of compassionate concern. It is still the welfare of the other that is sought in acting. What would change is the impact of the motive in the deliberative field. A natural motive is effective as it is strong. A normalized motive is effective as a function of its place in the deliberative field: expressing more than the natural impulse at its origin, standing aside (not pressing its claim) as there are more important concerns present, but also drawing strength from its place in an overall practical conception.[28]

There is great complexity here. Motives can be embedded in or connected to other motives. Some concerns can absorb deep constraints without damage; others are fragile. Requiring civility while doing the grocery shopping introduces no grave distortions in the activity. A demand

---

27. The psychological models moral theorists use in these contexts are frequently unwarrantedly simple. We might want to think about sublimation, or other strategies of object-shifting (the mechanism of delayed gratification involves not just a willingness to wait for some [often indefinite] good, but also a release of focused task-oriented energy).

28. Bishop Butler's distinction between the strength and the authority of a motive might help here (*Five Sermons* [Indianapolis: Hackett, 1983], p. 39).

that one justify all nonnecessary expenses from the point of view of world hunger might well interfere with reasonable enjoyments. But this is a problem, if it is, of a substantive moral requirement. It does not follow from the formal fact that motives (or interests or concerns) are normalized to impartial moral principles.

Let me be clear about what I am *not* trying to say. The normalization of a natural motive does not eliminate the possibility of conflict with other moral considerations and claims. This discussion has been about the structure of deliberative commitments. The likelihood that the world will throw up difficulties is not diminished, though perhaps one will be, in a manner of speaking, better prepared when they occur.

Still, one might worry that too little is left for deliberation to do because the process of "normalizing" has covertly usurped its work. If one thinks that deliberation brings its principles to bear on raw data, this would be so. Part of what I have wanted to present here are reasons for thinking this is not true to experience. Two larger theoretical concerns give me confidence that this way of treating deliberation is appropriate. First is the fact that Kantian deliberation, if it in any way engages with the Categorical Imperative procedure, applies to maxims, and maxims require exactly the normalized input I have described.[29] Second is a view about what a practical commitment to morality amounts to. The moral agent (certainly the Kantian moral agent) is not one who has some set of desires and interests and then introduces an onlay of controlling principles and rules (with a new motive to get the regulative authority right). She is rather someone who takes the fact of morality to be constitutive of herself (or her identity as a moral person) and for whom the normalization of desires and interests is a way of making them her own.

Deliberation is not called for unless the agent finds reasons in her circumstances of action or choice to believe that normal moral constraints should not apply. So, for example, in cases of threat, or danger, or pressing need, one may need to deliberate to determine whether such facts ground a rebuttal of the moral prohibition on, say, deceit. But such facts ground a rebuttal, if they do, not because of the degree of one's concern but because they mark the presence of additional moral facts in an agent's deliberative field.

The upshot of this discussion for the questions with which we started can be put somewhat simply. When understood within the deliberative field model, the regulative or transformative priority of impartial morality does not cause the loss or corruption of motives of connection. We can resist the idea that any constraint of a natural motive, any move to relocate it in a structure of justification, gives it a new object. Once attachment is moved into the deliberative field, however, we must acknowledge that strength or intimacy of attachment alone does not provide grounds to rebut the demands of moral requirement.

29. This is argued in sec. 1 of my "The Practice of Moral Judgment."

If in deliberation moral requirement is not external to other motives, and if our understanding of morality and attachment are mutually transformative, then the motives of connection themselves can come to express the fact that attachment takes place in a world attachment alone does not create.

III

Having argued that there is no obvious or necessary incompatibility between impartial ethics and the value of attachment, we still need to consider arguments that claim the particular assumptions of Kantian ethics make it inimical to a sound notion of the person as moral subject.

A typical argument goes this way. In Kantian ethics, we are moral agents insofar as we have practical reason (an autonomous will). Other facts about us—what we feel, how we are connected to others, that we are empirically, socially, and historically situated—are not what make us moral agents. Since "Kantian" persons have moral value insofar as they are moral agents, the moral value persons have does not reflect their situation or attachments (neither that we in general have them, nor how, in particular, having them makes a difference). If these omitted features are central to our ideas of what a person is (and of the good for persons), then the substantive normative claims of Kantian ethics are derived from an inadequate and impoverished concept of the person as moral agent.[30] If this is true, it is a serious problem. For even if, as argued in Section II, moral deliberation is informed by the facts of our attachments, interests, and specific needs, the moral principles that construct the deliberative field have their source in the "pure" autonmous self.

Kantian autonomy is the property the rational will has of being self-legislating. This is a metaphysical claim about the nature of rational agency. Its role is to explain both the possibility and authority of morality. Nothing follows from it to the effect that persons are radically separate, nor that insofar as we take the moral point of view we are not to pay attention to the distinctive features of other persons. As I need not, because I am an agent with interests, look out at the world and others from a fortress of own-interests and desires, so equally, as a moral agent, I do not look out on a world of featureless moral agents because I have an autonomous will. Whether I am preoccupied with myself or engaged with others and sensitive to differences depends on my circumstances and my conception of the Good. Perhaps it is this last bit that is the source of the problem.

Kantian ethics constrains a conception of the Good by requiring that one's deliberative field be given a certain structure (a structure implied

---

30. As one critic writes, "Why assume that the sole form of human autonomy adequate to support our moral theory is one that an agent [has] in isolation from her contingent ends, her culture, history, and relations to others?" (Sally Sedgwick, "Can Kant's Ethics Survive the Feminist Critique?" *Pacific Philosophical Quarterly* 71 [1990]: 60–79, p. 22).

by the nature of rational agency itself). In particular, we are never to act on a maxim that we cannot will all rational beings act on. But, it is argued, this cannot be the right way to derive moral principles for persons, since filtering for what is possible for all rational beings (or even all human beings) cannot tell the full moral story about fully embodied and socially connected persons in specific historical settings.

We can see some of the force of this concern by looking at a second kind of criticism of Kantian autonomy. The identification of Kantian autonomy as the property of a rational will seems to ignore morally important ways in which we judge that human beings are or can fail to be autonomous. If one has Kantian autonomy just in case one is a rational being (able to act on self-given principles), Kantian autonomy may be a necessary but not a sufficient condition for "real" moral autonomy. Ordinarily, we have reason to think that the autonomous person is not merely one who can act on principles but is, rather, the person whose situation and/or upbringing yields not only a character capable of practically effective critical reflection but also a character moved by desires and interests that are in some important sense her own: that is, desires and interests that are neither the result of coercion nor the products of institutionalized oppression.[31] Lack of autonomy in this sense is compatible with Kantian autonomy. The question then is whether the Kantian conception of autonomy obscures a real issue of human autonomy, and, if it does, whether it implies that oppression cannot interfere with (the most important kind of) human freedom.

I want to argue that the Kantian conception of the autonomous agent neither elevates rationality to the only thing that really counts (morally) about persons nor forces us to deny that agency is compromised by the circumstances of oppression. It is true that the "worth-beyond-price" of the Kantian agent is in her autonomous will. This is the ground of the claim that persons are not to be valued only for use. The contested question is whether the constraints on action that follow from this ignore the real circumstances and full nature of persons.

The best way to answer the question is to look carefully at the way specific constraints work. What I will offer here is a summary examination of the restrictions on deceit and coercion: actions that are the archetypes of impermissible "use" of another. What the restrictions show is that the subject of moral protection is the fully situated human agent.

Deceit is an attempt to control the way another will choose to act through the introduction of relevant false beliefs into her deliberative circumstances. In coercion, threats or force alter deliberative circumstances by evoking or strengthening desires that will bring the victim to act as the coercer wills. In both cases, the impermissible actions constitute an

---

31. I do not mean to suggest that such desires are easy to identify, though at critical times they may come to the surface not only as plainly alien—not mine—but also as identifiably other (certain desires for approval, dispositions to defer, etc.).

assault on the situated integrity of the victim's agency. You would not, for what deceit or coercion do to you, cease being an autonomous agent. Deceit and coercion invade the morally supported boundaries between autonomous agents in that the aggressor regards the *situated* will—the will as it draws reasons from beliefs and desires—as a possible means to her ends.[32]

This story does not quite describe the moral wrong involved in deceit, since I look to control the will of another when I introduce true beliefs to get someone to act as I will.[33] The problem clearly is not control of the will in the sense of contributory cause to a deliberative outcome, since that is the case whether what I tell you is true or (known by me to be) false.

What others tell us is one of the normal ways we have access to the facts in our circumstances of action (and belief). This is an inescapable fact about human agency. Our reliance on what others say creates an area of vulnerability—a point of access to the will. Although what I want in telling you the truth can be the same as when what I say is false—that you do what I will—the full story about how I am acting can be, in morally important ways, different. In some cases when I say what is true, I tell the truth only as what I need to say in order to get you to do what I will. I have no commitment to telling you the truth in telling you the truth. If the truth will not bring you to do what I will, I am ready to tell you something else.[34] When, by contrast, I tell you the truth as truth, though I believe that if you know this truth you will do what I will (and I even tell it to you wanting you to act as I will), I tell you the truth as information of use to you as well as me. Insofar as I conceive of what I give you as information, the intent is not to control your will, though it is to contribute to the causal (here, deliberative) conditions of your action. On this principle of action, I would not tell you something if I believed it was not the case.

Of course things are not so simple. If I tell misleading partial truths, I am equally taking advantage of our situation in order to create a view of the circumstances of action which will lead you to act as I want. This kind of truth-telling is a kind of deceit. You take me to be giving relevant information, in part because I lead you to believe that is what I am doing, but also in part because it is a normal expectation that I know of and rely on. This expectation is for you a condition of belief formation. That is why you must not catch on that I am controlling the flow of information if I am to get you to act as I will. You are deceived in that you are brought (encouraged) to believe falsely that I have told you whatever I know that is relevant to your deliberation, choice, and action. And this is why when I tell you a partial truth I am manipulating your will.

---

32. The arguments for this interpretation of the Kantian objections to coercion and deceit can be found in "Moral Deliberation and the Derivation of Duties" (in my *The Practice of Moral Judgment* [Cambridge, Mass.: Harvard University Press, in press]).

33. The same problem arises with offers.

34. There are problems involving counterfactuals that we can ignore here.

The importance of this for our question about Kantian agency lies in the fact that what counts as deceit varies with the persons involved, the social conditions of expectations, particular practices, etc. That is, if impermissible actions are those which fail in respect for the value of the autonomous agent, respect for the autonomy of another person in cases where we wish to influence deliberation requires detailed attention to specific facts about them. This will include facts about relationships (where one person has authority over another, or responsibility for another, expectations are affected), as well as facts about the social world that bear on their circumstances of action.

The point of morality, one might say, is to regulate what can go on given the vulnerabilities of persons as agents—vulnerabilities we all share as human rational beings *and* vulnerabilities that are specific to our situations and relationships. Thus the constraints morality imposes reflect the real conditions of effective human rational agency: the aspects of a person's circumstances of action (or deliberation) that are situated, historical, empirical. As I read it, Kantian morality not only does not ignore these features, it makes them central to its "derivation of duties."

In effect, much of the critique of the Kantian conception of autonomy confuses autonomy and agency. Autonomy is the condition of the will that makes agency possible. If we were not rational beings we would not have wills that could be interfered with. But *agency* is not completely described by identifying a will as rational. As human agents we are not distinct from our contingent ends, our culture, our history, or our actual (and possible) relations to others. Agency is situated. The empirical and contingent conditions of effective agency set the terms of permissibility because it is through effective agency that autonomy is expressed (made real). Here is a place where consequences matter.

The implications of the idea of deriving Kantian duties from the situation of real agents are far-reaching. If agency is situated, the conditions of agency will not be uniform. Certain features will remain constant: that we have vulnerable bodies, are mortal, are capable of acquiring new skills, that we are deceivable and vulnerable to duress. Other features will be a function of the social world in which a person acts. Matters of institutionalized subordination, dependency, questions of gender, class, and race, will need to be taken into account. This encourages us to move beyond the "agent-to-agent" limitations of traditional interpretations of Kantian ethics, where everything that is morally relevant is found in the actions and intentions of single, separate persons.[35]

35. Textual support for such a move is not wanting. In elaborating the duties of beneficence, Kant attends to the special moral situation of the recipient of charity: a person receiving charity is in a position in which his or her dignity and sense of self-worth is fragile. Kant recommends that charity be given in such a way that the giver "make it felt that he is himself obliged by the other's acceptance or honored by it, hence that the duty is merely something that he owes" (*The Doctrine of Virtue,* trans. H. J. Gregor [Philadelphia: University of Pennsylvania Press, 1971], p. 121). And see Victor J. Seidler, *Kant, Respect, and Injustice* (London: Routledge & Kegan Paul, 1986) for a sensitive if highly critical treatment of Kant's views on these issues.

Suppose, for example, social circumstances are such that the possible range of successful activities is dramatically limited by inability to read and/or write (both in terms of opportunities to act but also for gaining skills and developing talents). Illiteracy prevents the acquisition of information necessary to effective action. In such circumstances, denial of opportunity to become literate could be judged an impermissible refusal (under mutual aid) to provide for agency-necessary needs. Since literacy is not normally a good that functions outside an institutional context—schools, publishers, etc.—the moral failure in providing real access to literacy skills will not be one that is best or completely described as occurring between individuals. (I think a similar argument can now be made for provision of a minimal standard of health care.) It does not follow that one is committed to viewing literacy as necessarily making people better off regardless of their cultural circumstances. The point is to explain the circumstances in which literacy could become a moral requirement: the ground of a moral claim.[36]

In analogous fashion, there is room to talk about institutional or cultural assaults on the conditions of agency. If agent-to-agent coercion controls choice by manipulating desires (introducing penalties in order to block permissible choices), then when institutions penalize permissible choices, they act no less coercively. (The chief difference in the moral analysis is, I think that in the institutional case there can be coercion without specific intent.) Quite apart from issues of dependency and lack of alternatives, it can be hard to understand the battered wife's refusal to leave her home, with its violence, without factoring in the effect of social pressures that measure adult success in terms of a woman's ability to maintain a marriage.[37]

On similar grounds I regard a recent controversy over the introduction of new brands of cigarettes targeted at particular, vulnerable groups as capturing the institutional variant of the wrong involved in agent-to-agent deceptive manipulation. Uptown and Dakota brand cigarettes were to be marketed to inner city blacks and "virile females," respectively. Now the fact that advertising works by playing on beliefs and desires is not news. But since the conditions which make deceit possible vary from person to person and group to group, it is precisely the fine-tuning of the ad campaign to trade on marks of social prestige among those both young and doubly disadvantaged that makes the moral case. (It is hard here not to see intent; but there will be other similar cases where the belief in the information conveyed is more credible. Certainly it was a stunning moment of the Uptown episode when a Philip Morris executive labeled as racist those who argued against the Uptown campaign on the grounds that it would exploit the special vulnerabilities of young blacks.)

36. Kant, of course, makes education as well as welfare a moral task of the state (and as such the grounds for coercion through taxation) (see *The Metaphysical Elements of Justice,* trans. J. Ladd [Indianapolis: Bobbs-Merrill, 1965], p. 93).

37. Lenore E. Walker, *The Battered Woman Syndrome* (New York: Springer, 1984).

On the basis of these brief remarks I want to offer two provisional conclusions. First, if agency is situated, then the fundamental moral equality of agents requires that we attend to difference when it affects the capacity for effective agency. And second, if agency is situated, and groups of people share vulnerabilities and needs that rise from institutional or nonuniversal cultural causes, then there are grounds for moral criticism of those causes that appeal to the same root values as ground agent-to-agent requirements.

This section began with a question about the relations among Kantian views of autonomy, rationality, and agential separateness. There has been no attempt to deny that autonomy and rationality are deeply connected and that both are the condition of our moral and practical capacities. On the other hand, the tremendous practical importance of autonomy and rationality in understanding the kind of agent we are does not force us to view ourselves as, from the moral point of view, wholly, or essentially, or even ideally, rational. As we are practical agents—human agents—we are constituted by our needs, our interests, our beliefs, and our connections to others. Different aspects of our agency will be peculiar to our "natural" condition, our social circumstances, and our particular histories. We will be free human agents—ones whose actions express autonomy—as the actual conditions of our agency allow us to deliberate and act according to a conception of the Good that is constructed not only by moral requirements but also by the pursuit and critical attention to interests that we can understand to be part of a good life.

Two Kinds of Respect*

Stephen L. Darwall

I

An appeal to respect as something to which all persons are entitled marks much recent thought on moral topics. The appeal is common both in writings on general moral theory and in work on particular moral problems. For example, such writers as John Rawls, Bernard Williams, David Gauthier, R. S. Downie, and Elizabeth Telfer refer to the respect which is due all persons, either in arguing for or in articulating various moral principles.[1] The idea is not particularly new, since one of the keystones of Kant's ethics is the view that respect for the moral law entails treating persons (oneself included) always as ends in themselves and never simply as means. Precisely what Kant meant, or should have meant, by this is a matter of some controversy, but it is generally thought that the same claim is expressed in saying that one must respect persons as such.[2]

The appeal to respect also figures in much recent discussion of more specific moral problems such as racism or sexism. For example, it is argued that various ways of regarding and behaving toward others, and social arrangements which encourage those ways, are inconsistent with the respect to which all persons are entitled.

* I am indebted to several of my colleagues at Chapel Hill, to Lawrence Crocker and Stephen Hudson, and to the editor of *Ethics* for help with this essay.

1. John Rawls, *A Theory of Justice* (Cambridge, Mass.: Harvard University Press, 1971); Bernard Williams, "The Idea of Equality," in *Moral Concepts,* ed. Joel Feinberg (Oxford: Oxford University Press, 1970), pp. 158–61; David Gauthier, *Practical Reasoning* (Oxford: Oxford University Press, 1963), pp. 119–20; R. S. Downie and Elizabeth Telfer, *Respect for Persons* (London: Allen & Unwin, 1969).

2. Kant, *Foundations of the Metaphysics of Morals,* trans. L. W. Beck (Indianapolis: Bobbs-Merrill Co., 1959), hereinafter *FMM.* See especially p. 46 (Ak. p. 428), where Kant claims that "rational beings are designated persons because their nature indicates that they are ends in themselves." See also *The Metaphysical Principles of Virtue,* trans. James Ellington (Indianapolis: Bobbs-Merrill Co., 1964), pp. 96–98, 112–14, 130–33. It is interesting to observe in this connection the rather different use that various writers have made of the Kantian principle. Both Rawls and Robert Nozick invoke it in support of quite different substantive conceptions of justice; see Rawls, passim; and Nozick, *Anarchy, State, and Utopia* (New York: Basic Books, 1974), p. 32.

This essay originally appeared in *Ethics,* vol. 88, no. 1, October 1977.

The claim that all persons are entitled to respect just by virtue of being persons may not seem wholly unproblematic, however. How could respect be something which is due to all persons? Do we not also think that persons can either deserve or fail to deserve our respect? Is the moralist who claims that all persons are entitled to respect advocating that we give up this idea? Questions of this sort should call into question just what respect itself is.

Other questions about respect appear as soon as one starts to press. Is respect a single kind of attitude? Is it primarily, or even solely, a moral attitude? Are persons the only sort of thing to which respect is appropriate? Everyone at least understands the coach who says that his team must respect the rebounding strength of the opposing team's front line. No moral attitude is involved here. Nor may persons be respected only as persons. Frank may be highly respected as a weaver, Sarah as a doctor.

II

Several writers have in fact given explicit attention to what constitutes respect for persons. On most such accounts it is a willingness to take into consideration one or another aspect of persons when one's actions affect them. Candidates for the relevant aspects of persons which are owed our consideration are their wants,[3] their point of view on a particular situation,[4] and the like. These accounts are not intended as general accounts of respect. They are only meant to give some more specific content to what it is that persons are entitled to by virtue of being persons.

One notable exception to such accounts is a recent attempt by Carl Cranor to give a general account of respect.[5] Cranor holds respect to be a complex relationship which obtains between two persons (the respecter and the respected), some characteristic (the basis of respect), and some evaluative point of view (from which the person is respected). This relationship consists, roughly, in the respecter's judging that the person's having the characteristic is a good thing (from the relevant point of view), his appreciating why it is a good thing, and his being disposed to do what is appropriate to the person's having that characteristic.

III

One problem that infects each of the accounts mentioned as a general theory of respect is that each fails to distinguish two rather different ways in which persons may be the object of respect. Or, as I am inclined to say, two rather different kinds of attitude which are both referred to by the term

---

3. Gauthier, p. 119; and Downie and Telfer, p. 29.
4. Williams, p. 159; and Rawls, p. 337.
5. Carl Cranor, "Toward a Theory of Respect for Persons," *American Philosophical Quarterly* 12 (October 1975): 303–19.

'respect.'[6] The two different ways in which a person may be respected provide but one instance of a more general difference between two attitudes which are both termed respect. Crudely put, the difference is this.

There is a kind of respect which can have any of a number of different sorts of things as its object and which consists, most generally, in a disposition to weigh appropriately in one's deliberations some feature of the thing in question and to act accordingly. The law, someone's feelings, and social institutions with their positions and roles are examples of things which can be the object of this sort of respect. Since this kind of respect consists in giving appropriate consideration or recognition to some feature of its object in deliberating about what to do, I shall call it *recognition respect*.

Persons can be the object of recognition respect. Indeed, it is just this sort of respect which is said to be owed to all persons. To say that persons as such are entitled to respect is to say that they are entitled to have other persons take seriously and weigh appropriately the fact that they are persons in deliberating about what to do. Such respect is recognition respect; but what it requires as appropriate is not a matter of general agreement, for this is just the question of what our moral obligations or duties to other persons consist in. The crucial point is that to conceive of all persons as entitled to respect is to have some conception of what sort of consideration the fact of being a person requires.

A person may not only be the object of recognition respect as a person. As Erving Goffman has shown in great detail, human beings play various roles, or present various "selves," both in their interactions with others and in private before imagined audiences.[7] Others may or may not respond appropriately to the presented self. To fail to take seriously the person as the presented self in one's responses to the person is to fail to give the person recognition respect as that presented self or in that role. It is this sort of respect to which Rodney Dangerfield refers when he bemoans the fact that neither his son nor his wife takes him seriously as a father or a husband with the complaint, "I can't get no respect."

There is another attitude which differs importantly from recognition respect but which we likewise refer to by the term 'respect.' Unlike recognition respect, its exclusive objects are persons or features which are held to manifest their excellence as persons or as engaged in some specific pursuit. For example, one may have such respect for someone's integrity, for someone's good qualities on the whole, or for someone as a musician. Such respect, then, consists in an attitude of positive appraisal of that person either as a person or as engaged in some particular pursuit. Accordingly the appropriate ground for such respect is that the person has manifested charac-

---

6.   Though I prefer to put the point in this way, nothing crucial hangs on it. I could as well speak throughout of two different ways in which persons may be the object of respect.

7.   Erving Goffman, *The Presentation of Self in Everyday Life* (Garden City, N.Y.: Doubleday & Co., 1959).

teristics which make him deserving of such positive appraisal. I shall later argue that the appropriate characteristics are those which are, or are based on, features of a person which we attribute to his *character*.

Because this sort of respect consists in a positive appraisal of a person, or his qualities, I shall call it *appraisal respect*. Unlike recognition respect, one may have appraisal respect for someone without having any particular conception of just what behavior *from oneself* would be required or made appropriate by that person's having the features meriting such respect. Appraisal respect is the positive appraisal itself. It is like esteem or a high regard for someone, although, as I shall argue later, the appropriate grounds for appraisal respect are not so broadly based as those of these latter attitudes.

Typically, when we speak of someone as meriting or deserving our respect, it is appraisal respect that we have in mind. We mean that the person is such as to merit our positive appraisal on the appropriate grounds. It is true that in order to indicate or express such respect, certain behavior from us will be appropriate. But unlike recognition respect, appraisal respect does not itself consist in that behavior or in the judgment that is appropriate. Rather, it consists in the appraisal itself.

In giving this characterization of appraisal respect, it would seem that I am giving no role to *feelings* of respect. Just as one ma, be said to have feelings of admiration so one may be said to feel respect for another. Although I won't pursue this point further, I suggest that such feelings may be understood as feelings which a person would explain by referring to his or her positive appraisal of their object. Just as we understand the feeling of fear to be that which is explained by one's belief in the presence of danger, so the feeling of respect for a person is the one which is occasioned by the positive appraisal which constitutes appraisal respect for that person.[8]

My project in this paper is to develop the initial distinction which I have drawn between recognition and appraisal respect into a more detailed and specific account of each. These accounts will not merely be of intrinsic interest. Ultimately I will use them to illuminate the puzzles with which this paper began and to understand the idea of self-respect.

IV

The most general characterization which I have given of recognition respect is that it is a disposition to weigh appropriately some feature or fact in one's deliberations. Strictly speaking, the object of recognition respect is a fact. And recognition respect for that fact consists in giving it the proper weight in deliberation. Thus to have recognition respect for persons is to give proper weight to the fact that they are persons.

One can have recognition respect for someone's feelings, for the law, for the judge (in a legal proceeding), for nature, and so on. In each case such

---

8. For a similar account of the moral sentiments see Rawls, pp. 481–82.

respect consists in giving the appropriate recognition to a fact in one's deliberations about how to act. It is to consider appropriately, respectively, the fact that a person feels a certain way, that such and such is the law, that the person one is addressing is the judge, that the object one is confronting is part of nature, and so forth. To respect something in this way is just to regard it as something to be reckoned with (in the appropriate way) and to act accordingly.

On this very general notion of recognition respect, any fact which is something that one ought to take into account in deliberation is an appropriate object. As it stands, then, the notion has somewhat wider application than what we would ordinarily understand as respect, even of the recognition sort.

One rather narrower notion of recognition respect conceives of it as essentially a moral attitude. That is, some fact or feature is an appropriate object of respect if inappropriate consideration or weighing of that fact or feature would result in behavior that is morally wrong. To respect something is thus to regard it as requiring restrictions on the moral acceptability of actions connected with it. And crucially, it is to regard such a restriction as not incidental, but as arising because of the feature or fact itself. One is not free, from a moral point of view, to act as one pleases in matters which concern something which is an appropriate object of moral recognition respect. To have such respect for the law, say, is to be disposed to regard the fact that something is the law as restricting the class of actions that would be morally permissible. It is plainly this notion which we have in mind when we speak of respect for persons as a moral requirement. Accordingly, when I speak of recognition respect below, I shall be referring specifically to moral recognition respect.

There are attitudes similar to moral recognition respect, and referred to as respect, but which differ importantly. A boxer talks of having respect for his opponent's left hook and an adventurer of respecting the rapids of the Colorado. Neither regards the range of morally permissible actions as restricted by the things in question. Rather each refers to something which he fails to consider appropriately at his peril. What is restricted here is the class of prudent actions. Thus a careful crook who has no moral recognition respect for the law per se may still be said to have this sort of respect for the power that the law can wield. Here again we have the idea that the object of respect (or some feature or fact regarding it) is such that the class of "eligible" actions is restricted. But in this case the restriction is not a moral but a prudential one. Some people hesitate to use the word 'respect' when speaking of such cases. That makes no difference. All that matters is that we understand what the attitude comes to and thus how it is like and unlike moral recognition respect.

As we are understanding recognition respect it includes a component of regard. To have recognition respect for something is to regard that fact as itself placing restrictions on what it is permissible for one to do. It is of course true that one can "be respectful" of something without having any respect for it (even of a recognitional sort). This will be the case if one behaves as one who does have respect would have behaved, but out of motives other than respect. For example, a person participating in a legal proceeding who in fact has no respect for the judge (i.e., for the position he occupies) may take great pains to be respectful in order to avoid a citation for contempt. Such a person will restrict his behavior toward the judge in ways appropriate to the role that he plays. But his reason for so doing is not that the mere fact of being the judge is itself deserving of consideration, but that the possibility of a contempt citation calls for caution.

Importantly, the sort of regard involved in recognition respect is a regard for a fact or feature as having some weight in deliberations about how one is to act. This is rather different from the sort of regard involved in appraisal respect.

V

The latter sort of respect is a positive appraisal of a person or his character-related features. As such it does not essentially involve any conception of how one's behavior toward that person is appropriately restricted.

I have distinguished appraisal respect for persons judged as persons from appraisal respect for persons assessed in more specific pursuits. As I shall later argue in more detail, those excellences of persons which are the appropriate grounds for appraisal respect for a person as such are those which we delimit as constituting character. I shall also have something more specific to say by way of a rudimentary account of character.

Appraisal respect for a person as such is perhaps a paradigm of what people have in mind when they speak of moral attitudes. On the other hand, appraisal respect for persons judged in more particular pursuits need not be. The particular virtues or excellences of a particular pursuit may either be irrelevant or even bear negatively on an overall appraisal of the person judged as a person. To be highly respected as a tennis player, for example, one must demonstrate excellence in tennis playing which is not primarily excellence of character. At the very least one must be a good tennis player and that will involve having abilities which are in themselves irrelevant to an appraisal of the tennis player as a person. Even in such cases, however, respect for a person assessed in a particular pursuit seems to depend on features of his character (or his excellence as a person) in at least two ways.

To begin with, somebody may be an excellent tennis player without being a highly respected one. He may be widely acclaimed as one of the best players in the world and not be widely respected by his fellows—though they may (in the extended recognition sense) respect his return of serve, his vicious backhand, and so on. Human pursuits within which a person may earn respect seem to involve some set of standards for appropriate and inappropriate behavior within that pursuit. In some professions this may be expressly articulated in a "code of ethics." In others it will be a more or less informal understanding, such as that of "honor among thieves." To earn respect within such a pursuit it is not enough to exercise the skills which define the pursuit.

One must also demonstrate some commitment to the (evolving) standards of the profession or pursuit.

Even in a game like tennis one can lose the respect of other players by paying no attention to such standards of behavior. If a player constantly heckles his opponent, disputes every close call to throw off his opponent's concentration, or laughs when his opponent misses shots, then even if his skill is such that he would be capable of beating everyone else without such tactics, he is not likely to be respected as a tennis player. Thus, insofar as respect within such a pursuit will depend on an appraisal of the participant from the perspective of whatever standards are held to be appropriate to the pursuit, such respect will depend on a judgment to which excellences of character are thought relevant. Note that exactly what aspect of the person's character is thought to be relevant in this instance is his recognition respect (or lack of it) for the standards of the pursuit.

Second, even when we attend to those features of a person which are the appropriate excellences of a particular pursuit and involve no explicit reference to features of character, the excellences must be thought to depend in some way or other on features of character. The point here is that purely "natural" capacities and behavior manifesting them are not appropriate objects of appraisal respect, although perhaps of recognition respect, even in the context of a fairly narrowly defined human pursuit.[9] If someone is capable of some feat (which may be widely admired) solely by virtue of, say, his height, then neither this feat nor the person's ability to perform it are appropriate objects of respect—just as one cannot respect an ant for its ability to carry comparatively large objects long distances to the anthill, though one may be appropriately amazed.

This is because it is almost never the case that human accomplishments are a result of simple natural ability. Talents and capacities of various sorts are prerequisites for various accomplishments, but almost invariably talents must be developed, disciplined, and exercised in the face of various obstacles, and this will call into play features of persons which we identify as part of their character.

Which features of persons are properly regarded as features of their characters and hence as appropriate grounds for appraisal respect? Being resolute and being honest are character traits. Being prone to sneeze in the presence of pepper is not. But there are difficult cases as well. How about being irascible? Or being good natured? Or prudent? Discerning? Sensitive?

The notion of character (whether of persons or other things) seems to involve the idea of relatively long-term dispositions. But not all long-term dispositions of persons are held to be parts of their characters. The question then becomes, which such dispositions constitute character?

I have suggested that those features of persons which we delimit as constituting character are those which we think relevant in appraising them

---

9. On this point see Cranor, p. 312.

as persons. Furthermore, those features of persons which form the basis of appraisal respect seem to be those which belong to them as moral *agents*. This much Kantianism is, I think, at the core of the conception of the person which we generally hold to be relevant to appraisal respect. If this is true, then there may be other features of human beings, for example their capacity for affective sympathy, which are not encapsulated in the conception of the person which is relevant to appraisal respect. As Kant wrote, "Rational beings are designated 'persons' because their nature indicates that they are ends in themselves."[10] Those features of persons which are appropriate grounds for appraisal respect are their features as agents—as beings capable of acting on maxims, and hence, for reasons.[11] Thus, there may well be characteristics of human beings which are regarded as *human* excellences but which are not appropriate grounds for appraisal respect. For example, warmth in one's dealings with other human beings is regarded as an excellence of humanity, but may be irrelevant in the appraisal of persons which constitutes appraisal respect. Compare lack of warmth or being stiff in one's relations to others to deliberate cruelty as a ground for failing to have appraisal respect for someone. Of course, lack of personal warmth is an appropriate ground for failing to have appraisal respect for someone to the extent that we conceive such a lack to be the result of insufficient effort on the person's part. But insofar as we so conceive it, we regard it as a lack in the person's agency: an unwillingness to do what is necessary to treat others warmly.

If the appropriate conception of the person which is relevant to appraisal respect is that of a moral *agent*, then one would expect our notion of character to be likewise tied to such a conception. I think that this is indeed the case. Those dispositions which constitute character (at least as it is relevant to appraisal respect) are dispositions to act for certain reasons, that is, to act, and in acting to have certain reasons for acting. For example, honesty is a disposition to do what one takes to be honest at least partly for the reason that it is what honesty requires. Aristotle's theory of virtue and Kant's theory of the moral worth of actions both stress that what is appropriate to the assessment of persons is not merely what they do, but as importantly, their reasons for doing it.[12]

As it stands the conception of character as constituted by our dispositions to act for *particular* reasons is inadequate. This account captures such par-

---

10. *FMM*, p. 46.

11. Thus Kant: "Only a rational being has the capacity of acting according to the conception of laws, i.e., according to principles" (*FMM*, p. 29).

12. Aristotle argues that character is constituted by our dispositions to *choose*, where the notion of choice is held to involve the idea of picking an alternative on some grounds or other (see, e.g., *Nicomachean Ethics*, 1112a15, and Book VI, chaps. 12–13). Especially relevant here is Aristotle's distinction between a "natural disposition" to virtuous qualities and virtue "in the strict sense" which involves a self-reflective habit of acting on the "right rule" (*Nicomachean Ethics*, 1144b1–28). Kant's famous discussion of the good will and the moral worth of actions as grounded in the "principle of the will," i.e., the agent's reason for acting, is in the first section of *FMM*.

ticular character traits as honesty, fairness, kindness, and the like. But there are other dispositions of persons which we hold to be part of their character, and thus relevant to appraisal respect, but which are not best thought of as dispositions to act for particular reasons. For example, we may fail to have appraisal respect for someone because we regard him to be weak of will or not sufficiently resolute. What is referred to here is not a disposition to act for any particular reason, but rather the higher-level disposition to act on what one takes to be the best reasons whatever they may be. Thus, the conception of character which is relevant to appraisal respect includes both rather more specific dispositions to act for certain reasons and the higher-level disposition to do that which one takes to be supported by the best reasons.

Two final points need to be made about appraisal respect. First, not every positive attitude toward a person on the ground of his or her character amounts to appraisal respect for that person. If I want to pull a bank heist and am looking for partners, I may look for someone who has no reservations about stealing (at least from banks) and who can be counted on to threaten violent action and, if need be, carry it out. Thus, I may have a favorable attitude toward such a person on the ground that he has those particular character traits. But my having that attitude toward such a person is not the same thing as my having appraisal respect for him for having those traits. This attitude fails of being appraisal respect in that my having it toward the person is *conditional* on those traits being such as to make him serve a particular purpose that I happen to have—heisting the bank. In order for the attitude toward the trait, or toward the person for having it, to constitute appraisal respect it must not be thus conditional on such an interest or purpose. We may employ some Kantian terminology here and say that it must be a *categorical* attitude, one which is unconditional on the fact that the traits in question happen to serve some particular purpose or interest *of mine*.[13]

The second point is that appraisal respect is something which one may have or fail to have for someone, *and* it is an attitude which admits of degree. One may respect someone more than someone else. When we speak of having or not having respect for someone what is implied is an appraisal of him as satisfactory with respect to the appropriate grounds. Many attitudes have this sort of structure. We speak alternatively of liking and not liking things as well as of liking something more than something else.

To sum up: Appraisal respect is an attitude of positive appraisal of a person either judged as a person or as engaged in some more specific pursuit. In the first case, the appropriate grounds are features of the person's char-

---

13. See Kant's distinction between hypothetical and categorical imperatives in *FMM*, sec. 2. This idea of unconditionality on one's interests (i.e., on the fact that they are one's interests) is involved in Hume's notion of "moral sense" and Butler's notion of the "principle of reflection." David Hume, *A Treatise of Human Nature*, ed. L. A. Selby-Bigge (Oxford: Oxford University Press, 1967), p. 472; Joseph Butler, *Sermons* (New York: Liberal Arts Press, 1950), p. 27.

acter: dispositions to act for particular reasons or a higher-level disposition to act for the best reasons. In the second case, though features of character do not exhaust the appropriate grounds for appraisal respect, some such character traits will be relevant (recognition respect for the standards of a particular pursuit). Also, the other features which constitute the appropriate excellences of the pursuit must be related to traits of character in the way specified. In both cases, the positive appraisal of the person, and of his traits, must be categorical. It cannot depend on the fact that the person, because of his traits, serves an interest or purpose of one's own.

Appraisal respect brings into focus the idea of virtue. Much of recent moral philosophy has been exclusively concerned with the assessment of actions or social institutions. However, an account of the appropriate grounds for appraising persons, the virtues, is also a proper concern of moral philosophers.

VI

Since appraisal respect and recognition respect may both have persons, conceived of as such, as their objects, it is important to distinguish them as attitudes.

To have recognition respect for someone as a person is to give appropriate weight to the fact that he or she is a person by being willing to constrain one's behavior in ways required by that fact. Thus, it is to recognition respect for persons that Kant refers when he writes, "Such a being is thus an object of respect *and, so far, restricts all (arbitrary) choice*."[14] Recognition respect for persons, then, is identical with recognition respect for the moral requirements that are placed on one by the existence of other persons.

This is rather different from having an attitude of appraisal respect for someone as a person. The latter is a positive appraisal of an individual made with regard to those features which are excellences of persons. As such, it is not owed to everyone, for it may or may not be merited. When it is, what is merited is just the positive appraisal itself.

To bring out the difference between recognition respect and appraisal respect for persons as such, consider the different ways in which the two attitudes may be said to admit of degree. When one person is said to be more highly respected as a person than someone else, the attitude involved is ap-

---

14. *FMM*, p. 428, emphasis added. Cranor is by no means alone in confusing recognition respect with appraisal respect. Hardy Jones faults Kant's identification of respect for persons with being disposed to treat persons as ends in themselves on the grounds that: "To respect a judge or a parent is not merely to behave in specific deferential (and thus 'respectful') ways. It is also to have a certain attitude toward them and to regard them in certain ways. 'To respect a person' is often properly used to mean 'to think well of him' " (Hardy Jones, *Kant's Principle of Personality* [Madison: University of Wisconsin Press, 1971], p. 75). If we interpret Kant as identifying recognition respect for persons as such with a willingness to treat persons as ends in themselves no such problem arises. See also Downie and Telfer, p. 18, for another instance of this confusion.

praisal respect. One's appraisal of a person, considered as a person, may be higher than of someone else. Consider the instruction to order a list of persons according to one's respect for them. The natural way to respond would be to rank the persons in the light of one's appraisal of them as persons.

What sense can be given, however, to degrees of recognition respect? For example, a person might think that we should have more respect for people's feelings than for social conventions. Presumably what such a person thinks is that we ought to weigh other people's feelings more heavily than we do considerations of social convention. Insofar as we can give a sense to having more recognition respect for one thing than another it involves a disposition to take certain considerations as more weighty than others in deciding how to act. There is, of course, a kind of appraisal involved here. But it is not an appraisal of a person as such, but of the weight that some fact or feature ought to have in one's deliberations about what to do, and if all persons as such should be treated equally, there can be no degrees of recognition respect for them, although one may be a greater or lesser respecter of persons.

The confusion between appraisal respect and recognition respect for persons as such infects the account of respect for persons given by Cranor. He intends his account to capture the sort of respect that it is claimed persons are entitled to by virtue of being persons. Part of his account is the claim that for one person to have respect for another there must be some characteristic that the respected person is believed to have, and the possession of which is held to be a good thing from some point of view. Cranor fleshes this out with the following remarks: "In respecting a person we are giving him credit for having some trait or characteristic . . . the believed characteristic in virtue of which one respects a person must be believed to be a good-making characteristic of persons or contingently connected to a good-making characteristic of them."[15]

These remarks apply only to appraisal respect for persons. When one is appraising an individual as a person, those features which merit a positive appraisal are good-making characteristics of persons. Or to use the language of Cranor's other remark, they are to his credit as a person. On the other hand, to have recognition respect for a person as such is not necessarily to give him *credit* for anything in particular, for in having recognition respect for a person as such we are not appraising him or her as a person at all. Rather we are judging that the fact that he or she is a person places moral constraints on our behavior.

The distinction between appraisal respect and recognition respect for persons enables us to see that there is no puzzle at all in thinking both that all persons are entitled to respect just by virtue of their being persons and that persons are deserving of more or less respect by virtue of their personal characteristics.

Though it is important to distinguish between these two kinds of respect,

15. Cranor, p. 312.

there are connections between them. I will mention two in particular. First, there will be connections between the grounds of one's appraisal respect, or lack of it, for particular persons and the considerations which one takes as appropriate objects of recognition respect. For example, if one judges that someone is not worthy of (appraisal) respect because he is dishonest, one is committed to recognition respect for considerations of honesty. Our appraisal of persons depends on whether they show the appropriate recognition respect for considerations which merit it. The account of character brings this out. Second, the only beings who are appropriate objects of appraisal respect are those who are capable of acting for reasons and hence capable of conceiving of various facts as meriting more or less consideration in deliberation. Once again, so much is entailed by the account of character. Because of the particular sorts of reasons which are relevant to our assessment of character, we may say that the only beings who are appropriate objects of appraisal respect are those who are themselves capable of recognition respect, that is, of acting deliberately.

VII

Both recognition respect for persons as such and appraisal respect for an individual as a person are attitudes which one can bear to oneself. Accordingly, these two kinds of self-respect must be distinguished.

Consider the following remark of Virginia Held's: "For persons to acquiesce in the avoidable denial of their own rights is to lack self-respect."[16] What 'self-respect' refers to here is recognition respect for oneself as a person. The passage is obviously false when we take it to refer to appraisal respect for oneself as a person. To acquiesce in the avoidable denial of one's rights is to fail to respect one's rights as a person. Exactly what such self-respect requires depends on what moral requirements are placed on one by the fact that one is a person.

It is recognition self-respect to which we appeal in such phrases as "have you no self-respect?" hoping thereby to guide behavior. This is not a matter of self-appraisal but a call to recognize the rights and responsibilities of being a person. As a person capable of recognition respect, one is liable to reflective appraisal of one's own behavior, and as such has a *stake* in it—that stake being appraisal self-respect or self-contempt.

One's behavior can express a lack of recognition self-respect in different ways. It may have a negative effect on one's ability to continue to function as a person. Such behavior is self-destructive, and therefore manifests a lack of appropriate regard for oneself as a person. If not actually self-destructive, behavior may be degrading in expressing a conception of oneself as something less than a person, a being with a certain moral status or dignity. Submitting to indignities, playing the fool, not caring about whether one is taken

---

16. Virginia Held, "Reasonable Progress and Self-Respect," *Monist* 57 (January 1973): 22.

seriously and being content to be treated as the plaything of others may or may not be actually self-destructive but nevertheless manifests lack of self-respect.[17] Exactly what behavior is so regarded depends both on the appropriate conception of persons and on what behaviors are taken to express this conception or the lack of it. Certainly the latter is something which can vary with society, convention, and context.

One may give adequate recognition to the fact that one is a person and still have a rather low opinion of oneself as a person. People appraise themselves as persons, and the attitude which results from a positive appraisal is appraisal self-respect. Like appraisal respect generally, the appropriate grounds for appraisal self-respect are those excellences of persons which we delimit as constituting character.

It is important, therefore, to distinguish appraisal self-respect from other attitudes of appraisal which one can bear to oneself. One such attitude is that which we normally refer to as *self-esteem*.[18] Those features of a person which form the basis for his self-esteem or lack of it are by no means limited to character traits, but include any feature such that one is pleased or downcast by a belief that one has or lacks it. One's self-esteem may suffer from a low opinion of, for example, one's appearance, temperament, wit, physical capacities, and so forth. One cannot always be what one would wish to be, and one's opinion of oneself may suffer. Such a failing by itself does not give rise to lack of appraisal self-respect, although it might suffer if one attributed the failing to a lack of will, an inability to bring oneself to do what one wanted most to do. So far forth the failing would be regarded as arising from a defect in one's character and not solely from, for example, a lack of physical ability.

The self-appraisal which constitutes self-respect is of oneself as a person, a being with a will who acts for reasons. The connection between respect and agency is striking. Recognition respect consists in being disposed to take certain considerations seriously as reasons for acting or forbearing to act. On the other hand, appraisal respect consists in an appraisal of a person on the basis of features which are part of, or are based on, his or her character. And we conceive a person's character to consist in dispositions to act for certain

17. Kant's writings on self-respect are especially useful here; see *Lectures on Ethics* (New York: Harper & Row, 1963), pp. 118–19. The place of respecting one's own autonomy is especially important in the Kantian idea of self-respect. For some illuminating comments about servility and its relation to a recognition of oneself as a person, see Thomas E. Hill, Jr., "Servility and Self-Respect," *Monist* 57 (January 1973): 87–104.

18. To some degree Rawls's remarks on self-respect in *A Theory of Justice* suffer from a confusion between self-respect and self-esteem. (This point is developed in Larry L. Thomas, "Morality and Our Self-Concept," forthcoming in the *Journal of Value Inquiry*.) Rawls's explicit account of self-respect (p. 440) is very close to my notion of appraisal self-respect. In other places, however, it seems to be the more broadly based attitude of self-esteem that he has in mind. This is especially clear in his remarks on the connection between natural shame and self-respect (p. 444). It is an interesting question to what extent this conflation affects his account of self-respect as a primary good and his argument for the proposed principles of justice.

sorts of reasons together with the higher order disposition to act for what one takes to be the weightiest reasons. Thus, the appropriate conception under which a person is appraised as worthy of respect is as a being capable of recognition respect for those things which are entitled to it. This is what connects the two kinds of respect. The one is the attitude which is appropriate for a person to bear, as an agent, toward those things which deserve his or her consideration in deliberation about what to do. The other is an attitude of appraisal of that person as just that sort of being, a being capable of expressing such consideration in action.

Integrity*

Lynne McFall

> Olaf (upon what were once knees)
> does almost ceaselessly repeat
> 'there is some shit I will not eat'
> [e. e. cummings][1]

Integrity is a complex concept with alliances to conventional standards of morality—especially those of truth telling, honesty, and fairness—as well as to personal ideals that may conflict with such standards.[2] When we speak of the integrity of a politician, for example, we mean that she keeps her campaign promises, does not lie to her constituents, is fair to adversaries, will not participate in shady deals, bribe taking, cover-ups, scams of any sort. On the other hand, when Stephen Dedalus declares his independence from all authority except his own, he does so in the name of integrity but without respect for conventional standards: "I will not serve that in which I no longer believe whether it call itself my home, my fatherland or my church: and I will try to express myself in some mode of life or art as freely as I can and as wholly as I can, using for my defense the only arms I allow myself to use—silence, exile, and cunning."[3] In the first case, conformity to conventional standards of truth telling, honesty, and fairness is required; in the second, it is not. Integrity in the sense of being true to oneself may require being false to others, in spite of Polonius's famous claim to the contrary.

* I would like to thank James Fishkin, Robert Fogelin, Bernard Gert, Rebecca Holsen, John Kekes, and Brent Spencer for valuable criticisms of an earlier draft of this paper.

1. e. e. cummings, *Complete Poems* (New York: Harcourt Brace Jovanovich, 1980), p. 339.
2. According to the *Oxford English Dictionary*, compact ed., "integrity" means "soundness of moral principle; the character of uncorrupted virtue, especially in relation to truth and fairdealing; uprightness, honesty, sincerity." The *American Heritage Dictionary* says that integrity is "strict personal honesty and independence." *Webster's Third New International Dictionary* defines "integrity" as "an uncompromising adherence to a code of moral, artistic, or other values; utter sincerity, honesty, and candor; avoidance of deception, expediency, artificiality, or shallowness of any kind."
3. James Joyce, *A Portrait of the Artist as a Young Man* (New York: Viking Press, 1968), pp. 246–47.

This essay originally appeared in *Ethics*, vol. 98, no. 1, October 1987.

My aim in this paper is to give an account of integrity that does justice to both senses, as well as clarifying the relation between them.

There is a temptation to make this task too easy by drawing a distinction between *moral* and *personal* integrity and saying that moral integrity requires truth telling, honesty, and fairness while personal integrity does not. I think this is a mistake, for two reasons.

First, integrity appears to be consistent with deception. If you are living in Germany in World War II and a Jew is hiding in your basement, no one except Kant would claim that you suffer a loss of moral integrity if you tell the Nazi at the door that you are the only one home.

Second, whether or not one's principles are conventional, one's relation to them cannot be. This is brought out in Tolstoy's story, "The Death of Ivan Ilych."[4] Ivan says, "Maybe I did not live as I ought to have done. . . . But how can that be, when I did everything properly?"[5] At first he dismisses the possibility that his life has been all wrong; he has, after all, lived in conformity with "legality, correctitude and propriety." It is only after his sickness and being cared for by the peasant Gerasim that he questions this: "It occurred to him that what had appeared perfectly impossible before, namely that he had not spent his life as he should have done, might after all be true. It occurred to him that his scarcely perceptible attempts to struggle against what was considered good by the most highly placed people, those scarcely noticeable impulses which he had immediately suppressed, might have been the real thing, and all the rest false."[6] The point is not that the principles he subscribed to were "false," although they probably were, but that his relation to them was false, that is, inauthentic. He simply bought "his" principles wholesale from those around them. A *merely* conventional relation to one's principles seems to rule out personal integrity. One must speak "in the first person," make one's principles, conventional or otherwise, one's own.[7]

The apparent centrality of honesty to the concept of integrity may reflect a general but defeasible commitment to what is taken to be a "sound moral principle,"[8] allowing for cases of deception where this is morally condoned or required, or it may be a reflection of a requirement that is fundamental to both personal and moral integrity: coherence.

4. Leo Tolstoy, "The Death of Ivan Ilych," in *The Short Novels of Tolstoy,* trans. Aylmer Maude (New York: Dial Press, 1946). There is a good discussion of this story in Ilham Dilman and D. Z. Phillips, *Sense and Delusion* (Atlantic Highlands, N.J.: Humanities Press, 1971).

5. Tolstoy, p. 462.

6. Ibid., p. 466.

7. "At the end of my lecture on ethics, I spoke in the first person. I believe that is quite essential. Here nothing more can be established, I can only appear as a person speaking for myself" (Ludwig Wittgenstein, quoted by Fredrich Waismann, "Notes on Talks with Wittgenstein," *Philosophical Review* 74 [1965]: 16). This passage is also quoted by Dilman (in Dilman and Phillips), who makes this point with respect to a person's moral beliefs (pp. 123–24).

8. See n. 2 above.

I shall begin with an account of integrity in its least value-laden sense—coherence—and attempt to build from there.

COHERENCE

Integrity is the state of being "undivided; an integral whole."[9] What sort of coherence is at issue here? I think there are several.

One kind of coherence is simple consistency: consistency within one's set of principles or commitments.[10] One cannot maintain one's integrity if one has unconditional commitments that conflict, for example, justice and personal happiness, or conditional commitments that cannot be ranked, for example, truth telling and kindness.

Another kind of coherence is coherence between principle and action. Integrity requires "sticking to one's principles," moral or otherwise, in the face of temptation, including the temptation to redescription.

Take the case of a woman with a commitment to marital fidelity. She is attracted to a man who is not her husband, and she is tempted. Suppose, for the purity of the example, that he wants her too but will do nothing to further the affair; the choice is hers. Now imagine your own favorite scene of seduction.

After the fact, she has two options. (There are always these two options, which makes the distinction between changing one's mind and weakness of the will problematic, but assume that this is a clear case.) She can (1) admit to having lost the courage of her convictions (retaining the courage of her mistakes) or (2) rewrite her principles in various ways (e.g., by making fidelity a general principle, with exceptions, or by retroactively canceling her "subscription"). Suppose she chooses the latter. Whatever she may have gained, she has lost some integrity. Weakness of the will is one contrary of integrity. Self-deception is another.[11] A person who admits to having succumbed to temptation has more integrity than the person who sells out, then fixes the books, but both suffer its loss.

A different sort of incoherence is exhibited in the case where someone does the right thing for (what he takes to be) the wrong reason. For example, in Dostoevsky's *The Devils*, Stepan Verkhovensky says, "All my life I've been lying. Even when I spoke the truth. I never spoke for the sake of the truth, but for my own sake."[12] Coherence between principle and action is necessary but not sufficient. One's action might *correspond* with one's principle, at some general level of description, but be inconsistent

9. *Oxford English Dictionary*, s.v. "integrity."

10. I say "principles or commitments" because I don't think it is necessary that one subscribe to some principle to have integrity, and one can have commitments other than to principles, e.g., to one's deepest impulse or to a person, without those being redescribable in terms of principles.

11. Gabriele Taylor makes this point more elaborately in "Integrity," *Proceedings of the Aristotelian Society Supplement* 55 (1971): 143–59.

12. Quoted by Dilman (in Dilman and Phillips), p. 70.

with that principle more fully specified. If one values not just honesty but honesty for its own sake, then honesty motivated by self-interest is not enough for integrity.

So the requirement of coherence is fairly complicated. In addition to simple consistency, it puts constraints on the way in which one's principles may be held (the "first-person" requirement), on how one may act given one's principles (coherence between principle and action), and on how one may be motivated in acting on them (coherence between principle and motivation). Call this *internal coherence*.

An appeal to dishonesty in these three cases—the inauthentic Ivan Ilych, the self-deceived adulterer, and the lying truth teller—is not necessary to justify the claim that these persons lack integrity; the internal incoherence of the inauthentic, the self-deceived, and the impurely motivated is sufficient.

Dishonesty to others might be characterized as a form of incoherence: between behavior and belief. There is a split between what one believes and what one says (or otherwise suggests) one believes. So it could be for this reason that dishonesty constitutes a lack of personal integrity.

This requirement, however, may be too strong. What about the *honest* deceiver, who says to himself "I am not what I am"? It may be thought that only internal coherence is required for integrity, so that there is no contradiction in speaking of the integrity of an Iago or of a Machiavelli. On the other hand, it seems odd to speak of a loss of integrity in the *failure* to lie, scheme, and murder or, in general, the failure to be ruthless. But if internal coherence were sufficient for integrity, then internal incoherence would be the only way it could be lost.

Similarly in the case of the weak-willed. Suppose one's *principle* is "Yield to temptation; it may not pass your way again." In a case where the promising adulterer goes home alone, not through any moral compunctions but for lack of nerve, it may sound strange to call it weakness of the *wanton* will. But our intuitions are pulled both ways.

One explanation of our conflicting intuitions is that we import our own evaluative judgments into judgments of integrity. Integrity is like happiness in this respect. We may refuse to *call* a person happy if his values seem to us shallow or corrupt, even if he has met his own standards and is satisfied as a consequence.[13] Thus the old dispute about whether the evil can be "truly" happy. There is a demand, legitimate or not, that he get his values right (or what we take to be right).

The same may be true of integrity. Consider the principled adulterer. Although it may seem linguistically odd to speak of weakness of the wanton will in her failure to yield to temptation, the oddness may come from the moral connotations of *temptation* or from a false assumption—that her principle is wantonness—rather than the value that is really at

13. See R. M. Hare, *Freedom and Reason* (Oxford: Oxford University Press, 1963), p. 128.

stake: romantic love. Most of us take love to be a great if not the greatest good. And it's rare enough. So the principle is not simply a joke. If she holds this value very highly, and if she is prepared to sacrifice social approval and all the other goods that go to the conventionally moral for it, then personal integrity may be consistent with adultery; may even require it. If, on the other hand, we reject this line of defense (as the adulterer's husband is likely to do), then we may want to deny an ascription of integrity altogether. Which way we are inclined to go will depend on our own moral beliefs and on our willingness to inflict our moral or personal standards on others.

To summarize the argument so far: personal integrity requires that an agent (1) subscribe to some consistent set of principles or commitments and (2), in the face of temptation or challenge, (3) uphold these principles or commitments, (4) for what the agent takes to be the right reasons.

These conditions are rather formal. Are there no constraints on the *content* of the principles or commitments a person of integrity may hold?

INTEGRITY AND IMPORTANCE

Consider the following statements.

Sally is a person of principle: pleasure.

Harold demonstrates great integrity in his single-minded pursuit of approval.

John was a man of uncommon integrity. He let nothing—not friendship, not justice, not truth—stand in the way of his amassment of wealth.

That none of these claims can be made with a straight face suggests that integrity is inconsistent with such principles.

A person of integrity is willing to bear the consequences of her convictions, even when this is difficult, that is, when the consequences are unpleasant. A person whose only principle is "Seek my own pleasure" is not a candidate for integrity because there is no possibility of con-flict—between pleasure and principle—in which integrity could be lost. Where there is no possibility of its loss, integrity cannot exist.

Similarly in the case of the approval seeker. The single-minded pursuit of approval is inconsistent with integrity. Someone who is de-scribable as an egg sucker, brownnose, fawning flatterer cannot have integrity, whatever he may think of the merits of such behavior. A com-mitment to spinelessness does not vitiate its spinelessness—another of integrity's contraries.

The same may be said for the ruthless seeker of wealth. A person whose only aim is to increase his bank balance is a person for whom nothing is ruled out: duplicity, theft, murder. Expedience is *contrasted* to a life of principle, so an ascription of integrity is out of place. Like the pleasure seeker and the approval seeker, he lacks a "core," the kind of commitments that give a person character and that make a loss of integrity possible. In order to sell one's soul, one must have something to sell.

The following objection might be raised.[14] Suppose my principle is "Seek my own pleasure," yet I cravenly yield to the temptation to act from moral conviction, which in calm moments I regard as an unfortunate residue of early socialization. Or I might fail to live up to my principle simply by sacrificing greater long-term pleasure, for example, putting my extra cash into an IRA, when tempted by lesser but more immediate satisfaction, buying cocaine, say. A similar case could be made for the approval seeker and the profit seeker.

This objection seems to me sound. Intuitively, though, these three are not even candidates for integrity. How, then, are we to support the intuition that integrity rules out adherence to certain principles or at least to explain it?

Most of us, when tempted to "sell out," are tempted by pleasure, approval, money, status, or personal gain of some other sort. The political prisoner under the thumbscrew wants relief, however committed he may be to the revolution. Less dramatically, most of us want the good opinion of others and a decent standard of living. Self-interest in these forms is a legitimate aim against which we weigh our other concerns. But most of us have other, "higher," commitments, and so those who honor most what we would resist are especially liable to scorn.

This tendency to objectify our own values in the name of personal integrity can best be seen, I think, in a more neutral case. Consider the following claim:

> The connoisseur showed real integrity in preferring the Montrachet to the Mountain Dew.

Even if he was sorely tempted to guzzle the Mountain Dew and forbore only with the greatest difficulty, the connoisseur, we would say, did not show integrity in preferring the better wine. Why? Resisting temptation is not the only test of integrity; the challenge must be to something *important*.

Important to whom? To him, one might reply; to his conception of himself, the sort of person he wants to be.

But a connoisseur of fine wines is, by definition, someone concerned with the quality of wine, and to such a person the preference for rotgut would be humiliating.

One may die for beauty, truth, justice, the objection might continue, but not for Montrachet. Wine is not that important.

Someone may have died for a bottle of wine (as in Poe's story, "The Cask of Amontillado"), but that is not the point: we (the enlightened majority) do not think wine is worthy of the importance that such an ascription of integrity implies.

14. I owe this objection, as well as other helpful criticism, to an anonymous reviewer for *Ethics*.

When we grant integrity to a person, we need not *approve* of his or her principles or commitments, but we must at least recognize them as ones a reasonable person might take to be of great importance and ones that a reasonable person might be tempted to sacrifice to some lesser yet still recognizable goods. It may not be possible to spell out these conditions without circularity, but that this is what underlies our judgments of integrity seems clear enough. Integrity is a personal virtue granted with social strings attached. By definition, it precludes "expediency, artificiality, or shallowness of any kind."[15] The pleasure seeker is guilty of shallowness, the approval seeker of artificiality, and the profit seeker of expedience of the worst sort.

Whether we grant or deny personal integrity, then, seems to depend on our own conceptions of what is important. And since most of our conceptions are informed if not dominated by moral conceptions of the good, it is natural that this should be reflected in our judgments of personal integrity.

Natural but not obviously justified. This, one might argue, only shows the coercive power language, which, along with other forms of coercion, a person of integrity will resist. Beyond internal coherence, the concept of integrity itself does not determine whether an ascription of integrity is justified; it merely reflects our tolerance or lack of it. (There may be a "glass house" factor as well: we buy tolerance for ourselves with our tolerance of others—so that even such tolerance may be badly motivated and therefore suspect.) I argue that this view is too liberal.

INTEGRITY, FRIENDSHIP, AND THE OLAF PRINCIPLE

An attitude essential to the notion of integrity is that there are some things that one is not prepared to do, or some things one *must* do.[16] I shall call this the "Olaf Principle," in honor of e. e. cummings's poem about Olaf, the "conscientious object-or." This principle requires that some of one's commitments be unconditional.

In what sense?

There are, in ordinary moral thought, expressions of the necessity or impossibility of certain actions or types of actions that do not neatly correspond to the notions of necessity and impossibility most often cat-alogued by moral theorists. "I *must* stand by my friend" (or "I *cannot* let him down") may have no claim to logical, psychological, rational, or moral necessity in any familiar sense. There is nothing logically inconsistent in the betrayal of friendship, or one could never be guilty of it. It is not psychologically impossible, since many have in fact done it and survived to do it again. Rationality does not require unconditional allegiance, without some additional assumptions, for one may have better reason to do a conflicting action, for example, where the choice is between betraying a friend and betraying one's country (although I am sympathetic to

15. See *Webster's Third New International Dictionary*, s.v. "integrity."
16. See Taylor.

E. M. Forster's famous statement to the contrary).[17] Nor is the necessity expressed one that has a claim to universality, for different persons may have different unconditional commitments. Impartiality and absoluteness are not what is at stake, for the choice may be between a friend and ten innocent strangers, and one person may have different unconditional commitments at different times. It is not clear, then, what sense of *unconditional commitment* is at issue.

Unless corrupted by philosophy, we all have things we think we would never do, under any imaginable circumstances, whatever we may give to survival or pleasure, power and the approval of strangers; some part of ourselves beyond which we will not retreat, some weakness however prevalent in others that we will not tolerate in ourselves. And if we do that thing, betray that weakness, we are not the persons we thought; there is nothing left that we may even in spite refer to as *I*.

I think it is in this sense that some commitments must be unconditional: they are conditions of continuing as ourselves.

Suppose, for example, that I take both friendship and professional advancement to be great goods, and my best friend and I are candidates for a promotion. Suppose, too, that I know the person who has the final decision has an unreasoned hatred of people who drink more than is socially required, as my friend does. I let this be known, not directly of course, with the predictable result that I am given the promotion.

Now in one sense I have not done anything dishonest. My friend may be the first to admit the pleasure he takes in alcohol. It may even be one of the reasons I value his friendship. (Loyal drinking companions are not easy to come by.) But this is clearly a betrayal of friendship. Is it so obviously a failure of integrity?

In *any* conflict between two great goods, I may argue, one must be "betrayed." And between you and me, I choose me.

What is wrong with this defense?

To beat someone out of a job by spreading vicious truths is proof that I am no friend. It is in the nature of friendship that one cannot intentionally hurt a friend in order to further one's own interests. So if I claim to be this person's friend, then I am guilty of incoherence, and therefore lack integrity.

Why does incoherence seem the wrong charge to make? The answer, I think, is that it is much too weak.

Some of our principles or commitments are more important to us than others. Those that can be sacrificed without remorse may be called *defeasible* commitments. For many of us, professional success is an important but defeasible commitment. I would like to be a successful philosopher, esteemed by my colleagues and widely published, but neither success nor failure will change my sense of personal worth.

17. What Forster said was: "If I had to choose between betraying my country and betraying my friends, I hope I should have the guts to betray my country."

Contrasted to defeasible commitments are *identity-conferring* commitments: they reflect what we take to be most important and so determine, to a large extent, our (moral) identities.[18] It is this sense of personal identity that explains Stephen Dedalus's remark, "I was someone else then," and Ivan Ilych's lament, "It was like a reminiscence of somebody else."[19]

For many of us, friendship is an identity-conferring commitment. If we betrayed a friend in order to advance our careers, we could not "live with" ourselves; we would not be the persons we thought we were. This is what it means to have a "core": a set of principles or commitments that makes us who we are. Such principles cannot be justified by reference to other values, because they are the most fundamental commitments we have; they determine what, for us, is to *count* as a reason.[20]

Different persons may of course have different commitments, and they need not be moral in nature. Nietzsche, for example, said that without music, life would be a mistake. Truth telling was an identity-conferring commitment for Thomas More; he went to his death for it. Family loyalty was such a commitment for Antigone. That one is willing to die for something does not make it true, but it is the clearest proof we have of such commitments. There are things we could not do without self-betrayal and personal disintegration. Here both kinds of coherence—logical and psychological—meet.

But is this requirement sufficient to discredit the pleasure seeker, the approval seeker, and the profit seeker? There *is* something each would not do: sacrifice pleasure, approval, profit to anything else.

Philosophers are fond of the fantastic case. Suppose it is your honor to either shoot Pedro or let Pedro and nineteen others be shot.[21] Or suppose some terrorists have poisoned the water supply in some large American city, you do not know which, and the only one who knows is John, the terrorists' "main man," and the only way to make him talk is to torture John Junior.[22] What should you do?

It has been suggested that in such circumstances suicide may be chosen, rationally and deliberately, as an act of rejecting both alternatives and a world in which these are our only choices as intolerable.[23] Whether or not such an act would be morally justified, this remark seems to me significant: whatever choice one makes in such circumstances is suicide

---

18. I owe the distinction between defeasible and identity-conferring commitments to John Kekes, "Constancy and Purity," *Mind* 92 (1983): 499–518.

19. Joyce, p. 240; Tolstoy, p. 460.

20. I owe this point to Kekes.

21. J. J. C. Smart and Bernard Williams, *Utilitarianism: For and Against* (Cambridge: Cambridge University Press, 1973). The example is Williams's, pp. 98–99.

22. This is a test question, slightly modified, of Robert Fogelin's, used in his ethics course at Dartmouth College.

23. S. I. Benn, "Persons and Values: Reasons in Conflict and Moral Disagreement," *Ethics* 95 (1984): 34.

of a sort; either action would, in the case of the morally normal, destroy us. Murder and torture are *things we could not do* and survive as the persons we are.

It might be objected, however, that to grant this point is to put too much moral weight on the word "integrity," when it more properly belongs to the qualified notion of *moral* integrity. There are conceivable cases in which we would want to grant that someone had *personal* integrity, even if we were to find his ideal morally abhorrent; if moral justification is what we are after, moral integrity is the place to look.

Suppose, for example, that the greater part of world literature is found obscene according to the prevailing moral code, and the remedy is, in the spirit of *Fahrenheit 451,* to burn all copies of the offending works. The only way to stop the book burners is to kill them, thereby creating a new moral majority. Faulkner once said that "The Ode on a Grecian Urn" is worth any number of old ladies, and this point could be generalized and raised to the status of a principle which would support a program of extermination: burn the book burners. (The justification for burning the book burners, instead of merely killing them, is utilitarian: once it is general knowledge that this is happening, the majority vote may change quite naturally, so that fewer book burners will in the end have to be killed.) Now suppose some lover of literature attempts to carry out this program, at great personal risk. Although we may find his actions morally abhorrent, we may still be inclined to grant him the virtue of personal integrity. We would not, however, hold him up as a paragon of moral integrity.

So if we want to justify the claim that the content of certain principles or commitments disqualifies their adherents as candidates for integrity, we should turn to moral integrity.

MORAL INTEGRITY

If integrity is a moral virtue, then it is a special sort of virtue. One cannot be solely concerned with one's own integrity, or there would be no object for one's concern. Thus integrity seems to be a higher-order virtue.[24] To have moral integrity, then, it is natural to suppose that one must have some lower-order moral commitments; that moral integrity adds a moral requirement to personal integrity.

One objection to this commonsense view is that there are two senses of "morality," one personal, the other social, and whatever a person takes to be most important *is* his personal morality.[25]

Where there is a conflict between personal and social morality, there are two ways of describing it: "Aestheticists think that one human activity, Art, is more important than any other. . . . We could describe them as

24. See Taylor.
25. Neil Cooper, "Morality and Importance," in *The Definition of Morality,* ed. G. Wallace and A. D. M. Walker (London: Methuen, Inc., 1970).

'subordinating' . . . morality to Art. But we could also say that their own autonomous morality consisted of putting Art first. As Gaunt says of the Bohemians, 'They had one law, one morality, one devotion and that was Art.' "[26]

If this were right, then a fundamental commitment to burning the book burners would be a *moral* stance; our book-loving exterminator, a paragon of moral integrity. So long as one acted on one's most important commitments, moral integrity would be guaranteed. Thus the consistent pleasure seeker, approval seeker, and profit seeker all would be clear possessors of moral integrity. One could have moral integrity without subscribing to any recognizable moral principle. Even an avowed subverter, not only of conventional morality but of all moral considerations as well, could have moral integrity. "Evil be thou my good" would be a moral stance. That the self-consciously immoral could be correctly described as paradigms of moral integrity seems paradoxical. An "autonomous morality" that exhibits autonomy in relation to all moral considerations does not seem to be a morality.

Further, the appeal to ordinary language does not appear to support this view. Gaunt's claim that the Bohemians had "one morality" seems to be metaphorical rather than literal. We say "Money is his God" without looking for another sense of "God" or assuming that a commitment to capitalism is a religious stance. Morality is one paradigm of an important concern; religion is another. So that when we want to say, in a metaphorical way, what a person takes to be most important, we can use either of these expressions. It does not follow that whatever a person takes to be most important—in this case, art—is a morality.

So it is more plausible to say that moral integrity adds a moral requirement to personal integrity: one must adhere to some set of recognizable moral principles or commitments. This rules out a singular commitment to art, as well as to personal pleasure, approval, and profit.

What makes something a moral principle?

One commonly accepted view is that moral principles are characterized by impartiality and universality. Assuming this is true, it follows that moral integrity will require that these conditions be met.

Is this plausible?

Let us return to the principled adulterer and look at it from the husband's point of view. At first he feels betrayed and is hurt. Then he stops to consider what impartiality requires. Perhaps my wife's new lover makes her happier than I can, he reasons, and the affair will certainly make her lover happier, so there is all that happiness to be weighed against my pain. The children are grown, so it is not hurting them. Impartiality seems to require that I grant her this freedom, even encourage it.

26. Ibid., p. 95.

Second example. Suppose you are having a bad day. The car breaks down on the way to teach a class in which three students fall asleep and the rest are bored or belligerent. Your latest philosophical masterpiece has come back in the mail with a note from the editor saying that the referees' comments were too abusive to decently pass on to you. During office hours your best student wonders aloud what moral theory has to do with anything that genuinely worries anyone. You have been worrying about that yourself. You wait an hour for a friend who was supposed to meet you at noon but who seems to have forgotten. On the way back from drinking your lunch, just as despair is about to take over for self-pity, you run into K. He sees by your wild eyes that you are in a bad way. He is just going to lunch, he says, and invites you along. You agree, having had nothing to eat since the English muffin your toaster burned for breakfast. While waiting to order, he listens sympathetically to your litany of unrelieved bad luck and real failure. He tries to cheer you up. Feeling better, you express your appreciation, tell him that he is a good friend. He says he is only doing his moral duty. You smile, thinking this philosophical irony. His blank expression suggests you are wrong. Over Caesar salad he tells you about his dear wife, whom he married because no one was more in need of love, nor so unlikely to find it. Somewhere between the main course and the coffee you realize he was not kidding. He is only doing for you what he would do for anyone in your sorry state—his duty.

The fairly simple point of these examples is that impartiality is incompatible with friendship and love, and so incompatible with personal integrity where friendship and love are identity-conferring commitments.

What does moral integrity require?

Any identity-conferring commitment *except* to impartiality will be inconsistent with impartiality. If moral integrity presupposes personal integrity, and personal integrity requires identity-conferring commitments, then moral integrity is, generally, inconsistent with impartiality.

So we must give up the claim (1) that personal integrity requires unconditional commitments, (2) that moral integrity presupposes personal integrity, or (3) that moral principles require impartiality. Which should it be?

The first claim seems to me a conceptual truth, so I won't argue for it, except to tell a story in closing that I hope will make it more vivid.

What about claim 2? On the view I have been defending, moral integrity presupposes personal integrity, but might moral integrity exist without it? I don't see how. If a minimum requirement of integrity is internal coherence, then moral integrity will require it as well. So one's moral and (nonmoral) personal principles could not be inconsistent. If one held personal but no moral principles, then one could have personal integrity without moral integrity. But the reverse does not hold because of the "first-person" requirement. Thus moral integrity presupposes personal integrity.

This leaves claim 3 to be rejected, which I think is right. If we accept that there are moral duties of friendship and love, then principles that govern such relations will be moral principles, and since friendship and love are characterized by partiality, some moral principles are characterized by partiality.

But this, one might object, begs the question of whether moral integrity requires impartiality. It may be true that there are moral principles that are characterized by partiality, but it doesn't follow that simply holding such principles is sufficient for moral integrity. Something stronger—moral *justification,* for example—may be required. And this possibility has been illegitimately ruled out.

We can reject claim 3 and resolve the inconsistency, without begging the question, by making a distinction: between personal and social morality.[27]

Say that a *personal morality* is that set of moral principles or commitments that I adhere to that I do not expect everyone to adhere to and that need not be characterized by impartiality.

The belief that friendship is more important than professional advancement might back some such principle: "Never harm a friend in order to further one's own professional interests." I could understand it if others (cancer researchers, say) put professional advancement above the claims of friendship, on the ground that it is likely to promote the general good (although I would not want them for friends). So I do not take my principle to be universal. Since by its very nature friendship is a relationship characterized by partiality, neither is my principle impartial. So "Never harm a friend . . ." is a moral principle that meets neither condition—universality or impartiality. Thus it is a personal moral principle.

A *social morality* is the set of principles that we adhere to that we expect everyone to adhere to and that are characterized by impartiality.

The difference between them is clearly seen in a case of conflict. Suppose, in my role as ship captain, that I am charged to take the safety of everyone equally into account. This would be true for anyone in my

---

27. Another way would be to distinguish, within morality, between *special* and *general* obligations (see H. L. A. Hart, "Are There Any Natural Rights?" in *Political Philosophy,* ed. Anthony Quinton [Oxford: Oxford University Press, 1967], pp. 53–66). Special obligations are based on a special history of relations among persons, e.g., friends, or on a particular role, e.g., ship captain. General obligations, grounded in impartiality, are owed by anyone to anyone, e.g., anyone who can save a stranger's life at small cost should. A conflict similar to the one I discuss arises where special and general obligations conflict (see James S. Fishkin, *The Limits of Obligation* [New Haven, Conn., and London: Yale University Press, 1982]). Although the conflict between love/friendship and impartiality could be recast in this way, in the example I discuss—the ship captain whose spouse is drowning—the conflict is between two *special* obligations, one requiring partiality, one impartiality. I think this makes the conflict more powerful, since it cannot be resolved by denying that we have any positive general obligations.

position, so the principle, "Guard the safety of all passengers equally" is both universal and impartial.

Now suppose I see that my husband and two other passengers are drowning. My husband weighs what the two others weigh put together. He is drowning on starboard, they are drowning at port. If I save my husband, the two will drown, and vice versa.

As a wife I should save my husband; as ship captain I should save the two strangers. The demands of personal morality conflict with those of social morality.

What does moral integrity require?

I want to raise another question in attempting to answer this one. What makes such conflicts possible?

For most of us, both relations of personal affection and social moral commitments have great if not identity-conferring importance. If they did not, we would recognize no dilemma.

A general argument either way—for the claims of social or personal morality at the expense of the other—would do violence to our intuitions. If we were to grant supreme importance to social morality, we could honor no personal moral commitments. (Can a utilitarian have friends? Yes, but not of his own.) And conversely. A dilemma, by definition, presupposes a commitment to both sides.

Recent attempts to mitigate such conflicts have been unsuccessful.

Lawrence Blum, for example, argues that "friendship does not typically involve us in situations in which impartiality between the interests of our friends and those of others is a moral requirement," so in acting to benefit a friend we do not typically violate a duty of impartiality.[28] What is involved in comforting a friend is particular to the friendship. "I cannot just pop over to someone's house who is in need of comfort and comfort him, in the way I can to my friend."[29]

This seems to me false. There are many institutional contexts—suicide prevention and rape crisis hotlines, "friendship" programs for the elderly—that employ volunteers twenty-four hours a day to meet such needs. It may be true that we cannot give to strangers what we can give to friends, because of our lack of intimate knowledge and personal affection, but there clearly are limited resources—time and sympathy—that render these concerns competitive and so lead to conflicts. Unless one's friends are numerous and especially needy, or one's obligation to help others is extremely minimal, one will, on a day-to-day basis, have to choose between benefiting a friend (child, lover) and what impartiality requires.

Another attempt to mitigate this conflict is made by John Cottingham.[30] Cottingham denies the requirement of impartiality except in cases where

28. Lawrence Blum, *Friendship, Altruism, and Morality* (New York: Routledge & Kegan Paul, 1980), p. 46.

29. Ibid., p. 56.

30. John Cottingham, "Ethics and Impartiality," *Philosophical Studies* 43 (1983): 83–99.

there is a "specific duty" not to show favoritism or partiality. The mistake that defenders of the "impartiality thesis" make is in generalizing from these special cases to every ethical situation. If, for example, one is the official in charge of the corn dole, then although it may be harsh, one must make one's son wait in line. If, however, it is one's own food to dispose of, then one morally ought to favor one's own child.

What about the case where the agent is the commodity: the ship captain whose spouse is drowning? Here there are two specific moral duties—one requiring impartiality, one requiring partiality—and it is not obvious that the first should be met.[31]

Cottingham's justification for this position is unconvincing: "I have suggested that the substantial and continuous favorable treatment which we all in fact bestow on ourselves and our loved ones is not only permissible but essential, since without it the very object of ethics, human fulfillment, would be defeated."[32] Whose human fulfillment? Strangers suffer and die very much like our own family and friends.

The existence, and persistence, of such cases of genuine moral conflict suggests that the claims of personal and social morality may be *equally* strong, so that no uniform resolution is possible.

I want to return now to my drowning husband. My own view is this. Whatever choice I make (further extraordinary complications excluded), I would not be morally blameworthy. (Praise we save for those who would do as we do or better.) If I save the two strangers, I am right from the social-moral point of view; if I save my husband, I am right from the personal-moral point of view. And whatever choice I make I am wrong from some point of view. Since both are moral requirements of comparable importance, I am free to choose, based on commitments particular to myself, what I could or could not "live with" (or without).

It may be said that I should not have put myself in the position where such a conflict is possible (ship captains should leave their spouses at home) and that I am therefore morally culpable for the conflict. But as a prescription for how to live, this is naive. By taking part in the wider community—through volunteer work, say, or even employment—we introduce the possibility of conflict, and the only way to avoid it would be to take up residence in our closets.

In trying to elucidate the relation between personal integrity and morality, I have used examples of love and friendship because they are commitments most of us have. But other examples could have been used to make the same point—which is this: if we grant that there are cases where the claims of personal and social morality conflict, and where the conflict may be justifiably resolved either way, without loss of moral integrity, then we do not claim (1) that every person should, under the same circumstances, do the same thing, nor (2) that there is a moral duty

31. See Bernard Williams, who argues eloquently for the second in "Persons, Character, and Morality," in his *Moral Luck* (Cambridge: Cambridge University Press, 1981), pp. 1–19.

32. Cottingham, p. 94.

to be impartial. It follows that every morality is, fundamentally, a personal morality.

CONCLUSION

Moral integrity is as much a threat to social morality as personal integrity. The difference is that the attack comes from *within* the moral point of view, and its target is impartiality. Perhaps, then, integrity should be given up, as having a moral cost that is too great.

I think this would be a mistake. The reason is made graphically clear in a story by the science fiction writer Theodore Sturgeon, called "The Dark Room."[33] In this story the narrator, Conway, has a friend named Beck who regularly gives cocktail parties at which everyone who attends is eventually humiliated. A sweet old woman, the author of children's books, tells an obscene story. A man who prides himself on his dignity and decorum urinates on the living room floor. An undercover agent walks up to a CIA man and spills his guts. And at the most recent party, Conway's loyal wife ends up in bed with one of the other guests. This gets his attention; on reflection he sees the pattern of humiliation and resolves to find out what's going on. Breaking into Beck's house while he's out of town Conway comes upon an alien being who has the ability to take on any form, to be whatever people want to see. The alien confesses that he feeds on the humiliation of humans. Without it he will die. He finances the parties for Beck in order to get new victims, whose humiliation he causes. This explanation satisfies Conway except for one thing: why, having attended every party, has *he* never been humiliated? The alien explains that Conway is an "immune": a creature who cannot be humiliated because there is nothing he would not do.

Without integrity, and the identity-conferring commitments it assumes, there would be nothing to fear the loss of, not because we are safe but because we have nothing to lose.

33. Theodore Sturgeon, "The Dark Room," in *The Golden Helix and Other Stories* (Garden City, N.Y.: Doubleday & Co., 1979), pp. 191–227.

Appeals to Conscience*

James F. Childress

Unfortunately the phrase "appeals to conscience" is ambiguous. First, it may indicate an appeal to another person's conscience in order to convince him to act in certain ways. Second, it may mean the invocation of one's own conscience to interpret and justify one's conduct to others. Third, it may indicate the invocation of conscience in debates with oneself about the right course of action, conscience being understood as a participant in the debate, a referee, or a final arbiter. Although it is possible to distinguish these three meanings of "appeals to conscience," they are usually intertwined in our moral discourse. Nevertheless, I shall concentrate on the second meaning, referring to the other two only when it is necessary to fill out the picture.[1] Appeals to conscience in the second sense raise important issues of justification and public policy which can be considered apart from the other meanings of appeals to conscience.

My concern is with what we might call "conscientious objection"

*I owe a debt of thanks to audiences at Brown University, the University of Notre Dame, the American University, and the American Society of Christian Ethics, to colleagues in the Department of Religious Studies at the University of Virginia and in the Kennedy Institute of Ethics at Georgetown University, and particularly to Stanley Hauerwas and Dorle Vawter for their helpful comments on earlier drafts of this paper. I wrote the first draft while I was a fellow in law and religion at the Harvard Law School in 1972–73 under a study fellowship from the American Council of Learned Societies and a sesquicentennial associateship from the University of Virginia. I am grateful to these institutions for their support.

1. For aspects of the appeal to another person's conscience, see James F. Childress, *Civil Disobedience and Political Obligation* (New Haven, Conn.: Yale University Press, 1971), and "Nonviolent Resistance: Trust and Risk-Taking," *Journal of Religious Ethics* 1 (Fall 1973): 87–112. For a theological interpretation of the third meaning, see Karl Rahner, "The Appeal to Conscience," *Nature and Grace* (New York: Sheed & Ward, 1964), chap. 2.

This essay originally appeared in *Ethics*, vol. 90, no. 4, July 1979.

(broader than objection to participation in war), or what John Rawls calls "conscientious refusal."[2] What is involved in a person's description and evaluation of his own or others' acts as "conscientious"? What should our public policy be toward those who appeal to their consciences when they violate customs, established expectations, and laws? In suggesting some answers to these questions, I shall focus on the most general and least disputed aspects of the experiences to which we apply the terms conscience and conscientious, leaving aside many of the issues raised by various philosophical, psychological, sociological, and theological theories of conscience.[3] My phenomenological description of conscience and interpretation of the logic of appeals to conscience (in the second sense) will, of course, provide *elements* of a theory of conscience, but I do not intend to develop such a theory in this discussion. I shall, rather, examine the phenomena that we express in the language of conscience and related notions and try to determine how these enter into appeals to conscience (in the second sense) before discussing some public policies toward conscientious objection. Three cases of appeals to conscience and related notions are useful points of reference for our discussion.

1. On June 21, 1956, Arthur Miller, the playwright, appeared before the House Committee on Un-American Activities (HUAC) which was examining the unauthorized use of passports, and he was asked who had been present at meetings with Communist writers in New York City. Here is part of the dialogue:

Mr. Arens: Can you tell us who was there when you walked into the room?
Mr. Miller: Mr. Chairman, I understand the philosophy behind this question and I want you to understand mine. When I say this, I want you to understand that I am not protecting the Communists or the Communist Party. I am trying to, and I will, *protect my sense of myself.* I could not use the name of another person and bring trouble on him. These were writers, poets, as far as I could see, and the life of a writer, despite what it sometimes seems, is pretty tough. I wouldn't make it any tougher for anybody. I ask you not to ask me that question. . . .
Mr. Jackson: May I say that moral scruples, however laudable, do not constitute legal reason for refusing to answer the question. . . .
Mr. Scherer: We do not accept the reason you gave for refusing to answer the question, and . . . if you do not answer . . . you are placing yourself in contempt. . . .

2. John Rawls, *A Theory of Justice* (Cambridge, Mass.: Harvard University Press, 1971), pp. 368–71.
3. For a discussion of many of these theories, see Eric Mount, Jr., *Conscience and Responsibility* (Richmond, Va.: John Knox Press, 1969). For a broader view of conscience than the one I am developing, see Eleanor Haney, "Conscience and Law," *Dialog* 9 (Autumn 1970): 284–94.

Mr. Miller: All I can say, sir, is that *my conscience* will not permit me to use the name of another person.[4]

2. On December 29, 1970, Governor Winthrop Rockefeller of Arkansas commuted to life imprisonment the death sentences of the fifteen prisoners then on death row. He said, "I cannot and will not turn my back on life-long Christian teachings and beliefs, merely to let history run out its course on a fallible and failing theory of punitive justice." Understanding his decision as "purely personal and philosophical," he insisted that the records of the prisoners were irrelevant to it. He continued, "I am aware that there will be reaction to my decision. However, failing to take this action while it is within my power, *I could not live with myself.*"[5]

3. In late December 1972, Captain Michael Heck refused to carry out orders to fly more bombing missions in Vietnam. He wrote his parents: "I've taken a very drastic step. I've refused to take part in this war any longer. *I cannot in good conscience* be a part of it." He also said, "I can live with prison easier than I can with taking part in the war." "I would refuse even a ground job supervising the loading of bombs or refueling aircraft. I cannot be a participant . . . *a man has to answer to himself first.*"[6]

Conscience is a mode of consciousness and thought about one's own acts and their value or disvalue. It is often retrospective; in being conscious of and thinking about his past acts, an agent's conscience comes into play. It appears primarily as a bad conscience, as the feelings of guilt and shame that accompany this consciousness of one's own acts as wrong or bad. Hannah Arendt insists that "only good people are ever bothered by a bad conscience whereas it is a

4. Eric Bentley, ed., *Thirty Years of Treason: Excerpts from Hearings before the House Committee on Un-American Activities, 1938–1968* (New York: Viking Press, 1971), pp. 819–22 (italics added). See also, Eric Bentley, *Are You Now or Have You Ever Been?* (New York: Harper & Row, 1972), excerpts from which appeared in *Yale Alumni Magazine* (January 1973). Miller's moral objections to "informing" can also be seen in his creative writings such as *The Crucible* (for some of the contemporary discussion of Miller's stand, see John Steinbeck, "The Trial of Arthur Miller," and Richard Rovere, "Arthur Miller's Conscience," in *Contemporary Moral Issues*, ed. Harry Girvetz, 2d ed. [Belmont, Calif.: Wadsworth Publishing Co., 1968], pp. 97–105). In addition to conscience, Miller felt that the question about who was present at meetings with Communist writers was not germane to the issue of the use of passports, the alleged subject of inquiry. His conviction for contempt was overturned by the Supreme Court.

5. Reproduced materials for course in criminal law, Professor Alan Dershowitz's section, Harvard Law School, 1972.

6. On Heck, see *Newsweek* (January 22, 1973), p. 18; *Boston Globe* (January 13, 1973), and Steven V. Roberts, "2 Pilots, 2 Wars," *New York Times Magazine* (June 10, 1973).

very rare phenomenon among real criminals. A good conscience does not exist except as the absence of a bad one."[7] Most often the good conscience is described by nouns such as "peace," "wholeness," and "integrity," or by adjectives such as "quiet," "clear," "clean," and "easy." Job (27:6) affirmed this peace of the good conscience when he said (using one of the Hebrew words for the experience that we call conscience): "My heart shall not reproach me so long as I live."

When a person appeals to his conscience or describes his act as conscientious, he makes a hypothetical and prospective claim. He claims that if he were to commit the act in question, he would violate his conscience. This violation would result not only in such unpleasant feelings as guilt and/or shame but also in a fundamental loss of integrity, wholeness, and harmony in the self. He thus makes a prediction about what would happen to him if he were to commit such an act, a prediction based on the imaginative projection of concrete courses of action in the light of his fundamental standards. His appeal to conscience constitutes a motive-statement about his refusal, an indication of why he is doing it. In order to clarify this motive, let's look at the marks of conscience, including feelings of guilt and shame. I shall emphasize that conscience functions as a sanction, and I shall delineate the context of appeals to conscience.

MARKS OF CONSCIENCE AND APPEALS TO CONSCIENCE

Some of the marks of conscience are implicit in my comments about a good and a bad conscience. Conscience is personal and subjective; it is a person's consciousnes of and reflection on his own acts in relation to his standards of judgment. It is a first-person claim, deriving from standards that he may or may not also apply to the conduct of others. As Hannah Arendt indicates, "when Socrates stated that 'it is better to suffer wrong than to do wrong,' he clearly meant that it was better *for him,* just as it was better for him 'to be in disagreement with multitudes than, being one, to be in disagreement with [himself].' "[8] In the three cases presented above, the agents held that their consciences required certain actions from them. While it is likely that they would have raised moral questions about others who acted differently, it would have been odd and ever absurd for one of them to have said, "My conscience indicates that you should not do that" (e.g., continue to fight in Vietnam or be an informer). In judging others or advising them about their conduct, may consult my conscience but only in the sense of imagining what would think and feel if I acted in a certain way. I may then say tha

7. Hannah Arendt, "Thinking and Moral Considerations: A Lecture," *Socia Research* 38 (Autumn 1971): 418.

8. Hannah Arendt, *Crises of the Republic* (New York: Harcourt Brac Jovanovich, 1972), p. 62.

someone else ought not to engage in that conduct, but I cannot logically justify this admonition by saying "I would have a guilty conscience if he did that." Perhaps I would have a guilty conscience if I failed to warn him, but my reasons for his abstention from that conduct must involve more than an appeal to my conscience; they must invoke the moral values, principles, and rules that are determinative for my conscience.[9]

Although a person's appeal to his conscience usually involves an appeal to moral standards, conscience is not itself the standard. It is the mode of consciousness resulting from the application of standards to his conduct. For example, the retrospective bad conscience emerges after the moral judgment about the act. Even in the prospective bad conscience, a matter of the imagination, conscience still comes after the judgment of rightness and wrongness. C. A. Pierce in *Conscience in the New Testament* comments on "conscience" in 1 Corinthians: ". . . here conscience is to some extent regarded as dependent on an assessment on other grounds of the quality of acts. In this case it is knowledge of the source of the meat eaten that brings on the pain, not the eating of the meat. Even in its negative and limited function, conscience does not so much indicate that an act committed is wrong, as that an act 'known' (by other means, and rightly or wrongly) to be wrong, has been committed."[10]

To appeal to conscience thus is not necessarily to assert that moral rightness and wrongness are determined by the need for a good conscience or that moral integrity serves, in effect, as the source and ground of obligation. As Thomas Nagel suggests, "For if by committing murder one sacrifices one's moral purity or integrity, that can only be because there is *already* something wrong with murder. The general reason against committing murder cannot therefore be merely that it makes one an immoral person."[11]

A number of puzzles appear at this point. If conscience emerges

9. Two other issues emerge from the discussion of conscience as personal and subjective: (1) the duality of the self and (2) the social context and formation of conscience. On both issues, see H. R. Niebuhr, "The Ego-Alter Dialectic and the Conscience," *Journal of Philosophy* 42 (1945): 352–59.

10. C. A. Pierce, *Conscience in the New Testament* (London: SCM Press, 1955), p. 77. But his analysis of contemporary interpretations of conscience, especially in ordinary language, differs from mine: "Conscience, then, is taken today as justifying, in advance or in general principle, actions or attitudes of others as well as one's self. But in the New Testament it cannot justify; it refers only to the past and particular; and to the acts of a man's own self alone" (p. 117). (For a view, similar to mine, that conscience follows judgment, see Martin C. McGuire's fine article, "On Conscience," *Journal of Philosophy* 60 [May 9, 1963]: 253–63; also see Gilbert Ryle, "Conscience and Moral Convictions," in *Philosophy and Analysis*, ed. Margaret Mac-Donald [Oxford: Basil Blackwell, 1954], pp. 156–65.)

11. Thomas Nagel, "War and Massacre," *Philosophy and Public Affairs* 1 (Winter 1972): 132.

after a moral judgment or after the application of moral standards, what does it mean to consult one's conscience, to have a conflict of conscience, and to say "I believe that I ought to do that but my conscience tells me not to." When a person consults his conscience, from the perspective that I am developing, he examines his moral convictions to determine what he really thinks and feels, even reconsidering his values, principles, and rules, their weight, and their relevance to the situation at hand. When he consults his conscience, it will only give him one answer: Do what you believe you ought to do. This appeal to conscience (in the third sense of the phrase) is thus only one step in the examination of one's moral convictions.

A "conflict of conscience" appears when a person faces two conflicting moral demands, neither of which can be met without at least partially violating the other one. This is a conflict of conscience because there is a firm judgment, right or wrong, that both courses of action are required. Conscience gives conflicting directives because it follows conflicting judgments. Perhaps the agent has misconstrued his situation and the relevant moral standards, and the only way out is to reconsider them. This may also be the situation of a "doubtful conscience," unsure about the operative standards and their weight.

More difficult in terms of the perspective that I am developing is the statement, "I believe that this act is right and that I ought to do it, but my conscience prevents me from doing it." What sense can one make of this statement if conscience follows rather than authorizes moral judgments? First, it may be another version of the conflict-of-conscience situation that I just described. Second, it may be an example of what John Rawls calls "residue guilt feelings" that persist after a person has changed his moral convictions (e.g., about some "vice" that was prohibited in his earlier religious training). Third, perhaps the situation is closer to that of the doubtful conscience since uncertainty may result from changes in a person's moral convictions so that he is not sure what he now believes. For example, as a person surrenders his pacifism and becomes a defender of justified violence, he may not be able at some points in time to say that he does or does not believe that violence is wrong for him and that his conscience does or does not provide a sanction against his participation in war.[12]

Another important mark of conscience is often overlooked: The appeal to conscience asserts a personal sanction rather than an authority. This mark is frequently overlooked because first-person appeals to conscience most often appear in the explanation of acts

12. For a similar view, see McGuire, p. 262.

that contravene the demands of an established authority such as a religious community or a legal-political order. I shall return to this point later, but now I want to analyze this sanction. J. Glen Gray describes what happens when soldiers discover that they cannot continue obeying certain orders: "Suddenly the soldier feels himself abandoned and cast off from all security. Conscience has isolated him, and its voice is a warning. *If you do this, you will not be at peace with me in the future.*"[13] This threatened "ache of guilt," as Gray describes it, is a fearful sanction for those with an interest in the self and its welfare. In the words of Shakespeare, "It fills a man full of obstacles" (*Richard III,* act 1, sc. 4, line 142).

The agents in the three cases mentioned earlier emphasize this personal sanction. They fear the loss of selfhood, integrity, and wholeness in the anticipated judgment of the future self on the present self's acts, and they express this fear in several dramatic ways: "I could not live with myself"; "A man has to answer to himself first"; "I must protect my sense of self." Others have said, "I could answer it, but if I did, I would hate myself in the morning."[14] Or, "I could not look myself in the mirror."[15] Hannah Arendt summarizes the rules or logic of conscience drawn from Socrates: "These are the rules of conscience, and they are—like those Thoreau announced in his essay—entirely negative. They do not say what to do; they say what not to do. They do not spell out certain principles for taking action; they lay down boundaries no act should transgress. They say: Don't do wrong, for then you will have to live together with a wrongdoer."[16]

Furthermore, these dictates of conscience are purely formal, not material. "Let your conscience be your guide," but its advice is formal: "Do what you believe to be right and avoid what you believe to be wrong, or else." Let there be consistency and harmony between belief and action under the threat that inconsistency will undermine integrity and occasion a bad conscience.

This claim about the formal nature of the dictates of conscience may seem at first glance to be contrary to our experiences. Conscience is awakened, consulted, or invoked only when there is some difficulty, some perplexity, or some temptation; retrospectively, it

13. J. Glenn Gray, *The Warriors* (New York: Harper & Row, 1970), pp. 184–85 (italics added).

14. Ring Lardner, Jr., before HUAC, October 30, 1947; see Bentley, *Thirty Years of Treason,* pp. 187, 189.

15. For a very interesting discussion of the relation between the widespread use of mirrors and a sense of individuality and selfhood, see Lionel Trilling, *Sincerity and Authenticity* (Cambridge, Mass.: Harvard University Press, 1972).

16. Arendt, *Crises of the Republic,* p. 63.

appears when a person has violated some of his standards. This perplexity or temptation is not general but specific; it relates to standards in specific circumstances, whether real or imagined. Conscience thus appears in envisioning (or remembering) a concrete course of action. Yet its admonition remains constant: Do what you believe is right or suffer the consequences. As agents we do not experience conscience as a general and indefinite call to integrity but only as a call to integrity in the face of situations that offer some temptation to depart from standards. The self over time acting in real situations and imagining others comes to associate this admonition about integrity with particular moral requirements that it has identified as matters of conscience. Thus conscience, whose warning is formal, appears to have material content because it is experienced only in situations that raise specific moral questions and because the self usually has stable values, principles, and rules that, in part, constitute its character.[17]

I have emphasized the sanction of the loss of integrity or wholeness which is closely connected with the feelings of guilt and/or shame. When a person appeals to his conscience he indicates his liability to certain feelings which he predicts will result from acting in certain ways. The phrase "bad conscience" especially indicates the feelings of guilt and shame.[18]

It is not fruitful or even possible to distinguish natural and moral feelings in terms of sensations or behavioral manifestations; rather, the distinction is to be found in the type of explanation that is offered for the feelings. When an agent explains why he experiences certain feelings, he will sometimes offer a moral explanation. Moral feelings, then, are those feelings that are explained by moral notions. Both feelings of guilt and feelings of shame are involved in conscience (although we tend to emphasize "guilt" perhaps because of the Jewish and Christian traditions), but the moral notions that explain them come, roughly, from different parts of morality. As Rawls puts it, "In general, guilt, resentment, and indignation invoke the concept of right, whereas shame, contempt, and derision appeal to the concept of goodness."[19] In the former we have the society's basic morality, its stations, duties, and obligations; in the latter we

17. See Peter Fuss, "Conscience," *Ethics* 74 (January 1964): 111–20, esp. 116–17.

18. In my analysis of these feelings of guilt and shame, I draw heavily on Rawls, esp. pp. 479–85, and on David A. J. Richards, *A Theory of Reasons for Action* (Oxford: Clarendon Press, 1971). See also, Herbert Morris, ed., *Guilt and Shame* (Belmont, Calif.: Wadsworth Publishing Co., 1971).

19. Rawls, p. 484. A number of debates are involved in these matters, although I cannot try to resolve them here; e.g., between the intellectualistic and pragmatic interpretations of conscience (see Bernard Wand, "The Content and Function of Conscience," *Journal of Philosophy* 58 [November 23, 1961]: 765–72).

have the morality of aspiration, ideals, and supererogation. If an agent feels guilty, he invokes a moral concept of right, expects others to feel resentment and indignation, and can relieve his feelings by acts of reparation or by forgiveness. If he feels shame, he invokes an ideal (e.g., self-control or love), expects others to feel contempt for his shortcomings, and can overcome the feeling of shame for his failures only by improving in the future.

The same act may, of course, evoke both feelings of guilt and shame. Take, for example, the act of yielding to the state's demand that one serve in the armed forces. A person who thinks that a war violates the principles of just war may feel guilty about his involvement in it. But he may also have an image of himself as one who can withstand social pressures, and he may be ashamed that he submitted to family and community pressures to serve in the army. In our earlier cases, Rockefeller's statement seems to put greater emphasis on shame than on guilt. His image of himself as a person who acts when he has the opportunity despite social pressures is critical as is his understanding of himself as a Christian, but he also invokes the moral concept of right (e.g., in his reference to barbarism and a "fallible and failing theory" of punishment).

Occasionally within a religious framework, one finds another explanation for a feeling that is close to guilt and shame although it is probably distinct from both: impurity or unworthiness, particularly vis-à-vis God and whatever else is holy. Basil the Great (the fourth century after Christ) said, "Killing in war was differentiated by our fathers from murder . . . nevertheless perhaps it would be well that those whose hands are unclean abstain from communion for three years."[20] This attitude was part of a general aversion to bloodshed.

A person who appeals to his conscience indicates not only that the refused act is prima facie wrong, given his moral convictions, but also actually wrong in these circumstances, at least for him. This apparently trivial observation is very important, for the conscientious agent claims that none of the available public descriptions, justifications, or excuses for the act will ease the anguish of his conscience if he performs it. First, the appellant to conscience claims that he can find no justification for the act in question, at least none that will satisfy his conscience. Sometimes it is suggested that a moral absolutist should be willing to sacrifice his moral purity for the sake of some greater good. Thomas Nagel rightly indicates that such a notion is incoherent: "For if one were justified in making such a sacrifice (or even morally required to make it), then one would not be sacrificing one's moral integrity by adopting that course: one

20. See Roland H. Bainton, *Christian Attitudes toward War and Peace* (New York: Abingdon Press, 1960), p. 78.

would be preserving it."[21] At any rate, the appeal to conscience is a denial that such a justification is present. The moral issue, nevertheless, is an important one, especially since it can be argued that in some genuine conflicts of conscience a violation of a moral principle or rule is necessary and justified. But this issue of the assumption of guilt or "dirty hands" is not identical with the issue of a "bad conscience," for the agent may consider his act to be justified (and hence not subversive of his moral integrity), although the violated moral principle still exerts its influence, for example, in the feeling of guilt and in the duty of reparation.

Second, the appellant to conscience claims that he will not be able to forget the act in question if he performs it. Conscience is sometimes depicted as a still, small voice, but it is perhaps more accurate to view it as a voice that is heard only when one is still and quiet, when one, in effect, stops and thinks. Perhaps this is the basis of Goethe's statement: "The actor is always without conscience; only the spectator has a conscience."[22] This inner witness can be avoided if a person continues his activity and never stops to think; then his crimes can be committed with impunity as far as his conscience is concerned.[23] But the agent who appeals to his conscience claims that this route is closed, for he will not be able to forget the act in question if he performs it.

Third, he claims that he will not be able to deny that the act is his if he performs it. Sometimes a denial of responsibility for an act is used to silence conscience. Instead of trying to show that the deed, apparently against conscience, is actually justified, one might try to show that it is excused. A more common strategy is to attempt to shift the responsibility for the deed and its consequences to someone else. Many soldiers apparently deny not only legal responsibility but also moral responsibility for their deeds by pointing to their oaths as

21. Nagel, pp. 132–33. R. M. Hare responds, "Though Nagel is perfectly right in saying that it is incoherent to suggest that one might 'sacrifice one's moral integrity justifiably, in the service of a sufficiently worthy end,' it is not incoherent to suggest that one might so sacrifice one's peace of mind. And moral integrity and peace of mind are easily confused if one equates having sinned with having a sense of having sinned" ("Rules of War and Moral Reasoning," *Philosophy and Public Affairs* 1 [Winter 1972]: 180). See also Michael Walzer's superb discussion of "dirty hands" in "Political Action: The Problem of Dirty Hands," *Philosophy and Public Affairs* 2 (Winter 1973): 160–80.

22. Johann Wolfgang Goethe, "Maximen und Reflexionen," in *Gedenkausgabe der Werke, Briefe und Gespräche,* ed. Ernst Beutler (Zürich: Artemis Verlags-AG, 1949), p. 522 (maxim no. 241).

23. See Shakespeare's *Richard III* and Arendt's discussion in "Thinking and Moral Considerations: A Lecture," pp. 417–66. Also of interest on this and other matters is Edward Engelberg, *The Unknown Distance: From Consciousness to Conscience, Goethe to Camus* (Cambridge, Mass.: Harvard University Press, 1972).

soldiers and by pleading superior orders.[24] In the traditional under-standing of the order of the universe, the king could absolve his subjects of their misdeeds. In Shakespeare's *Henry V* (act 4, sc. 1, line 137), one of the soldiers says, "we know enough if we know we are the King's subjects. If his cause be wrong, our obedience to the king wipes the crime of it out of us." The appellant to conscience insists that he will not only be unable to forget the act in question but that he will also remember and think about it as his own. Even if others do not hold him responsible for it, he still has to answer to himself.

I can amplify this point by reference to a legal case, *Application of President and Directors of Georgetown College* (331 F. 2d 1000 [D.C. Cir.], *cert. denied*, 377 U.S. 978 [1964]). The Georgetown University Hospital applied for an order to authorize blood transfusions to save a woman's life although she and her husband, both Jehovah's Wit-nesses, conscientiously opposed the transfusions which, they said, would violate the Biblical prohibition against consuming blood. The order was granted by Judge J. Skelly Wright, who indicated that both the husband and the wife conceded that court-ordered transfu-sions would not be their responsibility although they could not con-sent to them. Wright was thus able to protect their consciences and to save the woman's life. In most cases of conscientious objection, however, the agents hold that even coercion does not relieve them of their responsibility.

Having looked at some of the marks of appeals to conscience, we need now to inquire into the context of such appeals: When are they made? Such appeals are made only when there is a need or demand to explain one's past, present, or future acts. Although this demand may emerge either from the internal dialogue of the self or from the inquiries of other persons ("Why are you doing that?"), I am more concerned with the public forum. Especially for acts that contravene customary and conventional expectations and standards, the appeal to conscience functions as a motive-statement, an expla-nation, which may be taken to justify or excuse the act, mitigate its guilt, or even bring it under a recognized exemption (e.g., conscien-tious objection to participation in war in any form). R. S. Peters stresses the important feature of the contexts of such appeals when he says that we seek or ascribe motives only "when a breach with an established expectation has occurred and there is need to justify some action."[25]

The agent accepts the demand for explanation because this is required by his sociality or perhaps because he recognizes that a

---

24. Gray, pp. 181–83.
25. R. S. Peters, "Motives and Motivation," *Philosophy* 31 (April 1956): 118.

plausible case can be made for a different act on grounds of prudence or morality. In the latter instance he may recognize (1) a conflict between moral claims and other desires (e.g., the desire for survival or security) or (2) a conflict between different moral claims. Such conflict situations emerge with special urgency when traditional authority structures are losing their power. As Pierce remarks, "It is clear that *conscience* only came into its own in the Greek world after the collapse of the city-state. The close integration of politics with ethics, with the former predominant, was no longer possible: there was no sufficiently close authority, external to the individual, effectively to direct conduct. Consequently, as a *pis aller*, men fell back on the internal chastisement of *conscience* as the only authority."[26] A similar historical point can be made about seventeenth-century England and the crisis of authority that Christopher Hill has described as "the world turned upside down" in his book by that title. But even in times of less dramatic social conflict, appeals to conscience are also common.

What are we to make of the appeal to conscience as a motive-statement in this sort of context? In *Human Acts,* Eric D'Arcy offers a helpful analysis of types of motive-statements and their logic; all of them are explanations in terms of the agent's objective for the sake of which he acts.[27] They are offered and ascribed when there is reason to think that the act (X) is good and the motive (M) is bad, or that M is good and X bad. The first type of motive-statement (type 1) is forward looking; it explains an act in terms of its function as a means to an end. The agent says, "What I really want is not the natural accompaniment or outcome of the act X, but the end M to which X is simply a means. I do X for the sake of M" (p. 158). For example, "I am working at this job in order to please my wife." The second type of motive-statement (type 2) shows why a course of action that has "no intrinsic attractiveness, has been in some way rendered an objective worthy of pursuit by some circumstance *not naturally or necessarily connected with it*" (p. 155). This may be a past circumstance (leading, for example, to acts of revenge, gratitude, or reparation), or a present circumstance (for example, love or a sense of duty). One says, "What I want is indeed the natural outcome or accompaniment of the action; but I want it, not because of its intrinsic attractiveness, but because of its being made worth while by some extrinsic circumstance C. I do X because of C" (p. 158). For example, "I am laying down my life for him out of a sense of gratitude." The third type of motive-statement (type 3) is not properly a motive-statement at all but, rather, functions to deny that any mo-

26. Pierce, p. 76.
27. Eric D'Arcy, *Human Acts: An Essay in Their Moral Evaluation* (Oxford: Clarendon Press, 1963).

tives other than the natural outcome of the act are present; it asserts that no "ulterior" motives are at work. For example, "I am caring for my elderly father simply and solely out of love." Such a statement adds nothing to an account of the conduct; it only dispels suspicion.

What type of motive-statement is the appeal to conscience? D'Arcy located this appeal under type 2: to say that a person acted "for conscience' sake" or out of a sense of duty is to explain his act in terms of an extrinsic circumstance. It is to say that he did X not because doing X was attractive or because the natural outcome was attractive but because an extrinsic circumstance was operative. Yet most cases of conscientious refusal are more complex and interesting than D' Arcy's analysis of type 2 suggests. For often, as in the case of conscientious objection to participation in war, act X (refusing to fight) and the natural accompaniment or outcome (avoiding the risks of being killed) are not totally unattractive. Indeed, others suspect that precisely this outcome is sought, and they consider X to be unworthy, cowardly, or unfair to others. Hence they are hostile to those who refuse to serve. Such charges and hostility obviously make X and its outcome less attractive to the objector. His appeal to his conscience is designed to dispel suspicion about his motives, not to indicate, as in type 3, that the natural outcome is the only motive but to deny that this attractive outcome (not dying) is the motive of X (not fighting) and to assert that an extrinsic circumstance (not killing as required by conscience) is the motive.

If my analysis is correct, the appeal to conscience is also a motive-statement of Type 1, the forward-looking, means-to-end type (although this terminology is not entirely appropriate). In appealing to conscience I indicate that I am trying to preserve a sense of myself, my wholeness and integrity, my good conscience, and that I cannot preserve these qualities if I submit to certain requirements of the state or society. While X (obedience or submission) is not naturally or necessarily associated with a negative outcome (loss of integrity) for many or most people, it would have this result in my life. I must avoid the sanction of a bad conscience. An analysis of Arthur Miller's refusal to give information to HUAC suggests that his motive-statement about conscience not only invokes conscience as an extrinsic present circumstance but also as an end to be attained or, negatively, a sanction to be avoided.

Against either my approach or D'Arcy's, there is the contention that "conscientious" applies to a person and a procedural policy of decision making rather than to the motive of acts. "Conscientious" refers not only to acts done from a sense of duty or "for conscience' sake" but also to a person's orientation and procedural policy when these can be characterized as scrupulous, painstaking, and serious. Although we consider all acts done from a sense of duty as conscientious, the converse does not hold. We also consider an act to be conscientious when the actor has seriously tried to discern his duty by considering the views of others and by testing his criteria of rightness and wrongness.[28]

Now, the critical point for this view developed, for example, by John Llewelyn is that "The conscientious man invokes conscience when he wishes to disclaim the capacity to *justify* an action and yet reserve the right to deny that the action was unconsidered."[29] Although the Rockefeller statement is somewhat ambiguous, it seems to be a candidate for such analysis. His reasons were "Christian" and "personal and philosophical." Perhaps he considered them somewhat inappropriate for public policy, or perhaps he thought that others would not find them convincing. If he had thought that his reasons would be acceptable to the people in his state, his appeal to conscience would have been unnecessary. To this extent Llewelyn's point is correct, for then the appeal to conscience would have added nothing but an indication of how deeply Rockefeller felt about reasons that would have been sufficient by themselves. Although Rockefeller appealed to a private framework, he hinted at another social framework of justification when he referred to "barbarism" and "a fallible and failing theory of punitive justice." He also could have drawn on a wide range of arguments against capital punishment, some of which have since been employed to exclude some laws authorizing capital punishment. But even so, I do not think that Rockefeller's invocation of conscience really was a disclaimer of the capacity to justify his act. Moral justification is, as Sidney Hook suggests, "a matter of reasons not of conscience."[30] But the appeal to conscience presupposes justification to oneself if my argument about conscience following judgments of moral worth is correct.

Typically a person invokes conscience in the course of explaining acts that require explanation because they contravene normal and established expectations. He invokes conscience not only to indicate that he made his decision "all things considered," including the reassessment of his standards, but also to indicate his motive for acting. That motive is, in part, avoidance of a sanction imposed by the self on itself, but the sanction comes into play only if there is a

28. For this second sense of "conscientious" as applying to decision-making procedures, see Albert R. Jonsen, *Christian Decision and Action* (New York: Bruce Publishing Co., 1970), and David Little, "A View of Conscience within the Protestant Theological Tradition," in *Conscience: Its Freedom and Limitations,* ed. William C. Bier, S. J. (New York: Fordham University Press, 1971), pp. 20–28.

29. John E. Llewelyn, "Conscientiousness," *Australasian Journal of Philosophy* 38 (December 1960): 221.

30. Sidney Hook, "Social Protest and Civil Disobedience," in *Moral Problems in Contemporary Society: Essays in Humanistic Ethics,* ed. Paul Kurtz (Englewood Cliffs, N.J.: Prentice-Hall, 1969), p. 165.

judgment of the act in terms that the self accepts. A person's appeal to conscience thus presupposes justification to himself if not to others.

The agent typically views his appeal to conscience as a last resort to be employed only when he thinks that he has exhausted other arguments for justifying or excusing his conduct. For the appeal to conscience is unnecessary if other reasons are acceptable, and it appears to constitute a cloture of debate. Usually the agent has given up the attempt to convince others of the objective rightness of his act and is content to assert its subjective rightness, perhaps to secure some positive treatment such as an exemption from ordinary duties. He cannot make an appeal to conscience until he has made a moral judgment because conscience follows judgment, and he does not need to make that appeal if the grounds for the judgment are acceptable to others. (I hardly need to emphasize that these stages are rarely clearly demarcated in actual moral discourse.) And yet if our observations about "consulting one's conscience" and "conscientiousness" are accurate, a person of conscience can never view the case as irrevocably closed. He or she must be willing to reopen it in the light of new evidence.

THE KEEPER OF CONSCIENCE: CONSCIENTIOUS OBJECTION AND PUBLIC POLICY

I think that this understanding of conscience and appeals to conscience has several important implications for public policies toward conscientious objection and refusal. I can only suggest a few of these implications at this point, but they revolve around the issue of the "keeper of conscience." In an exchange with Governor Winthrop in the seventeenth century, Anne Hutchinson defended entertaining "saints" in her home by insisting "That's a matter of conscience, Sir." Governor Winthrop responded, "Your conscience you must keep or it must be kept for you." Anne Hutchinson: "Must not I then entertain the saints because I must keep my conscience?" I do not propose to treat this matter of the "keeper of conscience" in terms of either the state or the individual. Indeed, my approach suggests that such an ultimate perspective, while sometimes helpful and even indispensable, often involves the wrong question for public policy: Which of the two authorities, state or conscience, is final? This question is too broad and must be specified in particular areas or particular laws, but it is also the wrong question in some contexts because conscience is more usefully understood not as an authority but as a sanction. When we ask as citizens and legislators, "What ought to be our policy toward conscientious claims for exemptions from laws?" we are asking, "When should (or may) we force a person to choose between the severe personal sanction of conscience and some legal sanction?" This is a question of public policy toward a class of genuine conscientious objectors to some particular law; it is a different question as to whether any particular individual belongs to that class, that is, whether he is able to pass the threshold test of sincerity.

My procedure will be to utilize a number of principles and distinctions that are mutually consistent although their coherence in a general political philosophy is not indicated. Many of these principles and distinctions are already at work (although not necessarily decisively) in the liberal, constitutional, democratic polity of the United States—in public policies, legal decisions, etc.—and my concern is to use and criticize some of them rather than to offer a constructive political philosophy as an alternative. Probably this level of discussion is most useful for criticism and direction of public policy.

Obviously public policy judgments involve balancing several values and principles, but in the area of the protection of conscience, some guidelines for such balancing seem to be possible and appropriate, especially in terms of setting presumptions and burdens of proof. If my analysis of conscience is correct, a state is a better and more desirable one if it puts the presumption in favor of exemption for conscientious objectors (not merely to war). It is prima facie a moral evil to force a person to act against his conscience, although it may often be justified and even necessary. And it is unfair to the conscientious person to give him the alternative of obedience to the law or criminal classification.[31]

My proposal can be seen more clearly by a comparison between two traditions in the interpretation of the free exercise of religion. Prior to *Sherbert* v. *Verner* (374 U.S. 398 [1963]), freedom of religion was seen primarily as the freedom of religious belief; religion was protected from the intentional and direct discrimination of the state. To determine whether the free-exercise clause had been violated, the courts only had to consider the question from the standpoint of the legislators (not the conscientious objectors) to see whether there was a valid secular legislative intent. With *Sherbert* v. *Verner* there was a shift in the interpretation of the free-exercise clause, although all its ramifications are far from clear.[32] A Seventh Day Adventist in

31. See the arguments by John Mansfield, "Conscientious Objection—1964 Term," in *Religion and the Public Order 1965*, ed. Donald A. Giannella (Chicago: University of Chicago Press, 1966); J. Morris Clark, "Guidelines for the Free Exercise Clause," *Harvard Law Review* 83 (1969): 337, 351; and the exchange between Gerald C. MacCallum, Jr., and Hugo Adam Bedau in *Issues in Law and Morality*, ed. Norman S. Care and Thomas K. Trelogan (Cleveland: Press of Case Western Reserve University, 1973), pp. 141–68.

32. For a superb discussion, from which I have drawn, of Sherbert v. Verner, see Alfred G. Killilea, "Standards for Expanding Freedom of Conscience," *Univer-*

South Carolina was denied state unemployment benefits because she refused to take employment that required her to work on Saturday, her Sabbath day, and the Supreme Court held that South Carolina could not "constitutionally apply the eligibility provisions so as to constrain a worker to abandon his religious convictions respecting the day of rest." The decision incorporated action along with belief under the protection of the free-exercise clause, and it also considered incidental effects of secular policies apart from legislative intent. According to this interpretation, it is not enough to see whether there is valid secular intent; the state also should consider the effects of the law from the standpoint of those who raise conscientious objections. Only in this way can it be determined whether conscience is affected. Furthermore, if conscience is affected, the state has to show that a compelling interest cannot be met in alternative ways to avoid the injury to conscience. That is, once there is evidence that conscience is affected, the state has the burden of proof; it must show its overriding interests in the legislation and policy and the absence of alternative means to achieve its ends. It is not enough to show a compelling interest of a general sort in the regulation; in effect, the state must show a compelling interest in denying the exemption to conscientious objectors. For example, if the possibility of spurious claims threatened to dilute the unemployment compensation fund and disrupt the scheduling of work, the state would have "to demonstrate that no alternative forms of regulation would combat such abuses without infringing First Amendment rights." The point is not that the state must not discriminate against conscience or intend to injure it (for this was already accepted) but that the state must intend that conscience not be injured even to the extent of assuming some burdens and costs to prevent such injury.

This general contention may be illuminated by a closer examination of types of conscientious objection and types of governmental interest. In one type of situation, the state may demand that a person perform some positive action to which he is conscientiously opposed; for example, it may impose on him the positive duty of military service. If the conscientious objector refuses to carry it out, should criminal penalties be imposed? (Later I will contrast these duties with negative ones—duties to refrain from certain conduct.)[33]

The government has a variety of possible responses short of applying criminal sanctions (against which my argument has estab-

---

sity of Pittsburgh Law Review 34 (Summer 1973): 531–55. But contrast Trans World Airlines, Inc. v. Hardison 97 (S. Ct.) 2264 (1977).

33. Although I recognize that this distinction and the related distinction between act and omission are not wholly satisfactory, they serve useful analytic functions in this essay.

lished a presumption). Its role as teacher and educator should not be underestimated. But when conscience opposes these positive duties, the state can often yield without any serious cost; or it can sometimes perform the act for the objector, thereby accomplishing its end and relieving the objector of the burden of conscience; or it can impose an alternative duty that will preserve fairness to other citizens (by preventing economic and other advantages) while protecting the objector's conscience.

The government can usually yield to conscientious objectors to jury duty (the only other conscription besides the military in the United States) without any serious cost.[34] Scruples against judging others can simply be accommodated along with numerous existing grounds for exemption, although it may be desirable to ask for alternative service.

Sometimes (e.g., in some medical treatments, inoculations, and tax collection) the government can protect the individual's conscience by performing the act in question for him. In such cases the agent may not consider his conscience violated because he did not consent to the act; an example is the case of the Jehovah's Witnesses whose consciences would not permit them to consent to a blood transfusion although they could live with a court-ordered transfusion. Also faced with the conscientious refusal to pay taxes for military expenditures, the government may attach the CO's salary or bank account. This obviously achieves the government's end, and it may avoid offense to conscience by eliminating the agent's responsibility. But this removal of responsibility will not work for all CO's even in the areas of medical treatment and taxes, for they may view conscience as imposing strict liabilities. It also will not work in some other cases, such as military service, where "the government cannot obtain its ends through the objector without violating his conscience."[35] Regarding inoculations, the government should determine whether its interest in public health and safety really requires that each individual be inoculated, for the unprotected individual may not be a threat to anyone else. My argument is not that conscience should be satisfied in every instance, but that the government should show that it cannot secure its legitimate interests, specific as well as general, by alternative means.

Finally, the government may be able to impose some substitute or alternative service and thus respect conscience. This is especially true of noncombatant or alternative service in the national interest in lieu of military service. Such a requirement not only offers some test of the objector's sincerity, but it also respects the principle of

34. See In re Jenison 375 U.S. 14 (1963).
35. Clarke, p. 348.

fairness in relation to other citizens by imposing burdens on all who are drafted even if the burdens are not exactly the same. Some cases of conflict between conscience and the law are not susceptible to these approaches; they probably include the refusal to testify in courts of law and the stance of noncooperation with the government in any of its positive requirements, such as registration for the draft.[36]

Several important issues emerge from these cases of conscientious objection to positive legal duties. First, in some instances, there is an important distinction between service and obedience or subjection. In the range of positive duties, a few are clear examples of service, as when individuals are selected for military service or jury duty in order to carry out the law; they are the law's instruments. Also there has been a duty to assist the police in the suppression of crime. Some have contended that a refusal of service is not a nullification of the law, although disobedience might be.[37] Thus the government need not treat conscientious refusals of service and conscientious disobedience in the same way.

Second, the nature of the service is also important, especially since some acts are closer to the core of some religious and moral traditions as well as personal character than others, and the state itself may have reasons for encouraging the attitudes reflected in some conscientious refusals: for example, the centrality of pacifism to the Historic Peace Churches and its affinities to dominant attitudes in day-to-day life. It might even be possible to single out military service for special treatment because killing human beings is considered prima facie wrong from practically all moral standpoints.

Third, the question of the number of persons seeking exemption is very important. If the state could not get enough servants for juries and military operations, it could justifiably deny the exemptions. But a better procedure would be to limit the number of exemptions for conscience, determining by means of a lottery who would be exempted and who would be forced to serve or face criminal penalties. There are, however, practical reasons for exempting conscientious objectors from jury duty and military service, for forced participation may be detrimental to the enterprise as a whole and many would choose jail or exile rather than participate in the military. Pacifist consciences are perhaps protected, in part, because their numbers are more or less predictable, while the number of just-war objectors cannot be estimated in advance of a particular war. Nevertheless, a lottery would be possible for selective objectors

36. Ibid., pp. 357–58.
37. See Michael Walzer, *Obligations: Essays on Disobedience, War, and Citizenship* (Cambridge, Mass.: Harvard University Press, 1970), p. 136.

as well as for pacifists if the state faced serious shortages of manpower, and it would obviate one of the main difficulties feared by opponents of selective conscientious objection.[38]

Now we can look briefly at conscientious objection to and violation of a negative legal duty, the prohibition of some conduct that the agent considers essential to his religious or moral convictions. Several examples are proselytizing, polygamy, and sacraments involving prohibited substances. The Volstead Act had an exemption for wine used by churches for communion, and the California Supreme Court has held that the Native American Church may use peyote in its religious ceremonies. Again, the state should yield to conscience in matters that do not involve harm to persons outside a consenting moral or religious community (or minors within the community). When the conflict is only between the state and the individual conscience over negative duties, the state's interest in paternalism should be rejected and the state should grant conscience this freedom.

If these proposals are to be sufficiently concrete and feasible, there must be fuller specification of two elements that I can only identify here and plan to discuss elsewhere: (1) the distinction between conscientious and nonconscientious objection, and (2) the test of conscientiousness or sincerity in claiming conscientiousness. It is somewhat artificial to separate these two questions, but it is useful to do so for analytic purposes. Furthermore, it is possible to say that where there is a claim of conscientious objection to a particular law, the government should bear the burden of proof in showing that an exemption should not be allowed to this class of objectors. But an individual who claims to be a conscientious objector should bear the burden of proof that he really holds the beliefs in question and that he holds them deeply.

A number of attempts have been made to distinguish between conscientious and nonconscientious objection in terms of source of convictions (e.g., religious training), function, content, and psychological effects or consequences of such convictions. But regardless of the ground of the distinction between conscientious and nonconscientious objection (and I tend to favor a combination of functional and psychological), sincerity remains a "threshold" question which should be answered by the objector.

Liberal society is primarily a society of strangers—friendly strangers, but strangers nonetheless. Its members are strangers because of differences regarding fundamental values; they are

---

38. These fears were expressed by the National Advisory Commission on Selective Service, *In Pursuit of Equity: Who Serves When Not All Serve?* (1967), pp. 48–51. John Mansfield also argues for such a lottery (see Mansfield, p. 46, n. 59; and p. 73).

friendly because they agree on some general and vague values (such as life, liberty, and happiness) and on certain rules and procedures. The consensus, if such exists, is primarily about rules and procedures. Critical is the point that values are experienced mainly as subjective and individual. In the absence of agreement about values, the state becomes the bearer of social order to a great extent through the rules it enforces by its various sanctions. When individuals take it upon themselves to violate the legal rules or to ignore the procedures in the name of some higher, broader, or different conception of morality, how are such conflicts adjudicated? Often by falling back on secondary virtues, which concern the "how," rather than primary virtues, which concern the "what."[39] Secondary virtues include conscientiousness and sincerity. As John Rawls notes, "in times of social doubt and loss of faith in long established values, there is a tendency to fall back on the virtues of integrity: truthfulness and sincerity, lucidity and commitment, or, as some say, authenticity."[40] When values, ends, and primary virtues are experienced as subjective, trust is preserved by maintaining confidence in procedures and secondary virtues.[41] Trust may be confidence in and reliance on others to respect their commitments to a principle (e.g., pacifism) even if the truster disagrees with the principle.

When such scepticism about values prevails, the state, especially through the courts, will probably handle many of its religious and moral questions by means of secondary concepts, especially those that seem to offer some value neutrality. Such concepts and standards (e.g., the distinctions between action and belief and between public and private) have the virtue of establishing regularity over time and a stable basis of expectations—important for any rule of law. But they often obscure the real policy issue: the value question of how much room conscience should have, how much freedom and protection it should have in relation to other interests. My argument, grounded in an understanding of conscience as a sanction, is that we should start with the presumptive liberty of conscience, which then forces the state to bear the burden of proof to show that its interests are compelling and can be realized through no other means than a denial of the exemption.

39. Alasdair MacIntyre, *Secularization and Moral Change* (London: Oxford University Press, 1967), p. 24.
40. Rawls, p. 519.
41. See Childress, "Nonviolent Resistance: Trust and Risk-Taking," pp. 87–112.

The Decline of Guilt

Herbert Morris

With over thirty years of psychoanalytic reflection behind him, Freud observed in the concluding chapter of *Civilization and Its Discontents* that it was his "intention to represent the sense of guilt as the most important problem in the development of civilization and to show that the price we pay for our advance in civilization is a loss of happiness through the heightening of the sense of guilt."[1] This sense of guilt to which Freud refers, and to whose influence he assigns so significant and baneful an effect, generally becomes activated because of a belief that one is or would be, if one were to act in a certain way, in fact, guilty. This concept of guilt plays, of course, a major role in our moral life. Without it our morality would significantly differ from that with which we are now familiar. But the idea of one's being guilty, though integral to morality as we know it, seems even more central to law. We can imagine moral forms of life without guilt, but deep puzzlement confronts us when we make this attempt with the idea of law. In law, guilt clearly assumes its most systematic, its most recurrently public deployment.

While central to our idea of law and while a concept with the most serious legal and social implications, guilt remains, quite surprisingly, little examined. To be sure, much scholarly attention has been bestowed upon concepts closely linked with it, concepts such as responsibility, causation, and culpability, but guilt itself has largely escaped notice. In this paper I hope to go some way toward remedying this neglect. I first describe in some detail the nature and role of guilt and the sense of guilt in law, and I compare this with the situation in morality. I then set out a variety of theoretical critiques of guilt, each of which has in some way disturbed the comfort of mind of many who employ the concept, and I also draw attention to certain forces at work within society that I believe may slowly be transforming guilt's role. These critiques and these forces, reinforcing each other, strike at the very heart of law and create a crisis for guilt, posing what we might describe as "the problem of guilt in law." I intend to represent this problem, to echo Freud's formulation, as "the most important problem" presently before us in the development of law.

---

1. S. Freud, *Civilization and Its Discontents*, in *The Standard Edition of the Complete Psychological Works of Sigmund Freud* (London: Hogarth, 1961), vol. 21, p. 134.

This essay originally appeared in *Ethics*, vol. 99, no. 1, October 1988.

Finally, I argue—and here my position contrasts sharply with Freud's though not in its speculative character—that the erosion of guilt within law, coupled with a narrowed and weakened compass for our sense of guilt, both with respect to law and more generally, may carry a cost comparable to the lost happiness which Freud attributes to guilt.

Let us now turn to the first issue: the nature and role of guilt within law. While it may be impossible to imagine law without guilt, its role there has always been circumscribed. Judgments of guilt should neither be identified with, nor thought of as implied by, judgments of invalidity or judgments of liability. A marriage or a will, or, for that matter, a verdict of guilt itself, might be invalid, but this implies nothing about one's guilt in failing to satisfy the conditions required for a valid marriage or will or verdict. And in a civil action, judgment rendered for plaintiff and against defendant, establishing defendant's liability, implies nothing by itself about defendant's guilt, and this is so regardless of defendant's fault. Verdicts of guilt are rendered within and restricted to criminal proceedings or other proceedings, such as court-martials, which are criminal in character.

What, then, does legal guilt imply? No simple answer to this apparently simple question will suffice. I divide my discussion as follows: I first set out those conditions which legal systems generally require—exceptions will be addressed later—for a person to be guilty. With these conditions satisfied and the person in, what I shall label, "the state of guilt," I then attempt to answer the question, What is implied by being in that state? I then turn attention to those general beliefs about the world presupposed by application of the concept. I conclude this first major section of my discussion by offering an analysis of the sense of guilt that differs significantly from Freud's, and I offer for consideration some contrasts between law and morality.

What conditions characteristically must be satisfied if one can truthfully be said to be legally guilty? These are quite familiar. I shall enumerate them briefly, though the meaning of each, of course, deserves fuller discussion as does the respect accorded them by actual legal systems. First, legal guilt requires conduct. This means several things: first, a person must do something rather than merely, for example, desire or intend to do it; second, a person must do something rather than merely have something happen that involves one's body that results in harm—causing damage, for example, as a result of being lifted up by the wind; and, third, a person must do something rather than simply have a status of a certain kind such as being a member of a certain race. Each of these conditions is, of course, consistent with guilt attaching to omissive conduct. A second point is this: guilt requires conscious conduct; consequently, conduct while asleep precludes guilt. Third, legal guilt requires fault or culpability with respect to wrongdoing, what criminal lawyers refer to as a "guilty mind" or "the mens rea of an offense." The absence of a requisite culpability state or one's fair opportunity to behave otherwise than one did, precludes guilt. Fourth, legal guilt is individual, never vicarious, and requires a culpable relationship of the guilty person to the wrongful conduct. If guilty because of what another has done, some culpable relationship to that other's conduct must be present. Fifth, one must possess the capacity to appreciate the significance of the norms applicable to one. Immunizing, as we do, animals and infants from guilt reflects this requirement as does exculpation of at least some individuals suffering from mental illness. Sixth, legal guilt requires legal wrongdoing. Even the most egregious moral wrong, if unaccompanied by legal wrongdoing, does not incur legal guilt. Finally, "guilty" is a predicate that attaches to acts, states of mind, and persons. To be a guilty person (the particular focus of my concern in this study) requires satisfaction of all of the above conditions and a further condition that one be the self-same person as the one who satisfied all the above conditions. Puzzlement felt over guilty verdicts returned against those suffering severe amnesia at the time of conviction, or suffering any other condition that deprives them of a sense of continuity with the person who has committed the offense, would reflect one's attachment to this condition for guilt.

Important issues for my purposes arise if, within a system of criminal law, legal guilt is incurred when one or more of these conditions do not obtain. I shall address these issues shortly, but I want now to suppose that a particular person satisfies all these conditions. It would then be true to say of such a person that he or she was, to use a rough summary description, "culpably responsible for legal wrongdoing." And as such, the person would be legally guilty. But for an understanding of guilt, one must, I believe, keep in mind the distinction between two closely related, and therefore easily confused, concepts. To say of a person that he or she is "culpably responsible for legal wrongdoing" implies only that those conditions I have listed bearing on wrongdoing and culpability and causation have been satisfied, while to ascribe guilt to someone, though presupposing these conditions, implies more.

First, a guilty person is in a state deserving of some negative attitude, condemnation appearing the most apt term for this attitude, and the delivered verdict of guilt provides a formal expression of this attitude by an authoritative social organ. In declaring people guilty, we label them, perhaps more accurately, "brand" them, and thereby transform their status into that of the legally condemned. Second, being in the state of guilt implies that one has, through one's guilty act, set oneself apart from the community, membership in which we partly define by commitment to communal norms. Again, the verdict of guilt, with its branding one as guilty, reflects this fact of separateness, mirroring, through its setting the guilty apart from others, their having set themselves apart. Third, the state of guilt implies a special kind of separateness, for persons in this state have arrogated to themselves that to which they are not entitled, thereby placing themselves in a position of superiority to others who have complied with the norms. Thus, being guilty, one deserves a response that operates to cancel this improper arrogation. Again, branding one "guilty" supplies some of this, and the actual visiting of punishment upon the guilty provides more. Next, nothing seems more fundamental to guilt than the idea that being guilty one owes something. Of course, within law no formal legal obligation necessarily attaches to guilt, but we nevertheless believe that we are entitled to take from the guilty something they owe. It is from this that the imagery of "a debt owed to society" derives. Next, closely connected with this is the idea that the guilty are subject to a sentence of punishment and to its imposition which constitutes the "exacting of the debt." Any legal practice restricted to establishing one's liability to make reparations or restitution or to providing compensation would differ fundamentally from a legal practice involving guilt. None of these alternative practices implies that wrongdoers are deserving of condemnation, that they are insufficiently committed to the norms or that their conduct has caused injury to society, not just to a particular person. Finally, guilt admits of degrees, some persons being more, some less, guilty, and each of the above responses is guided by concepts of proportionality or fittingness or both.

If this analysis has validity, certain quite general beliefs would seem to be held by those who internalize this practice. There would appear to be, for example, beliefs in an established order of things where limits are respected and relationships among people are as they ought to be, beliefs in an imbalance to that order caused by the guilty, beliefs in individuals being together and apart, determined to some significant degree by their conduct with respect to norms, beliefs in the possibility of restoration—matters in the world of guilt may, after all, be righted—beliefs in one's being tainted because of one's guilt, and even beliefs, perhaps, residues from times when the conception of pollution was dominant, of society remaining itself not quite right, somewhat unclean, until through punishment purification is achieved.

Punishment, while certainly having other explanations as well is, on this conception, highly overdetermined, at once a means of righting wrongs, correcting imbalances, reordering disturbed relationships, promoting restoration, and cleansing both the criminal and society. As a response to guilt, punishment must be seen, then, as freighted with rich symbolic significance, and in considering what might justify punishment we risk, I believe, incompleteness in our theories if we neglect this symbolic baggage.

For the above to hold true, for there to be in effect a practice of the kind I have described, it would also appear necessary that there exist throughout society a general commitment to norms established by law, to the values they support and to the legitimacy of the practice that has been established to determine violations and guilt. Widespread disaffection among the populace from the norms or lack of belief in the legitimacy of tribunals established to judge people would transform the legal practice into one in which individuals with power merely enforced their will upon others. In such circumstances, the normative basis of the practice would crumble; condemnation would inevitably fall upon deaf ears and lose its point; punishment would become merely a matter of pain inflicted or freedom limited. Our conduct might be, in such circumstances, much as it presently is, but we should be going through the motions only—our world would have dramatically changed. If this is correct, a certain correspondence exists within society—and this hardly seems surprising—between being guilty and feeling guilty. Among the matters that seem presupposed by the practice would appear a generally pervasive vulnerability within the population covered by the legal norms to having their sense of guilt activated when contemplating or engaging in violative conduct. It is but the flip side of the disposition to feel indignation when others violate the law. To imagine that it was generally otherwise would throw into question central elements in the practice. But, if this is so, something needs to be said about the nature of our sense of guilt and its principal mark—one's feeling guilty.

Our sense of guilt reveals itself in our feeling inhibited from doing what we believe wrong and feeling guilty when we do it. Thus, it operates in a forward-looking and backward-looking manner. Freud's views about guilt are most thoroughly formulated in *Civilization and Its Discontents*. He there concentrates upon the sense of guilt as it operates in a forward-looking manner, conceiving of guilt as internalized anxiety, the incorporation or internalization by children of a threat of loss of love or attack embodied in parental attitudes. This view reduces guilt to anxiety, and clouds, I believe, our understanding of the former.[2] Let us see why this is so by looking first at what it is to feel guilty and then at the sense of guilt as inhibiting conduct.

A person who feels guilt holds to beliefs of a certain kind, feels a certain way, and is disposed to feel and act in certain specific ways. I believe we come at a clearer view of what it is to feel guilty by focusing on the distress that is intimately connected with it. It cannot—we shall then see—be reduced to anxiety, though if one experiences guilt, anxiety might accidentally be associated with it. A person feels such distress because of a unique set of beliefs, none of which implies either fear or anxiety. First, one has internalized norms and, as such, is committed to avoiding wrong. The mere fact that wrong is believed to have occurred, regardless of who bears responsibility for it, naturally causes distress. When we are attached to a person, injury to that person causes us pain regardless of who or what has occasioned the injury. But just as a special satisfaction attaches to thinking of oneself as the creator of what is valuable—we feel a special pleasure in our being the source of a loved

---

2. The fullest treatment of which I am aware of this topic is to be found in Michael Friedman, "Toward a Reconceptualization of Guilt," *Contemporary Psychoanalysis* 21 (1985): 501–45. For an early essay of mine setting out views that correspond to Friedman's, see "Guilt and Suffering," *Philosophy of East and West*, vol. 21 (1971), reprinted in *On Guilt and Innocence* (Berkeley: University of California Press, 1976).

one's pleasure—so thinking of oneself as responsible for wrongdoing arouses a special dissatisfaction. Further, in feeling guilt one turns on oneself the criticism and hostility that one would have visited upon others had they done wrong. Still another aspect of one's distress is one's feeling apart from those with whom one was attached. Indeed, another element of the distress derives from one's sense of fragmentation. Finally, in feeling guilty one feels burdened until steps are taken. One feels obliged to confess, to make amends, to repair, and to restore.

The painful feelings, then, associated with feeling guilt belong to those attendant upon damaging what we value, and not to anxiety, whether it be internalized or not. The impulse, for example, to confess reveals attachment and a desire to restore bonds. This must be kept distinct from any fear attendant upon the thought of not confessing. Likewise, to turn briefly to guilt as inhibiting wrongdoing, as a motive it derives from a desire to remain attached to what one values (with conscience, e.g., it is one's integrity). This should not be confused with the desire to avoid pain for oneself that would be attendant on damaging or betraying that to which one is attached. I am suggesting, then, that guilt is a nonegoistic motive, more like love than fear. Just as, when considering love, we should avoid confusing acting out of love for another with acting out of a desire for our own pleasure (easily confused because in achieving love's aim we derive pleasure), so we should avoid confusing guilt with a desire to avoid pain for ourselves.

This concludes my examination of the nature of guilt within law and our sense of guilt. I want now to return to an issue I raised a short while ago, namely, the status of the conditions I listed for one to be guilty, what I summarized in the phrase "culpably responsible for legal wrongdoing." Legal systems, however unjust, insist generally upon proof that these conditions obtain before judging one guilty. But we also know that our own law occasionally allows for a finding of guilt without proof in a particular case of any mens rea, and ignorance of law, which certainly bears upon culpability as I have defined it, is commonly not recognized as a defense. In these cases, though we might feel a pull to say of an individual without the requisite state that he or she was not "really guilty," we also seem prepared to affirm the existence of legal guilt if the person has been found guilty under the applicable rules. In what sense, then, are these conditions required if systems disregard them in making determinations of guilt?

To be sure, these conditions appear to embody constraints that justice places upon law and so their disregard may ground judgments of injustice. But there is still another sense in which the conditions may be viewed as required. This sense may be captured by putting the following question, How far might legal systems go in disregarding these conditions when making determinations of guilt and still be concerned with guilt?

Just so far, I would say. A system could, imaginably, impose suffering upon individuals just because of their racial characteristics. Or the law might, for example, treat relatives of escaped felons harshly in an attempt to reduce the number of escapes. In these cases, basic conditions for guilt do not obtain, the practices are unjust, and, in addition, we should find talk of guilt, talk of punishing because of guilt, talk of verdicts of guilt as entirely inappropriate. Determinations of fact, not judgments of guilt, underlie the visiting of pain upon people in these circumstances, and puzzlement would result from any insistence upon claiming that legal guilt attaches to such persons. Some criteria for legal guilt would appear, then, to connect with the idea of guilt so tightly that failure to satisfy them would imply inapplicability of the concept.

But the examples suggested above are extreme. What shall we say about the more common instances presented to us of legal disregard of conditions for guilt? For guidance on this issue, we must turn attention to some connections between legal guilt and our moral conception of guilt.

No mere linguistic oddity lies behind the fact that the same term 'guilt' applies in these spheres of human life, and it would be surprising if within law and morality the rules governing the term's application differed markedly. No formal, depsychologized analysis of legal guilt, of the sort some legal positivists might offer, will capture its nature. As we have seen, guilt has special significance. Individuals who are guilty are viewed as justifiably condemned, justifiably punished, as having set themselves apart from the community through insufficient attachment to its values. If this is so, a number of conditions for being morally guilty—among them conditions related to a fair opportunity to behave otherwise than one did—must be presuppositions of legal guilt as well, for we should be at a loss otherwise to understand what it meant to speak of justifiable condemnation, justifiable punishment, and the like. Scattered exceptions to this might exist, and where they do, it deserves noting, we deploy justifications that commonly invoke "presumptions" that a person must, say, know the law or in fact be culpable. By doing this, we reveal our attachment to one's being guilty as a basis for one's being legally guilty.

My claim, then, is that a system that generally allowed for findings of guilt in conflict with basic moral constraints on the concept of guilt would be one that used existing institutions of the criminal law in a way fundamentally at odds with certain of its basic presuppositions. As with marked alienation by the community from the norms applicable to them, significant disregard of the conditions for guilt would transform the practice. Prevention and social control would replace crime and punishment as these are now understood.

I want now to address the question, Supposing the existence of a practice of the kind I have described, what functions does it perform in the lives of people who have internalized it? The universal fascination with crime and punishment, the mystery, illumination, conflict, the pain and suffering and violence there to be found, betray a deep emotional need satisfied by this recurrently enacted drama. I shall draw attention to certain familiar facts and engage in some psychological speculation.

First, determinations of guilt and the infliction of punishment upon the guilty, vividly communicate, in a way no other social practice can, the community's values, serving both to instruct and to reinforce. Among law's clearest lessons are that norms exist and that they are to be taken seriously. These in turn provide reassurance that our social world is orderly and not chaotic, that it is a structured space in which not everything is permitted, where there are limits to conduct, a role for rational argumentation over who has crossed these limits, and, equally important psychologically, that closure exists as a possibility once these limits have been breached. When issues of guilt and innocence arise outside the law, we commonly meet with complexity and ambiguity. Law reduces life's murkiness, making matters somewhat neater than elsewhere. Law repeatedly enacts a compelling drama in which a person is either guilty or not guilty, in which light, so often sought and so generally elusive, is shed upon initial mystery, and in which conflict meets with resolution and guilt with its just deserts. Life, of course, is quite unlike that—indeed this is an idealized picture of law—but law, because of its relative definiteness and its institutionalized means of closure, nicely allows our indulging in this gratifying illusion. The world of guilt, then, contrary to Freud's suggestion, would appear to reduce rather than promote anxiety. This is so for still another important reason.

Guilt, perhaps more than any other concept, serves our need to believe ourselves capable of some effectiveness in the world, a need all the more insistent as conditions of modern life promote feelings of helplessness. Intimately involved as it is with responsibility, guilt testifies to human freedom and agency and, as such, it may serve to counteract one's sense of victimization. It is for this reason, I would suggest, that guilty feelings may operate for a person defensively, serving to hide from one something felt to be far more distressing than guilt.[3]

Something more needs to be said about how moral and legal guilt relate to one another. There can, of course, be moral guilt without legal guilt, legal guilt without moral guilt, and a range of instances in which the two overlap. Many lies and broken promises find no legal redress, and nothing is more evident than moral evil outside the law's compass. That legal guilt might exist without moral guilt is equally evident. Here one need only point to the moral rightness of violating an iniquitous law. That the two overlap is evident because of crimes such as murder where the legally guilty must commonly be morally guilty as well.

I earlier suggested that a conceptual connection also existed between the two kinds of guilt, with law constrained to some extent, if guilt is our concern, by moral considerations. While connected, moral and legal guilt

3. For a similar view, see W. R. D. Fairbairn, "The Repression and the Return of Bad Objects," in *Psychoanalytic Studies of the Personality* (London: Routledge & Kegan Paul, 1952).

also differ in significant ways. Legal systems may, and obviously frequently do, lay down norms devoid of moral justification. Just so long as there exists general societal acceptance of the procedures that generate those norms and commitment to acting in accord with them, the moral credentials of any particular norm are not an issue in determining guilt. There also remains, as we have seen, some latitude within law in specifying the circumstances under which violation of legal norms incurs guilt. But with moral guilt, the norms and the conditions to be satisfied for incurring guilt by violating them are immune from deliberate human modification. It would not follow, for example, that a society's acceptance of the authority of legal organs and the enactment by these organs of a morally iniquitous law converted a morally innocent wrongdoer into a morally guilty one because the criteria for legal guilt had been satisfied. Further, for the most part, guilt within moral situations arises when one has violated the rights of another individual, and society is not viewed as having an interest in the affair. Thus, those in a position to condemn or forgive are those whose rights have been violated and no others. Neither is there within morality the connection between punishment and guilt that one finds in law. Within morality one may criticize and resent, but commonly with moral guilt—think of guilt arising in close personal relationships—punishment would be viewed as inappropriate and entirely inconsistent with restoring the damaged relationship. Within the moral sphere essential for restoration are emotions and attitudes such as guilt, contrition, and repentance. Law and morality also differ through the objects taken for scrutiny. Maxims such as "the law aims at a minimum; morality at a maximum" and "law is concerned with external conduct; morality with internal conduct" draw attention to contrasting moral and legal emphases.

This richly textured practice of guilt, whose nature I have made an attempt to depict, did not instantaneously appear fully appareled in its customary garb in human culture. Ideas such as value and the wrongful had first to enter and assume their present hegemony in human consciousness. The story of Adam and Eve's scandalous flirtation with dreams of glory and inevitable horrifying fall condenses into a few vivid and chilling moments a long period of human development. Again, Ezekiel, signaling a shift toward the individualization of guilt, collapsed into a single edict, "the righteousness of the righteous shall be upon him, and the wickedness of the wicked upon him," a truth we now take for granted but whose acceptance surely evolved gradually. With Christianity we can record still another dramatic change, for the inner life of the moral agent assumed an importance it earlier did not have. But the words of Jesus, and the radical thoughts they embodied, fell upon receptive ears, suggesting a ground slowly tilled and made ready for the seed that flowered into a central tenet of the way in which we presently think.

I mention these few moments in guilt's history because, as I have suggested in my introductory remarks, we may ourselves be in the midst of a transformation—ironically guilt's slow demise after its slow ascendancy.

Through a confluence of factors—philosophical determinism, the development of the behavioral sciences, the ideology of sickness and therapy—the truth, indeed the rationality, of conceptions undergirding the practice of guilt have been thrown into question. And powerful social forces and an accommodating social ideology are also, even more influentially, at work, adding to the instability produced by the above views. Guilt is in the eye of a storm.

The assault on the rationality of the practice of guilt has moved along a number of parallel fronts. First, some challenge the presuppositions upon which guilt rests. Here we encounter either metaphysical lines of argument or more empirically grounded theories which claim that behind any instance of wrongdoing lie causative factors that should exempt wrongdoers from blame. Connected with these lines of argumentation are tendencies toward viewing antisocial conduct as pathological, a matter for therapy, not punishment. Sickness in our modern ways of thinking gradually occupies territory formerly governed by moral categories. Further, some have urged, taking a more epistemological than metaphysical line, that, even were we to acknowledge the possibility that people were sometimes guilty, we cannot have reasonable grounds for such belief. After all, when guilt is at issue, we make determinations about mental states and about the past, each of which presents its own epistemological difficulties, difficulties compounded when the factors are conjoined. Skepticism of this kind naturally inclines its adherents to urge forgoing concern with culpability at the time of the offense charged. Barbara Wootton's views nicely illustrate such thinking.[4] She has proposed a two-stage process in which attention would focus initially and exclusively upon what was in fact done, something observable. With this determined, focus would then shift to the responsible party's condition at the time of conviction and our concern limited to the most effective disposition of the offender. Moves to abolish the defense of insanity, a defense requiring inquiry into the state of the defendant's mind at the time of the wrongful act alleged, often reflect such a viewpoint.

These, then, are some familiar themes of discontent with guilt. It is not always evident what would practically follow from taking a particular critique seriously. For example, those who deny the existence of free will do not customarily advocate abandoning the criminal law and its distinction between those who act voluntarily and those, say, because of an epileptic seizure, who do not. It also deserves noting that these critiques have not gone unanswered; they have, in fact, mobilized tenacious defenses of customary ways of thinking about human beings. If this accumulation of critiques distinguishes the modern age so, too, do the number of defenses of human freedom and guilt made by those who have insisted that humans are free and that they often choose their own enslavement.

---

4. Barbara Wootton, *Crime and the Criminal Law* (London: Sweet & Maxwell, 1963).

What importance, then, outside of philosophy, do these various critiques of guilt possess? Sometimes, of course, they may directly influence the law, as when they serve to support abolition of the insanity defense or, to an entirely contrary purpose, when they serve to support exculpation on grounds of early and formative childhood experiences. They are also, of course, so to speak "in the air," elements in the intellectual climate, available to those who might seek support for the common human disposition to flee guilt with some justification or excuse. If there is merit in this speculation, critiques of guilt might occasionally be drawn upon to quiet an aroused sense of guilt. This is a powerful motivation with which to be aligned, and we should be cautious before discounting the potential this combination of theory and motivation has for fundamentally altering the ways in which we view ourselves and others.

Still, allowing that these negative views about guilt may have seeped into our consciousness and already even to some degree altered our practices, it seems evident, if change is occurring, that more powerful factors would have to be at work. Ideas may indeed ignite change, but to do so they obviously require combustible social conditions upon which to operate. Before entering upon some personal speculation, in no way grounded I must confess on careful empirical study, as to what other factors might be present and more effective, I should delay no further in indicating what I view as some noteworthy exceptions to the model of guilt within law.

I have in mind the following types of phenomena: (1) the practice of plea bargaining and the exercise of prosecutorial discretion more generally which operate to avoid inquiry into and determination of guilt with respect to particular offenses; (2) the employment of excessive punishments, violating the principle of proportionality that is tied to concern over degrees of guilt; (3) doctrines of strict and vicarious liability interpreted in such a way that an individual's culpability with respect to a particular matter ceases to be a material element in determining guilt; (4) constriction of or abolition of the defense of insanity; and (5) the proliferation of laws and regulations whose connection with wrongdoing, as generally conceived, is attenuated.

I must immediately acknowledge that the aspects of law to which this list draws attention have for a considerable period of time been familiar parts of the legal landscape. Our own law has always, of course, in some of its principal doctrines diverged in striking ways from basic principles governing attribution of guilt. I have in mind, to provide some greater specificity than the above list, the unavailability of certain defenses, such as reasonable ignorance or mistake of law, the pockets of strict liability with regard to certain sexual and regulatory offenses, the employment of objective standards to ground a finding of culpability, and the existence of narrow definitions of the defense of insanity which assure the conviction of those who are in fact not guilty. Those who believe that the criminal law should in its determinations of guilt reflect a person's actual guilt, that to disregard such a constraint implies injustice, have always subjected these doctrines to criticism. Their views have at least occasionally altered practice, witness the influence of the American Law Institute's *Model Penal Code* upon the criminal law of a number of jurisdictions. If there has been some movement away from guilt, it cannot be regarded as without powerful reactive tendencies, reflecting the grip of this concept upon our thinking.

If I claim, then, that something novel may now be underway, I can hardly rest my case upon the presence of new doctrines and practices. It must rather be, as is so often the case, a question of degree, a result of a conjunction of influences promoting different emphases and because of that, a drift, a tendency to assign less importance to guilt. What might these influences be? I have already referred to certain theoretical views that question the rationality of guilt. To these must now be added a familiar and seductive mode of thinking with far more evident impact upon law and our attitudes toward it than metaphysics and epistemology. To put it most succinctly, it is an approach that subordinates principle to the realization of social goals, a mode of thinking that focuses, not upon exculpation of the innocent and conviction of the guilty, that is, upon justice, but upon keeping social disruption at an acceptable level. It promotes the slow transformation of law into administration. Such an ideology provides the justification for conviction of the innocent, non-prosecution of the guilty, and disregard for principles of proportionality. It smacks of Wilde's cynic knowing the price of everything and the value of nothing. But this, too, is hardly novel. Coupled with certain contemporary social conditions, however, I believe it may be bringing about significant change.

What are some of these social conditions? First, I would list the pervasively held belief that crime has increased. It is a belief that also corresponds to reality, for while the rate of crime proportionate to the population may have varied only slightly over the last one hundred years, more laws on the books and more people in existence to violate them inevitably result in more crime. Again, whatever the reality might be, people generally believe that mass murders and crimes involving sadism and gratuitous violence are more prevalent today than ever before. The consequence of this is evident—increased fear. Another factor of importance enters in, feeding fear—growth of the news media and instantaneous coverage of events. Were there not more crime, such coverage would create the contrary impression. But, of course, along with this sense of more crime are media focus and elaboration upon it and upon particular kinds of crimes. Commonly, either crimes of violence or crimes perpetrated by governmental officials receive widest publicity. This phenomenon must be conjoined with a major growth in the entertainment industry and the obvious marketability of crime. It hardly deserves comment that our social consciousness is immersed in crime.

I would next draw attention to the enormous increase in the number of laws and legal regulations, that familiar accompaniment to a heavily populated modern industrial society. These laws result in more offenders and offenders whose crimes often diverge from traditional instances of wrongdoing. A consequence of legal wrongdoing diverging from accepted conceptions of wrongdoing is the dilution of respect for the law's norms generally. A consequence, of course, of many more laws and many more offenders is that those charged with responsibility for investigating crime, for finding, trying, and punishing wrongdoers, become burdened beyond their capacity to effectuate tasks assigned to them. Reported offenses commonly go uninvestigated for want of resources, and those individuals arrested, more often than not, go through a speedy, automated-like process bearing only the most distant resemblance to a solemn determination of guilt or innocence. The increase, then, of the number of laws tends, as inflation generally does, to devaluation of the currency of law generally.

Along with these familiar phenomena must be included the common belief that a sizable number of individuals within society are alienated from its values, that they do not accept the norms, that they are predators, more like enemies within than wayward citizens who have given into temptation. This perception may not accord with reality, but its source, again, lies in media focus upon such offenders, for they often excite greater interest, and incidentally stir up more intense feelings of helplessness, than one's common variety wrongdoer. What in the past has allowed for identification with wrongdoers seems, then, less operative today.

I shall only add one further speculation. It is a familiar truth that there is a pull to banalize evil. It is an effective, understandable way to survive. Almost each day, bombarded by horrifying evil and alive in a century where the scope of evil lies beyond true comprehension, we naturally defend ourselves from full emotional awareness. But in adopting this defensive maneuver, in understandably not experiencing its full impact, we cease to see new occurrences of evil for what they are. We become jaded, for we have, after all, seen everything. And so, tragically, we may purchase relief by sacrificing some of our humanity, that essential part of it that consists in emotional responsiveness to evil. But then we also run the risk that evil attendant upon departure from principles of justice, the violation, say, of the rights of a single innocent person, particularly when justified by minimization of social harm, has for us a rather banal character. The ideology of cost-effective analysis then reinforces these powerful defensive forces. And so just as the significance of violating any law may become less as there are so many laws, including morally suspect ones, around to violate, so the frequency of evil, our knowledge of it, our desensitizing ourselves to it, our attention to efficiency, lessens the seriousness of any particular instance of evil, including what we or our representatives perpetrate.

Now these factors—increased anxiety, increased crime, diminished capacity for identification with criminals, alienation, devaluation of law, and devaluation of justice—all put pressure upon guilt and pull us powerfully toward responding to wrongdoing and wrongdoers from the perspective of social efficiency and social control. This is, of course, a familiar disposition with respect to the procedural safeguards embodied in the Bill of Rights to the U.S. Constitution. Those who initially proposed the rights embodied in that document easily imagined that they might one day directly benefit from their invocation. As this capacity for identification lessens, as anxiety intensifies, support for the rights weakens. My hypothesis is that a similar process occurs with guilt.

All this also, of course, has relevance to the vitality of our sense of guilt with respect to law. When law begins to be viewed as a system of social control, intent upon keeping costs down and increasing gains, rather than a system of rules to effectuate justice, the risk is inevitably run that one's sense of guilt with regard to law becomes less a factor in one's conduct. One feels less the constraints of justice in responding to wrongdoers, less the constraint, indeed, in responding to the innocent whom we might see as justifiably sacrificed to the greater good. As those in authority with greater frequency act to further policy rather than promote justice, their moral authority diminishes, respect for the institutions generating norms and implementing them lessens, and in its train there is a lessened regard for complying with law because it is law. Further, where the criminals focused upon, as is frequently the case, are themselves officials, we can anticipate some erosion in respect for law. Commitment to law compliance becomes strained when noncompliance appears in our interest, and rationalization is readily available. And, if anything goes in law, why not elsewhere.

If these speculations have merit, if we are witnessing lessened respect for guilt and a lessening of our sense of guilt, we must then go on to ask whether good or evil attend the change.

At the beginning of this paper, I suggested that the lessened role for guilt in law and the erosion of our sense of guilt might have consequences equal in seriousness to those Freud associated with the heightening of our sense of guilt. I shall mention several such possible consequences. First, departing from the model of guilt I have set out, we do offense to principles of justice, and we do offense by punishing the innocent, disregarding the constraint of proportionality in punishment, and disregarding the guilt of the guilty. Second, departures from the practice of guilt, because they imply indifference to individual responsibility, carry an inevitable and heavy cost, for individuals come to be both looked upon and treated as justifiably serving some higher social goal rather than in response to choices they have made. Added to injustice, then, is the evil of objectifying human beings.

Finally, I offer this speculation. A powerful force at work in putting pressure on our customary ways of responding to alleged and actual wrongdoers is anxiety. We are prepared to sacrifice elements of the practice of guilt to allay it. An irony lurks in this. I have suggested that guilt functions in society to provide a sense of order. Limits are set; rules are followed in determining violations; some closure is achieved. Guilt is hardly pleasant, but there is some comfort in it. Now departures from this practice, inevitably, I believe, reintroduce into our social world a sense of disorder. A world governed by principles and respect for individual choice is transformed into a world with no fixed limits where anything goes provided some conception of a socially optimal result is foreseen. But this can only increase, not diminish, our feelings of helplessness and attendant anxiety. I believe that in our rush to quiet our fears we may be acting so as, in fact, to increase them.

To return to Freud. Because guilt constrained the instinctual, he saw it diminishing happiness. He had sex and aggression in mind when formulating his view. And, indeed, it has superficial appeal. What he failed adequately to note—and maybe it was because sex was rather too much on his mind—were the important respects in which guilt and our sense of guilt mark our attachment to others, to values outside ourselves, and how bleak life would be were these absent. He did not sufficiently note that happiness would be thrown into jeopardy in any world given over to the free play of the instinctual. Guilt also, as often as not, reduces rather than promotes anxiety. Returning to my theme, I have suggested that much is lost in any world given over to the dominance of social policy unregulated by respect for persons embodied in the idea of guilt. Pulled toward social policy and away from guilt, because we flee our anxiety, we shall end up facing a monster more fearful than the one from which we have fled.

Shame and Self-Esteem: A Critique*

John Deigh

Twenty-five years ago the psychoanalyst Gerhart Piers offered what remains the most influential way of distinguishing shame from guilt. Reformulated without terms special to psychoanalytic theory, Piers's distinction is that shame is occasioned when one fails to achieve a goal or an ideal that is integral to one's self-conception whereas guilt is occasioned when one transgresses a boundary or limit on one's conduct set by an authority under whose governance one lives. Succinctly, shame goes to failure, guilt to transgression. Shame is felt over shortcomings, guilt over wrong-doings.[1]

More recently, writers who have addressed themselves to the way shame differs from guilt, notably, among philosophers, John Rawls, have characterized shame as an emotion one feels upon loss of self-esteem and have analyzed self-esteem and its loss in a way that bears out Piers's influence.[2] Rawls plainly is in Piers's debt. He explains self-esteem in terms of the goals and ideals one incorporates into one's life plans, and he makes this explanation central to his account of our moral personality, in particular, our capacity to feel shame.

A characterization of shame like Rawls's, when set in the context of distinguishing shame from guilt, we are likely to find intuitively appealing. And we may feel a further pull in its direction when we think of shame in comparison with other emotions to which it is thought similar—for instance, embarrassment. For we associate both shame and embarrassment with an experience of discomfiture, a sudden shock that short-circuits one's composure and self-possession; yet we would agree, I think, that

* I am indebted to Herbert Morris for helpful comments on an earlier draft of this article.

1. Gerhart Piers and Milton B. Singer, *Shame and Guilt: A Psychoanalytic and a Cultural Study* (Springfield, Ill.: Charles C. Thomas, 1953), pp. 11–12.

2. John Rawls, *A Theory of Justice* (Cambridge, Mass.: Harvard University Press, 1971), pp. 440–46. For similar views see Helen Merrell Lynd, *On Shame and the Search for Identity* (New York: Harcourt Brace & Co., 1958), pp. 23–24; Robert W. White, "Competence and the Psychosexual Stages of Development," in *Nebraska Symposium on Motivation1960*, ed. Marshall Jones (Lincoln: University of Nebraska Press, 1960), pp. 125–27; and David A. J. Richards, *A Theory of Reasons for Action* (Oxford: Oxford University Press, 1971), pp. 250–59.

This essay originally appeared in *Ethics*, vol. 93, no. 2, January 1983.

embarrassment is an experience of discomfiture that, unlike shame, does not include a diminishment in one's sense of worth. An experience of shame, by contrast, strikes at one's sense of worth. Here we may be reminded of times when things were going well and we were somewhat inflated by the good opinion we had of ourselves, when suddenly, quite unexpectedly, we did something that gave the lie to our favorable self-assessment, and we were shocked to see ourselves in far less flattering light. Such are the circumstances for shame, and the positive self-image that disappears in these circumstances and is replaced by a negative one spells loss of self-esteem.

These contrasts between shame and guilt and shame and embarrassment present the bare outlines of a characterization of shame, which, when filled out, appears rather attractive. It is the topic of this article. My thesis is that this characterization, though attractive at first appearance, is unsatisfactory. It represents, I contend, a dubious conception of shame. In particular, I mean to call into question its central idea that shame signifies loss of self-esteem.

The paper is divided into three parts. In the first I lay out what I shall call the Rawlsian characterization of shame, Rawlsian in that I retain the controlling thesis and overall structure of Rawls's account but do not concern myself with its specifics, an exact rendering of Rawls being unnecessary for my purposes. Though my approach here is largely uncritical, my aim is to set up a well-defined target for subsequent criticism. In the second, then, I begin that criticism. I set forth a case of loss of self-esteem and some cases of shame that pose problems for the characterization. By themselves these cases stand as counterexamples to it, but my hope is that they will have a more illuminating effect, that they will produce a sense or spark an intuition that its central idea is problematic. Accordingly, in the third part I complete the criticism. I draw from the cases two lessons about shame intended to give definition to the intuition I hope will already have been sparked. Each lesson points to a key feature of shame that the characterization leaves out or misrepresents, its central idea being implicated as the source of these failures. Thus, while the criticism of this third part is aimed at the target set up in the first, the force of the criticism should lead us to consider rejecting the idea at the target's center.

I

We need at the start to fix our understanding of self-esteem, since the concept is at the base of the Rawlsian characterization. To this end I shall present some considerations leading up to a definition of self-esteem, from which an explanation of its loss will follow directly. This will then yield the characterization of shame we seek. Let us begin with the general idea that self-esteem relates to what one makes of oneself or does with one's life. One has self-esteem if one's spirits are high because one believes that one has made or will make something of oneself, that one has been or will be successful in one's life pursuits. Conversely, one lacks self-esteem if one is downcast because of a judgment that one has failed to make or never will make something of oneself, that one doesn't or won't ever amount to much. Something of this idea is suggested in William James's equation that sets self-esteem equal to the ratio of one's successes to one's pretensions.[3]

The first thing to note in this general idea is that self-esteem connects up with the condition of one's spirits. We speak of vicissitudes of self-esteem: highs and lows. One's self-esteem can plummet. It can also be boosted or bolstered. Indolence and languishing in doldrums are signs that one's self-esteem is at a low ebb. Enthusiasm for and vigorous engagement in activities in which one chooses to participate are signs of an opposite condition. We also describe persons in these conditions as having or lacking self-esteem. And though subtle differences may exist between a person's having self-esteem and his self-esteem's being high and between his lacking self-esteem and his self-esteem's being low, I shall treat the two in each pair as equivalent.

A second point of note, which is corollary to the first, is that self-esteem goes with activity. But to assert that having self-esteem requires that one be active would be an overstatement. We should allow that the esteem a person has for himself is relative to that period in his life with which he identifies for the purpose of self-assessment. Thus, a person may retain his self-esteem after having retired from active life if he looks back on his endeavors and accomplishments with pride while content to take it easy. He maintains a high opinion of himself while leading a rather leisurely and unproductive life because his self-assessment proceeds from recollections of an earlier period when he was active and successful. Or, to take the viewpoint of a youth looking forward in time, he may have esteem for himself in view of the life he aspires to lead if he believes in the accuracy of the picture he has of his future. He identifies, for the purpose of self-assessment, with the person he believes he will become, his present self having little bearing. Consequently, he may even at the time be leading an altogether easygoing and frivolous life while exuding self-esteem. I mention these possibilities only to set them aside. We simplify our task of explaining self-esteem if we restrict the discussion to self-esteem had in view of one's current doings and development.

Besides this simplifying restriction, we must also add a qualification to the statement that being active is a condition of having self-esteem. As a third point, then, one's actions, if they are signs of self-esteem, must have direction. They must be channeled into pursuits or projects and reflect one's goals and ideals. A wayward vagabond does not present a picture of someone who has self-esteem. Nor do we ascribe self-esteem to someone who, having no settled conception of himself, tries on this

3. William James, *The Principles of Psychology*, 2 vols. (1890; reprint ed., New York: Dover Publications, 1950), vol. 1, p. 310.

and that trait of personality, as he would sunglasses of different styles, to see which gives him the most comfortable look. Self-esteem is had by persons whose lives have a fairly definite direction and some fairly well-defined shape, which is to say that self-esteem requires that one have values and organize one's life around them.

One's values translate into one's aims and ideals, and a settled constellation of these is necessary for self-esteem. Specifically, we may take this as a precondition of self-esteem. For, arguably, someone who had no aims or ideals in life, whose life lacked the direction and coherence that such aims and ideals would bring, would be neither an appropriate object of our esteem nor of our disesteem. We would understand his behavior as the product of primitive urges and desires that impelled him at the time of action. Having given no order or design to his life, he would act more or less at random or for short-lived purposes. We should recognize in him a figure who frequents recent philosophic literature on human freedom: the man assailed by a battery of desires and urges, who is helpless to overpower them because he lacks a clear definition of himself.[4] Such a man is impelled in many directions at once but moves in no particular one for any great distance. Frustrated and disoriented by inner turmoil, he lapses into nonaction. He would, were we ever to encounter his like, properly evoke in us pathos indicating abeyance of judgment rather than scorn indicating low esteem for him.

By contrast, when a person has aims and ideals that give order and direction to his life, counterpoint between primitive forces that impel him and his wanting to fulfill those aims and ideals becomes possible. Thus, at those times when he acts in conflict with his aims and ideals, he may declare that he was caught in the grip of some emotion or was overpowered by some urge or desire. He would then convey the idea that he had been acted upon or compelled to act as opposed to doing the act or choosing to act. Undeniably, the emotion, urge, or desire is attributable to him; but by such declaration he disowns it and so disclaims authorship of the act it prompted. Authorship, not ownership, is the key notion here, that is, authorship in the general sense of being the originator or creator of something. When one has a settled constellation of aims and ideals, then one distinguishes between the acts of which one is the author and those in which one serves as an instrument of alien forces.[5] Without any such constellation, one is never the author of one's actions, though many times the instrument of alien forces that act on one, triggered by external events.

4. See Joel Feinberg, "The Idea of a Free Man," in *Educational Judgments: Papers in the Philosophy of Education*, ed. James Doyle (London: Routledge & Kegan Paul, 1975), pp. 148–49; Harry Frankfurt, "Freedom of the Will and the Concept of a Person," *Journal of Philosophy* 68 (1971): 5–20; Wright Neely, "Freedom and Desire," *Philosophical Review* 83 (1974): 32–54; and Gary Watson, "Free Agency," *Journal of Philosophy* 72 (1975): 205–20.
5. I have drawn here from Harry Frankfurt, "Identification and Externality," in *The Identities of Persons*, ed. Amélie Rorty (Berkeley: University of California Press, 1976), pp. 239–51.

It is in view of this contrast that I suggest we take one's having a settled constellation of aims and ideals as a precondition of self-esteem: when one is the author of one's actions, one is an appropriate object for esteem or disesteem; when one is only an instrument of alien forces, one is not. We can then look to this precondition for the defining conditions of self-esteem. So while we would have said, loosely speaking, that self-esteem came from one's having a good opinion of oneself, we may now say more strictly that it comes from a good opinion of oneself as the author of one's actions, more generally, one's life. Accordingly, this opinion comprises a favorable regard for one's aims and ideals in life and a favorable assessment of one's suitability for pursuing them. Lacking self-esteem, one would either regard one's aims and ideals as shoddy or believe that one hadn't the talent, ability, or other attributes necessary for achieving them. Either would mean that one lacked the good opinion of oneself that makes for self-esteem, and either would explain the dispirited condition that goes with one's lacking self-esteem.

These considerations then yield an understanding of self-esteem as requiring that two conditions jointly obtain. This we can formulate as a definition. Specifically, one *has self-esteem* if, first, one regards one's aims and ideals as worthy and, second, one believes that one is well suited to pursue them.[6] With reference to the first we say one has a sense that one's life has meaning. With reference to the second we speak of a confidence one has in the excellence of one's person. And this combination of a sense that one's life has meaning and a confidence in one's ability to achieve one's ends gives one impetus to go forward.

Turning then to loss of self-esteem and, in particular, the sudden loss taken on the Rawlsian characterization to be explicative of shame, we obtain immediately from the foregoing definition an account of this experience. One loses self-esteem if, because of a change in either one's regard for the worthiness of one's aims and ideals or one's belief in one's ability to achieve them, a once favorable self-assessment is overturned and supplanted by an unfavorable one. The loss here is the loss of a certain view of oneself. One had self-esteem and correspondingly a good opinion of oneself: one viewed oneself as having the attributes necessary for successfully pursuing worthy ends around which one had organized one's life. The change in judgment about the worthiness of one's ends or the excellence of one's person destroys that view. One's good opinion of oneself gives way to a poor one. This constitutes loss of self-esteem.

The Rawlsian characterization has it that shame is the emotion one feels when such loss occurs. Moreover, shame is to be understood as signifying such loss. Shame on this characterization is the shock to our sense of worth that comes either from realizing that our values are shoddy or from discovering that we are deficient in a way that had added to the confidence we had in our excellence. Either is a discovery of something

---

6. The definition matches Rawls's (see p. 440).

false in the good opinion we had of ourselves, and such self-discovery spells loss of self-esteem.

Of course, self-discovery of this sort does not figure in every experience of shame, for a person who has a poor opinion of himself is nonetheless liable to feel shame when the very defect that is his reason for the poor opinion is brought to his notice. Thus, as a last point, we must say something about shame felt by someone whose self-esteem is already low. While a schoolboy, Philip Carey, in Maugham's novel *Of Human Bondage*, feels shame innumerable times over his clubfoot. His feelings do not involve loss of self-esteem, since his self-esteem is low to begin with, nor, obviously, do they reflect any act of self-discovery. But it would be uncharitable to object to the Rawlsian characterization on the ground that it does not cover such cases, for they can be treated on analogy with cases it does cover. Philip does not always have his crippled foot on his mind; there are plenty of times when he is forgetful of it. On these occasions, especially when he is comfortable with himself, he is liable to feel shame when made conscious of his "freakish" condition, when, as it were, he rediscovers it. Then, while he does not lose any self-esteem, his being comfortable with himself is certainly lost to him.

II

In this section I shall set forth a case of loss of self-esteem and some cases of shame that present real problems for the Rawlsian characterization. I begin with the former. The case itself is quite straightforward. We have only to think of someone who suddenly loses self-esteem because he discovers that he lacks the ability to achieve some aim he has set for himself, who is crestfallen, dispirited, and deeply disappointed with himself, but owing to circumstances or a philosophical temperament, does not feel shame. And such a case is not hard to construct.[7]

Imagine, for example, some youth who is indisputably the best tennis player in his community. He defeats all challengers; he wins every local tournament; and he has recently led his high school team to a first-place finish in a league consisting of teams from the high schools of his and the neighboring towns. His coach rates him the most promising player to come along in a decade, and he is highly touted by other tennis enthusiasts in the area. Quite naturally, he comes to have a high opinion of his ability and visions of winning tournaments on the professional tour. At some point early in his high school years, he makes professional tennis a career goal and devotes much time to improving his game. In truth, though, the grounds for his high opinion of his ability and for his decision to make tennis a career are shaky. The competition in his and the neighboring towns is rather poor, these being rural and isolated from urban centers. And the aging coach's hopes have distorted his judgment

---

7. Examples similar to this first case were suggested to me by Herbert Morris and Rogers Albritton.

of his star player's talents. Thus, when this young player enters his first state tournament, he quickly discovers that his skills are below those of the top seeded players. His first defeat need not be humiliating, just convincing. And though he will surely lose some self-esteem, we need not suppose that he feels any shame.

One explanation of his losing self-esteem but not feeling shame is this. The first defeat is sufficiently convincing that it alters his view of himself as a tennis player, and given his aims, this means loss of self-esteem. But just as others close to him would respond that his defeat is nothing to be ashamed of, so his own attitude toward it may reflect such judgment. Accordingly, he would be deeply disappointed with himself but not ashamed. This possibility becomes even more vivid if we suppose that he has gone to the tournament alone or with friends who, unlike him, have only a passing rather than an abiding interest in tennis. For then he does not find himself having to face someone like his coach before whom feeling some shame would be natural, though even here the presence of the coach does not necessitate the emotion. This case thus broaches the question what distinguishes those cases of loss of self-esteem whose subjects feel shame from those whose subjects feel disappointment but no shame. The inability of the Rawlsian characterization to answer this question implies that the understanding of shame it gives is, at best, incomplete.

Let us next take up cases of shame. The first comes from an observation, made by several writers, that shame is commonly felt over trivial things. One writer instances experiences of shame had on account of "one's accent, one's ignorance, one's clothes, one's legs or teeth."[8] Another, to illustrate the same point, mentions shame felt over "an awkward gesture, a gaucherie in dress or table manners, . . . a mispronounced word."[9] To be sure, none of these examples poses a threat to the Rawlsian characterization, since each of the things mentioned could be for someone a shortcoming the apprehension of which would undercut the confidence he had in the excellence of his person. This would certainly be true of someone who consciously subscribed to ideals the achievement of which required that he not have the shortcoming. For then, though others would disparage these ideals as superficial or vulgar and accordingly think the shortcoming trivial, to him it would still appear as a serious flaw in himself. Naturally, the more interesting case is that in which the subject also thinks the shortcoming trivial and is surprised at having felt shame on its account. This case too can be understood as coming under the Rawlsian characterization. For one need not fully realize the extent to which one places value on certain things, and one may even deceive oneself about one's not being attached to certain ideals. We need, then,

8. Stanley Cavell, *Must We Mean What We Say?* (Cambridge: Cambridge University Press, 1976), p. 286.
9. Lynd, p. 40.

to distinguish between, on the one hand, what one would declare were one's aims and ideals and would list as one's important attributes if one were asked to describe oneself and, on the other, one's self-conception as it is reflected by one's behavior apart from or in addition to any explicit self-description. By one's self-conception I mean the aims and ideals around which one has organized one's life together with the beliefs one has about one's ability to pursue them. And what we understand is that these aims, ideals, and beliefs can guide one's behavior without one's being conscious of having subscribed to them. Consequently, a person who feels shame over crooked teeth or the slurping of soup, though he would have thought himself unconcerned with appearance and proper form, shows by his emotion that a pleasant-looking face or good table manners are important to him, that he subscribes to ideals of comeliness or social grace. Hence, we can easily understand his shame as signifying loss of self-esteem.

At the same time, such examples invite us to look for things over which someone might feel shame though he did not believe they made him ill suited to pursue his ends. Shame one feels over something one could not believe affected one's excellence, say, because one could not regard it as a fault in oneself, would present a problem for the Rawlsian characterization. Thus, consider shame felt over a humorous surname. The example comes from Gide. He describes to us the experience of a young French girl on her first day of school, who had been sheltered at home for the first ten years of her life, and in whose name, Mlle Péterat, something ridiculous is connoted, which might be rendered in English by calling her Miss Fartwell. "Arnica Péterat—guileless and helpless— had never until that moment suspected that there might be anything laughable in her name; on her first day at school its ridicule came upon her as a sudden revelation; she bowed her head, like some sluggish waterweed, to the jeers that flowed over her; she turned red; she turned pale; she wept."[10]

With this example we move from attributes that one can regard as minor flaws and insignificant defects to things about a person that leave him open to ridicule, though they do not add to or detract from his excellence. The morphemes of one's surname do not make one better or worse suited for pursuing the aims and ideals around which one has organized one's life. Hence, shame in this example, because it is felt over something that lies outside its subject's self-conception, opposes the Rawlsian characterization.

The second case of shame is cousin to the first. One finds oneself in a situation in which others scorn or ridicule one or express some deprecatory judgment of one, and apprehending this, one feels shame. Given only this general description, such a case presents no real problem

10. André Gide, *Lafcadio's Adventures*, trans. Dorothy Bussy (New York: Alfred A. Knopf, 1953), p. 100. The rendering of her name in English is suggested by the translator.

for the Rawlsian characterization. It serves to remind us that one's self-esteem depends to some extent on the esteem others accord one—certain others, anyway—and the greater that dependency the more readily one will feel shame in response to any deprecatory judgments they express. This can be understood by way of the amount of confidence one has in one's own independent judgments about the worthiness of one's aims and one's ability to fulfill them, for this, we might say, varies inversely with the strength of the dependency of one's self-esteem on the esteem of others. That is, the greater that dependency, the less one's confidence will be in independent judgments one makes about oneself and, concomitantly, the more accepting one will be of the judgments others make about one. Consequently, given a strong enough dependency, if they criticize or ridicule one for some fault, one accepts their criticism and thus makes the same judgment about oneself, where before one did not notice the fault or it did not much matter to one. This arouses shame inasmuch as the judgment issues in an unfavorable self-assessment that replaces a favorable one, that is, in loss of self-esteem. We have then an account of the case that is fully in line with the Rawlsian characterization.

But we must also admit cases of shame felt in response to another's criticism or ridicule in which the subjects do not accept the other person's judgment of them and so do not make the same judgment of themselves. And these cases do present a problem for the Rawlsian characterization. Consider Crito and his great concern for what the good citizens of Athens will think of him for failing to deter Socrates from meeting his demise. "I am ashamed," he says in vainly trying to argue Socrates out of accepting his fate, "both on your account and on ours your friends'; it will look as though we had played something like a coward's part all through this affair of yours."[11] And though Crito is in the end convinced that Socrates' course is the right one and knows all along that he has done everything one can expect of a friend, we still have, I think, no trouble picturing this good-hearted but thoroughly conventional man feeling ashamed when before some respectable Athenian, who reproaches him for what he believes was cowardice on Crito's part. Examples like this one demonstrate that shame is often more, when it is not exclusively, a response to the evident deprecatory opinion others have of one than an emotion aroused upon judgment that one's aims are shoddy or that one is deficient in talent or ability necessary to achieve them.

The third problematic case of shame is this. We commonly ascribe shame to small children. Shaming is a familiar practice in their upbringing; "Shame on you" and "You ought to be ashamed of yourself" are familiar admonishments. And, setting aside the question of the advisability of such responses to a child's misdemeanors, we do not think them nonsensical

11. Plato, *Crito* 45d–e. Quoted from the Hugh Tredennick translation, *The Collected Dialogues of Plato*, ed. Edith Hamilton and Huntington Cairns (Princeton, N.J.: Princeton University Press, 1961), p. 30.

or incongruous in view of the child's emotional capacities. Furthermore, close observers of small children do not hesitate to ascribe shame to them. Erik Erikson, writing about human development, observed that children acquired a sense of shame at the stage when they began to develop muscular control and coordination.[12] Charles Darwin, writing about blushing, noted that small children began to blush around the age of three and later remarked that he had "noticed on occasions that shyness or shamefacedness and real shame are exhibited in the eyes of young children before they have acquired the power of blushing."[13]

But it would certainly be a precocious child who at the age of four or five had a well-defined self-conception, who organized his life around the pursuit of certain discrete and relatively stable aims and ideals and measured himself by standards of what is necessary to achieve them. In other words, a child at this age, though capable of feeling shame, does not have self-esteem. Hence, the shame he experiences does not signify loss of self-esteem.

Finally, a fourth problematic case of shame emerges once we juxtapose the orientation of an aristocratic ethic and that of an achievement ethic. The Rawlsian characterization with its emphasis on making something of oneself, being successful in one's life pursuits, is tied to the latter. The experiences of shame it describes are at home in a meritocratic society, one in which social mobility is widespread, or, at any rate, the belief that it is constitutes a major article of faith. On the other hand, some experiences of shame reflect an aristocratic ethic; one feels shame over conduct unbecoming a person of one's rank or station. The experiences are better suited to a society with a rigidly stratified social structure like a caste society. And, as we shall see, they stand in marked contrast to experiences the Rawlsian characterization is designed to fit.

The contrast is this. With shame reflective of an achievement ethic, the subject is concerned with achieving his life's aims and ideals, and he measures himself against standards of excellence he believes he must meet to achieve them. So long as he regards his aims and ideals as worthy, they define for him a successful life, and accordingly he uses the standards to judge whether he has the excellence in ability or of character necessary for success. He is then liable to shame if he realizes that some of his aims and ideals are shoddy or that he has a defect portending failure where previously he had ascribed to himself an excellence indicating success. And this fits nicely the idea that shame signifies loss of self-esteem. On the other hand, with shame reflective of an aristocratic ethic, the subject's concern is with maintaining the deportment of his class and not necessarily with achieving aims and ideals that define success in life. He is concerned with conforming to the norms of propriety distinctive of his class, and

12. Erik Erikson, *Childhood and Society*, 2d ed. (New York: W. W. Norton & Co., 1963), pp. 251–54.

13. Charles Darwin, *The Expression of the Emotions in Man and Animal* (1872; reprint ed., Chicago: University of Chicago Press, 1965), p. 331.

conformity to these is neither a mark of achievement nor an excellence that forecasts achievement. In the usual case one is born into one's class and conforms to its norms as a matter of course. Failure to conform, that is, failure to deport oneself as becomes a member of one's class, invites comparison to persons of lower classes on whom the members of one's class look down. Thus, someone from a social class beneath which there are other classes may be liable to shame over such failure: someone wellborn may be liable to shame if he behaves like the vulgar. And such shame does not fit the Rawlsian characterization. For the subject neither realizes that his aims and ideals are shoddy nor discovers a defect in himself that makes him ill suited to pursue them. In other words, given the analysis we have laid out, he does not lose self-esteem.

But, one might ask, can't we say of someone who feels shame over conduct unbecoming a member of his class that he too has ideals that regulate his actions and emotions? After all, with his class we associate a way of life, and this implies an ideal or set of ideals. To feel constrained to act as becomes a member of one's class is to feel pressed to conform to its ideals, and conduct unbecoming a member is, in other words, conduct that falls short of an ideal. Granted, one doesn't so much achieve these ideals as conform to them, which shows perhaps that the conception of self-esteem on which the Rawlsian characterization is built must be modified. But supposing we make whatever modification is needed, isn't it sufficient to bring the experience under the Rawlsian characterization that we can redescribe it as shame felt over one's falling short of an ideal?

Something, however, gets lost in this redescription. When we redescribe the experience as shame felt over falling short of ideals around which one's life is organized, our focus shifts from who one is to how one conducts one's life. The subject's identity as a member of a certain class recedes into the background. We see it as the source of his ideals but do not assign it any further part. This, I think, is a mistake. In this experience the subject has a sense of having disgraced himself, which means he has an acute sense of who he is. We do not have an understanding of shame otherwise.

It is revealing that on the Rawlsian characterization this shift in focus does not register. For the characterization recognizes no distinction between questions of identity and questions of life pursuits, between who one is and how one conducts one's life. From its viewpoint, a person says who he is by telling what his aims in life are and what ideals guide him through life.[14] This makes it an attractive characterization of the shame felt by persons who are relatively free of constraints on their choice of life pursuits owing to class, race, ethnic origins, and the like. For such persons tend more to regard their aims and ideals as constituting their identity and their ancestry, race, class, and so forth as extrinsic facts about themselves. So the characterization explains the shame they feel as including

14. See Rawls, p. 408.

an acute sense of who they are. But because it restricts a person's identity to his aims and ideals in life, it fails to explain as including this sense the shame someone, living in a rigidly stratified society, feels when he does not act as befits a member of his class or the shame someone, living in a multiethnic society, feels when he acts beneath the dignity of his people. Granted, such a person recognizes that his conduct falls short of ideals members of his class or culture are expected to follow, but these ideals do not constitute his identity. Another, a pretender for instance, could have the same ideals as he but not the same identity, just as a tomboy has the ideals of a boy but not the identity of one. Hence, we fail to account for such shame if we describe it as being felt over one's having fallen short of ideals that regulate one's life.

Thus, about the following experience, which Earl Mills, a Mashpee Indian, relates, a defender of the Rawlsian characterization will insist that sometime during the episode Mills must have embraced the ideals of an Indian way of life or, alternatively, that he must have realized, though he nowhere suggests this, that the ideals he was then pursuing were shoddy. But ignoring the Rawlsian characterization, we can explain Mills's feeling shame without importing either of these assumptions: his having, in the circumstances he describes, to acknowledge his ignorance of Mashpee traditions disgraced him as an Indian, made him betray, as it were, his Indian identity, and this aroused shame. This explanation accepted, his experience directly opposes the Rawlsian characterization, for it suggests that, despite the aims and ideals around which a man organizes his life, circumstances may arise that make him, because of an identity he has that is independent of those aims and ideals, liable to experience shame.

> When I was a kid, I and the young fellows I ran around with couldn't have cared less about our Indian background. We never participated in any of the tribal ceremonies, we didn't know how to dance, and we wouldn't have been caught dead in regalia. We thought anyone who made a fuss about our heritage was old-fashioned, and we even used to make fun of the people who did. Well, when I came back from the Army in 1948, I had a different outlook on such matters. You see, there happened to be two other Indians in my basic-training company at Fort Dix. One of them was an Iroquois from Upper New York State, and the other was a Chippewa from Montana. I was nineteen years old, away from Mashpee for the first time in my life, and, like most soldiers, I was lonely. Then, one night, the Iroquois fellow got up and did an Indian dance in front of everyone in the barracks. The Chippewa got up and joined him, and when I had to admit I didn't know how, I felt terribly ashamed.[15]

15. Paul Brodeur, "A Reporter at Large: The Mashpees," *New Yorker* 54 (November 6, 1978): 62–150, p. 103.

III

Before drawing any lessons about shame from the discussion of Part II, I should say something to allay doubts about the import of the cases of shame presented there. Such doubts naturally arise because one might think that some, if not all, of those cases exemplify experiences of the emotion the subjects of which one could criticize for being irrational or unreasonable. That is, while agreeing that many persons are liable to such experiences, one might wonder whether they ought to be so liable and then note that a case's force as a counterexample lessens if it only describes an experience of irrational or unreasonable emotion. The first and last cases of shame are especially in point. To feel shame over one's surname and because of conduct unbecoming a person of one's class seem good examples of shame one ought not to experience. For one is not responsible for one's parentage and thus ought not to judge oneself according to facts wholly determined by it. Inasmuch as shame in these cases reflects such judgment, they exemplify experiences to which one ought not to be liable.

These doubts arise under the assumption that, in giving a characterization of an emotion, one specifies those conditions in which the emotion is experienced reasonably or rationally. Such an approach to characterizing an emotion requires that one regard as its standard cases those in which the subjects are fully rational individuals and not at the time of the experience in any irrational frame of mind. But we ought to question this requirement. Why should we restrict the class of standard cases to these? While there is, for instance, something absurd in the familiar picture of an elephant terrified at the sight of a mouse, why should this absurdity lead us to regard the elephant's terror as any less important a case to be considered in characterizing that emotion than the terror a lynch mob strikes in the person on whom it takes revenge? To be sure, the elephant is not a creature capable of bringing its emotions under rational control, whereas a human being, if sufficiently mature, is. And for this reason there is a point in criticizing the emotional experiences of human beings, whereas making similar criticisms of an elephant's emotional experiences is altogether idle. But this provides no reason to regard the class of rational or reasonable experiences of a given emotion as privileged for the purposes of conceptual inquiry. To have brought one's emotions under rational control means that the range of one's emotional experiences has been modified through development of one's rational capacities: one no longer responds with, say fear, to certain sensory stimuli that before the development provoked fear, and conversely. But far from instructing us to discount the elephant's or the toddler's emotions in our conceptual inquiries, this bids us to examine emotional experiences had in response to sensory stimuli unmediated by rational thought as well as experiences the occurrence of which we explain by reference to rational thought.

Similar points then apply to characterizing shame. To focus primarily on cases the subjects of which one would not criticize for being irrational or unreasonable is to risk introducing distortion into the characterization. Indeed, one might be well advised to examine closely those cases in which such criticism is forthcoming on the grounds that they may display more prominently than others certain characteristic features of the emotion. Thus, one might be well advised to examine closely the shame typical of *homo hierarchicus*, even though one thought that rigid, hierarchical social structures lacked rational foundations (i.e., even though one thought that the emotion indicated an irrational attachment to social class), on the grounds that in such shame one sees more clearly than in shame typical of persons living in an egalitarian society those parts of the subject's self-conception in virtue of which he is liable to the emotion. Moreover, though the resultant characterization rendered shame an emotion that, from the perspective of an egalitarian or meritocratic ethic, one never had good reason to feel, this would not in itself show the characterization to be faulty: no more than that gentlefolk like the Amish, because of certain theistic beliefs, regard resentment as an emotion one never has good reason to feel shows that they harbor misconceptions about resentment. Since we are capable of bringing our emotions under rational control, we may regard our feeling a specific emotion as incompatible with our moral principles and so try to make ourselves no longer liable to it. Alternatively, we may regard this emotion as essential to our humanity and so revise our principles. The conflict makes evident the importance of having a correct understanding of such emotions; at the same time we should see that altering the understanding one has in order simply to avoid such conflict or the criticism of irrationality would be misguided.

Turning then to lessons that come out of our discussion of the problematic cases, I shall draw two. The first is that a satisfactory characterization must include in a central role one's concern for the opinions of others. This is really a lesson in recall. From Aristotle onward, discussions of shame have focused attention on the subject's concern for the opinions others have of him.[16] Aquinas, Descartes, and Spinoza each incorporated this concern into his definition of shame.[17] And latter-day writers, Darwin and Sartre in particular, took the experience of shame before another as key to an understanding of the emotion.[18] Thus, we should not be surprised to find that the Rawlsian characterization founders, since it regards such concern as not internally related to shame.

Its failure, however, is not due to neglect. The characterization, through emphasis on the dependency of one's self-esteem on the esteem of others, can accord the concern an important role in an overall un-

16. For Aristotle's view see *Rhetoric*, bk. 2, chap. 6.
17. For Aquinas's definition see *Summa Theologiae* 1a2ae, 41,4. For Descartes's see *The Passions of the Soul*, pt. 2, article 66. For Spinoza's see *The Ethics*, pt. 3, definition 31.
18. See last chap. of Darwin. Sartre's view is found in *Being and Nothingness*, trans. Hazel E. Barnes (New York: Philosophical Library, Inc., 1956), pp. 252–302.

derstanding of shame.[19] But this makes the concern part of a mechanism that induces shame rather than part of our conception of shame. A mechanism exists which, when put into operation, transforms high self-esteem into low; part of that mechanism is the concern one has for the opinion of others; and one way in which the mechanism gets going is when others on whose good opinion one's self-esteem depends deprecate one and one apprehends this. In this way, the characterization gives one's concern for the opinion of others an important role. But it is only a supporting role and not the central one I think it deserves. And this is one reason for its failure.

Each of the first three problematic cases bears out this last point. It is evident in the second and third cases, where the subjects feel shame but do not lose self-esteem. In the third case shame is felt directly in response to another's scorn or reproach. Thus, an expressed low opinion of the subject induces in him shame without affecting his self-esteem. In other words, the mechanism is not engaged, though the subject's concern for the opinion of another is clearly operative. In the second, Mlle Péterat, even apart from the context in which she feels shame, jeering classmates, feels the emotion because of something about herself that is laughable. It invites deprecatory responses. Thus, she may feel ashamed because of it, even though it is not a deficiency. It is not a ground for reassessing her excellence, though, of course, the whole experience could cause her to think less of herself. Here, too, there is shame reflecting a concern for the opinion of others without the mechanism's being engaged.

We can also mine the first case to bring out the point that the Rawlsian characterization has misconstrued the role one's concern for the opinion of others has in shame. Consider again our young tennis phenom. In the circumstances described, he loses self-esteem, is disappointed with himself, but does not feel shame. On the other hand, as we noted, if the circumstances had been different, if he had had, say, to face his coach after the defeat, then his feeling shame would have well been imaginable. There would then have been someone at courtside whose look he could not meet. He would have averted his eyes, lowered his head, gulped to fight back tears. That the coach's presence could spell the difference between disappointment and shame cannot be explained by reference to the player's losing self-esteem, for the loss occurs in either case. The mechanism would be in operation whether or not the subject felt shame, so it would not account for the role his concern for the coach's opinion would have had in his experiencing shame. We can thus conclude from these three cases that one's concern for the opinion of others has a role in shame apart from the way in which their opinion can support or bring down one's self-esteem.

19. See, e.g., Rawls's discussion of the companion effect to the Aristotelian principle, pp. 440–41.

The second lesson is about our sense of worth. The Rawlsian characterization yields an understanding of a person's sense of worth according to which it has two sources. One is the person's conviction that he has given meaning to his life. The other is the confidence he has in his own excellence as a person. The first comes from his regarding his aims and ideals in life as worthy. The second comes from his belief that he is well suited to pursue them. Thus, according to the Rawlsian characterization, shame, since it is felt either upon a judgment that one's aims or ideals are shoddy or upon a judgment that one is deficient in a way that makes one ill suited to pursue them, is aptly described as a shock to one's sense of worth. One experiences a diminishment in one's sense of worth since either one's sense of having given meaning to one's life or one's confidence in one's excellence has been struck down.

There is difficulty in this, however, because, while the description of shame as a shock to one's sense of worth is apt, the account of the various ways in which the sense gets shocked is, at best, too meager. The reason for this is that the characterization omits important sources of our sense of worth. The point is directly evident in our last two cases. The child of four who feels shame over some misdemeanor has not given meaning to his life and does not have confidence in his excellence as a person. Hence, he has a sense of worth the source of which the characterization does not acknowledge. Similarly, we recognize in an aristocrat who feels shame over behaving like a plebian or in an American Indian who feels shame over betraying his Indian identity a sense of worth the source of which is neither a conviction about the worthiness of his ends nor a belief about his suitability to pursue them. A sense of worth that comes from knowledge that one is a member of the upper class or a noble people also lies beyond the sight of the Rawlsian characterization. To put the point generally, the Rawlsian characterization fails to recognize aspects of our identity that contribute to our sense of worth independently of the aims and ideals around which we organize our lives.

We should note here the structural, as well as the substantive, difference between the sense of worth the Rawlsian characterization recognizes and the one it excludes. We can get at this structural difference by looking at the theory of worth that underlies the characterization. That theory is based on a conception of us as the authors of our actions. We are authors in the sense discussed in Part I, that is, in virtue of having a constellation of aims and ideals according to which we live our lives. We have worth on this theory in accordance with the value of our lives, such as they are and such as they promise to be. An author has worth in view of his work, completed or in progress, and our lives, so to speak, are our work. This analogy can be pressed. Our work has value to the degree that it is the kind of thing that when well made has value and is itself well made. So we have worth to the degree that we produce such things or have directed our energies toward producing them and possess the talents and skills that augur successful production. Our lives, conceived as our work, thus have value to the degree that the ends that give them order and direction define a kind of life that has value and those ends have been realized. And we have worth as authors of our lives to the degree that we live lives of value or have directed our energies toward living such lives and possess the attributes that promise success.

In capsule form, what might be called the auteur theory of worth is that what a person does with his life, how well he directs it, determines his worth. On this theory, then, we attribute different degrees of worth to someone depending on how valuable we deem the kind of life he lives and how successful we think he has been in living it or how suitable we think he is for it. In other words, we attribute to him more or less worth according to how well or badly he conducts his life. Contrast this with attributions of worth made because of one's class or culture. Judging from these attributions, we might say that a person's worth is determined by his status in the context of some social hierarchy. The salient feature here is that one's status, and so one's worth, is fixed independently of one's conduct. To be sure, one can change classes through marriage or cultures through immigration, but short of this the general conduct of one's life, that is, however well or badly one conducts it, does not increase or decrease the worth that is attributed to one because of one's status. And pretty much the same holds of worth that is attributed to human beings because of their species or to persons because of the kind of beings they are conceived to be: rational ones, say, spiritual ones, or autonomous ones. That is, worth attributed to one because of one's essential nature is, like worth attributed to one because of one's status, fixed independently of how one conducts one's life.

Consequently, the dynamics of the sense of worth that comes from knowing the worth that goes with one's status or essential nature, that is, the understanding we give to augmentations and diminishments in that sense, are altogether different from those of the sense of worth the auteur theory recognizes. Statically, both kinds of sense correspond to the degree of worth one attributes to oneself. But an augmentation in one's sense of worth, as is experienced in pride, or a diminishment in it, as is experienced in shame, is not, if this sense originates in a recognition of one's status or essential nature, to be understood in terms of an attribution to oneself of greater or lesser worth than one attributed to oneself before the experience.[20] A college boy who wears his fraternity pin with pride does not regard himself as having greater worth for having worn it, and a man who feels ashamed of having eaten like a pig does not regard himself as having less worth than is attributed to human beings as such. This contrasts with the way the auteur theory would have us understand augmentations and diminishments in one's sense of worth. In particular, it would have us understand a diminishment in one's sense

20. Of course there are exceptions to this, e.g., the white supremecist who discovers he has a black ancestor.

of worth, as is experienced in shame, as amounting to loss of self-esteem and so corresponding to an assessment of oneself as having less worth.

On the auteur theory, a sense of worth reflects concern with one's real worth, and one takes one's conduct and appearance as evidence of or, more strongly, as the grounds for attributing to oneself that worth. By contrast, a sense of worth that comes from knowing one's status or essential nature reflects concern with the congruency between one's conduct or appearance and one's real worth. Here, we could say, one's concern is with the relation between appearance and reality. If one's status is high relative to that of others or one's nature is noble, then behavior that is congruent with one's worth and so displays it is occasion for pride, and behavior that is at variance with it and so gives appearance of lesser worth is occasion for shame.

This model better accommodates the idea that to have a sensibility to shame means that one is prepared to restrain oneself when one verges on the shameful and to cover up the shameful when it comes into the open. We speak in this regard of having shame as opposed to having no shame, and we connect this with modesty, particularly sexual modesty, which involves a sensibility to shame in matters of decorum. Having shame, that is, having a sensibility to shame, can be understood here as self-control that works to restrain one from giving the appearance of lesser worth and self-respect that works to cover up shameful things that, having come to light, give one such appearance.[21]

This suggests that we should conceive shame, not as a reaction to a loss, but as a reaction to a threat, specifically, the threat of demeaning treatment one would invite in giving the appearance of someone of lesser worth. Its analogues then are, not grief and sorrow, but fear and shyness.[22] Like fear, shame serves to protect one against and save one from unwanted exposure. Both are in this way self-protective emotions. Fear is self-protective in that it moves one to protect oneself against the danger one senses is present or approaching. From fear one draws back, shields oneself, or flees. Of course, it may also render one immobile, thereby putting one in greater danger, so the point does not hold without qual-

21. On these points, see Carl D. Schneider, *Shame, Exposure and Privacy* (Boston: Beacon Press, 1977), pp. 24–27.

22. Whether to pattern shame after grief and sorrow or after fear and shyness is an issue a review of the literature reveals. One often finds in the writings of those offering definitions of shame use of one or the other of these emotions as analogues, sometimes even as a generic emotion of which shame is defined as a specific type. For definitions of shame as a type of grief or sorrow see Hobbes (*Leviathan* chap. 6) and Descartes (pt. 3, article 205) (though the passage is equivocal since he also says there that shame is a species of modesty). For definition of shame as a type of fear see Aquinas; it is also suggested in Plato's *Euthyphro* 12a–d. In connection with this issue see Havelock Ellis's "The Evolution of Modesty," in *Studies in the Psychology of Sex*, 2 vols. 3d ed. (New York: Random House, 1942), vol. 1, p. 36, n. 1. Ellis himself appears to hold that shame is a kind of fear (see pp. 36–52, 72).

ification.[23] Still, the general idea is clear. Shame, too, is self-protective in that it moves one to protect one's worth.[24] Here the general idea is not so clear, though a trope may be useful. Shame inhibits one from doing things that would tarnish one's worth, and it moves one to cover up that which through continued exposure would tarnish one's worth. Less figuratively, we might say that the doing or exposure of something that makes one appear to have less worth than one has leaves one open to treatment appropriate only to persons or things that lack the worth one has, and shame in inhibiting one from doing such things and in moving one to cover them up thus protects one from appearing to be an unworthy creature and so from the degrading treatment such appearance would invite.

This idea that shame is a self-protective emotion brings together and explains two important features: first, that a liability to shame regulates conduct in that it inhibits one from doing certain things and, second, that experiences of shame are expressed by acts of concealment. The second is crucial. Covering one's face, covering up what one thinks is shameful, and hiding from others are, along with blushing, the most characteristic expressions of shame. Students of shame commonly note them. A quote from Darwin is representative, "Under a keen sense of shame there is a strong desire for concealment."[25] Moreover, etymology reinforces the point. According to many etymologists, a pre-Teutonic word meaning 'to cover' is the root of our word *shame*.[26]

Now the Rawlsian characterization, since it conceives shame as a reaction to a loss, can explain, on the model of fear of loss, how one's liability to shame regulates one's conduct. Where it has trouble is in explaining shame's moving one to cover up and hide. For it does not have in itself the materials needed to construct such an explanation. Because it conceives shame as a reaction to the loss of something one prizes, it yields an account of the emotion as at first giving way to low spirits and dejection and eventually moving one to attempt to recover what one lost, that is, to regain through self-improvement one's good opinion of oneself and so one's self-esteem.[27] Acts of concealment, however, are nowhere implicated in this account. Hence, if one adheres to the characterization, one must make use of supplementary materials to explain them. One must go outside the characterization by, say, citing certain fears associated with shame: fear of ridicule or rejection by those upon

23. I owe this point to John T. MacCurdy, "The Biological Significance of Blushing and Shame," *British Journal of Psychology* 21 (1930): 174–82.

24. The idea is one of the central themes of Max Scheler's essay "Über Scham und Schamgefühl," in *Gesammelte Werke*, ed. Maria Scheler and M. S. Frings, 11 vols. (Berne: Franke Verlag, 1954), vol. 10, pp. 65–154.

25. Darwin, p. 320.

26. See *Oxford English Dictionary*, s.v. "shame"; also Ernest Klein, *A Comprehensive Etymological Dictionary of the English Language* (Amsterdam: Elsevier, 1967).

27. See Rawls, p. 484; Lynd, pp. 50–51; and Richards, p. 256.

whose good opinion of one one's self-esteem depends.[28] But such an explanation would not be adequate, for it fails to explain acts of concealment as expressions of shame. Instead, it takes these as expressions of fears associated with shame. And the same objection would hold for any explanation one constructed from materials found outside the characterization. The characterization, in other words, is unable to explain, as expressions of shame, these acts. And this should tell us that something has gone wrong.

The adherent to the Rawlsian characterization thus appears to be in an untenable position. We would dismiss any suggestion that covering up and hiding were not really among shame's natural expressions. Reflection on shame, particularly shame concerning sexual improprieties, alone suffices to rule this out. And we should reject any characterization of an emotion that misrepresents its natural expressions. Faced with these objections, the adherent might retreat to a weaker thesis by proposing that the characterization gives an adequate account of some, but not all, experiences of shame. But this thesis is no more defensible than the original. For our adherent, as we saw from the first problematic case of Part II, has the burden of showing how the emotion the characterization describes is distinguishable from disappointment with oneself. Since he admits on this weaker thesis that some experiences of shame elude the characterization, he has, in other words, the burden of showing that the experiences of emotion the characterization captures are classifiable with these as shame. What reason could he give to show this? That they have the same feeling-tone is itself questionable, insistence on the point being question begging. That they involve a shock to one's sense of worth is insufficient. For the characterization identifies this shock with one's suffering loss of self-esteem, and this by itself does not qualify an experience as one of shame. The trouble with this proposal, I think, is that it would, in effect, divide shame into disparate kinds, one kind having fear as its analogue, the other grief. That is, we should suspect of any conception of shame the proposal spawned that it covered a mismatched set of experiences.

We can trace the characterization's problems back to the understanding it gives to the sense of worth that makes one liable to shame and ultimately to the auteur theory of worth, which grounds that understanding. On that theory one attributes to oneself worth according to how one conducts one's life, and so perceptions of that conduct determine one's sense of worth. Shame then, since it is felt upon discovery of shortcomings in oneself that falsify the worth one thought one had, includes a sense that one lacks worth. And this proves problematic because it leaves unexplained how shame motivates acts of concealment. By contrast, when we conceive shame as including a sense that one has worth, we can readily explain

---

28. See Piers and Singer, p. 16; and Rawls, p. 445. White, however, expresses reservations against connecting shame to such fears (pp. 125–27).

its motivating such acts: one covers up because one senses that the worth one has is threatened. This speaks in favor of the understanding of the sense of worth the idea that shame is a self-protective emotion entails, which understanding is grounded on a conception of worth that opposes the one the auteur theory yields. Consequently, we should suspect that the conception of worth the auteur theory yields is the wrong one for explaining the sense of worth that makes one liable to shame, and, because the Rawlsian characterization presupposes that conception, we should give up the view of the emotion it represents.

Norms of Revenge*

Jon Elster

I. INTRODUCTION

Revenge—the attempt, at some cost or risk to oneself, to impose suffering upon those who have made one suffer, because they have made one suffer—is a universal phenomenon. In this article I discuss proximate and ultimate causes of this behavior. I begin by sketching a typology of human motivations.[1]

First, people can act in a rational, outcome-oriented manner, choosing the best means to achieve their ends. Prima facie, this motivation is incompatible with revenge behavior. The very definition of revenge in the first sentence of this article shows that it involves only costs and risks, no benefits. Rational individuals follow the principles of letting bygones be bygones, cutting their losses and ignoring sunk costs, whereas the avenger typically refuses to forget an affront or harm to which he has been exposed. Later I discuss various arguments to the effect that revenge behavior can in fact be rational.

Second, people often act in impulsive, unreflective ways, under the sway of emotions too strong to be resisted. Impulsive behavior can be irrational, as in weakness of will, although it need not be so. Clearly, much revenge behavior is impulsive, conceived and executed in the rage of the moment. Often, it appears to be strongly against a person's interest to carry out an act of revenge. "Who sees not that vengeance, from the force alone of passion, may be so eagerly pursued as to make us knowingly neglect every consideration of ease, interest, or safety?"[2]

Third, people can act under the sway of social norms. These, too, are mediated by emotions—shame, embarrassment, anger, contempt. In this case, however, the role of the emotions is not to goad us into impulsive acts which we would not have carried out had we stopped to

* I would like to thank Lawrence Becker, Alan Hamlin, and William Miller for their detailed written comments on an earlier draft of this article. I am also grateful to Richard Arneson, Brian Barry, Allan Gibbard, and Jack Knight for comments made at the *Ethics* conference on norms. Acute observations by Aanund Hylland must also be acknowledged.

1. The typology derives from joint work with Stephen Holmes on Tocqueville's political psychology. For a preliminary report see chap. 4 of my *Psychologie Politique* (Editions de Minuit, in press).

2. D. Hume, *An Enquiry Concerning the Principles of Morals*, app. 2.

This essay originally appeared in *Ethics*, vol. 100, no. 4, July 1990.

consider our interest. Rather, they support judgments and expectations about what, in any given situation, is the appropriate thing to do. The main topic of this article is norms of revenge—socially shared and socially enforced rules governing the occasions for and the modalities of revenge. This will require a discussion of the relation of norms of revenge to (allegedly) rational revenge behavior and to revenge spurred by presocial emotions.

I shall discuss, then, interests, passions, and norms as proximate causes of revenge behavior. Yet many will feel unsatisfied with an explanation of revenge behavior in these terms. If revenge can be shown to be rational, no further explanation may be needed, but passions and norms do not seem to provide similarly self-contained accounts. We might want to ask, for instance, whether there is an evolutionary explanation of emotions such as anger or jealousy. Or one might want to explain a system of norms in terms of their contribution to some wider social end.

I now proceed as follows. Section II is a brief exposition and defense of the concept of social norms on which I shall be relying. Section III presents some evidence about norms of feuding in various societies. Section IV surveys arguments that have been made or could be made for the view that revenge behavior is rational. Section V shifts from individual to collective optimality, by considering some arguments that have been made for the social functions of feuding. Section VI considers the view that the maximand—and the explanation—for feuding behavior might be reproductive fitness. In Section VII, finally, I conclude that these reductionist arguments are of dubious value. The most plausible explanation for revenge behavior lies in psychological propensities that do not appear to serve any individual, social, or genetic purpose.

II. SOCIAL NORMS[3]

Rational action is concerned with outcomes. Rationality says: If you want Y, do X. I define social norms by the feature that they are not outcome oriented.[4] The simplest social norms are of the type: Do X (wear black for funerals), or: Don't do X (don't eat human flesh). More complex norms might say: If others have done Y, then do X (take revenge on those who insult you), or: If you have done Y, then do X (whoever proposes a topic for seminar discussion also has to introduce it). More complex norms still might say: Do X if it would be good if everyone did X. Rationality is conditional and future oriented. Its imperatives are hypothetical, that is, conditional on future outcomes one wants to realize. The imperatives expressed by social norms are either unconditional or,

3. This section draws heavily on my *The Cement of Society* (Cambridge: Cambridge University Press, 1989).

4. A related distinction between "terminal values" and "adjectival values" is made by A. O. Lovejoy, *Reflections on Human Nature* (Baltimore: Johns Hopkins University Press, 1968), pp. 79 ff. Terminal values are outcomes of actions, whereas adjectival values inhere in the actions themselves.

if conditional, are not future oriented. In the latter case, norms make the action contingent on past events or, more rarely, on hypothetical outcomes.

For norms to be social, they must be shared by other people and sustained by their approval and disapproval. Some norms, like those against cannibalism and incest, are shared by all members of society. Other norms are group specific. Managers and workers, or workers of different skill levels, do not have the same idea of what is a fair distribution of income. Also, norms are social because other people enforce them, by expressing approval or, especially, disapproval. These sanctions can be very strong, as we shall see later. In societies with a strict code of honor, the ostracism suffered by a person who fails to avenge an offense can be crippling.

In addition to being supported by the attitudes of other people, norms are also sustained by the feelings of embarrassment, anxiety, guilt, and shame that a person suffers by the prospect of violating them. As we shall see, emotions can also provide a positive emotion for following the norms. In my opinion, the emotive aspect of norms is fundamental. I do not deny that norms can have the cognitive function of coordinating expectations, nor that they can be understood as systems of sanctions. Yet if norms can regulate expectations and behavior it is ultimately because they have a grip on the mind that is due to the strong emotions they can trigger.

Even complex norms are simple to obey and follow, compared to the canons of rationality which often require us to make difficult and uncertain calculations. The operation of norms is to a large extent blind, compulsive, mechanical, or even unconscious. This point can be stressed too much. As we shall see, social norms offer considerable scope for skill, choice, manipulation, and interpretation. In some contexts, following the lodestar of outcome-oriented rationality is easy compared to finding one's way in a jungle of norms. I still want to retain the basic contrast between rationality and social norms. The force of norms—the feature that makes manipulation and interpretation possible and worthwhile—is that they have a grip on the mind; otherwise there would be nothing to manipulate. I return to this point.

Social norms must be distinguished from a number of related phenomena. First, social norms differ from moral norms. To bring out the difference, let us distinguish between obligation, permission, and interdiction. Social norms are nonconsequentialist obligations and interdictions, from which permissions can be derived. Some moral theories, like utilitarianism, rest on consequentialist obligations and interdictions. These are straightforwardly different from social norms. Other theories, like libertarianism, rest on nonconsequentialist permissions, from which certain interdictions can be derived. The basic notion in these theories is an assignment of rights to individuals, together with an injunction to others not to violate them. Still further theories, like Kant's moral philosophy, rest on nonconsequentialist obligations. These are quite similar to social norms.

Second, social norms differ from legal norms. For one thing, obedience to the law is often rational on purely outcome-oriented grounds. Although most people do not consider punishment as merely the price tag attached to a crime, laws are often designed as if it this were the case, so that legal sanctions will suffice to deter people from breaking the law. The law does not rest on informal sanctions and the voice of conscience but provides formal punishment. More important, it is individually rational for law enforcers to apply these sanctions: they will lose their jobs if they do not. By contrast, or so I shall argue, the enforcement of social norms is not in general individually rational.

Third, norms are not convention equilibria. Consider the social norms that are most similar to conventions, such as norms of dress, etiquette, and manners. One might argue that such norms are traffic rules of social life: it does not matter which set of rules is adopted, as long as there is agreement on one set. As in convention equilibria, one would not only want to follow the norm itself but also want others to follow it. The analogy is misleading, however. If I violate a traffic rule, two bad things can happen to me. I can get into an accident, and I may be blamed by bystanders because bad things can happen to them if I drive recklessly. But if I pick up the wrong fork at the dinner table, the only bad thing that can happen to me is that others blame me for my bad manners. Convention equilibria are guided by outcomes in a substantive sense, not just in the formal sense that people want to avoid disapproval.

Fourth, norm-guided behavior differs from habits and compulsive neuroses. Although similar in their mechanical character and lack of concern for consequences, they differ in several respects.[5] Unlike social norms, habits are private. Their violation does not generate blame or guilt. Unlike neuroses, they are not compulsive. The habit of washing one's hands after dinner is not like the neurotic's need to wash his hands fifty times every day. Habits begin as intentional behavior which later, as a result of repetition, loses its conscious, deliberate character. Compulsive neuroses are more complex and not well understood.[6]

The distinction between rationality and social norms does not coincide with the distinction between methodological individualism and holism. Although these distinctions go together in Durkheim, Bourdieu, and many others, one can define, discuss, and defend a theory of social norms within a wholly individualist framework.[7] A norm, in this perspective, is

5. Note, however, the far-reaching observation by O. Fenichel in *The Psychoanalytic Theory of Neurosis* (New York: Norton, 1945), p. 586, that "many forms of reaction which today are designated as compulsion neuroses are normal and institutionalized in other civilizations." The urge to seek revenge may be a case in point.

6. M. S. Gazzaniga, *Mind Matters* (Boston: Houghton Mifflin, 1988), pp. 125 ff.

7. Dan Sperber, "Anthropology and Psychology: Towards an Epidemiology of Representations," *Man* n.s. 20 (1984): 73–89, provides a useful starting point for an individualistic

the propensity to feel shame and to anticipate sanctions at the thought of behaving in a certain way. As explained above, the propensity becomes a social norm when it ·is shared with other people. The social character of the norm is also manifest in the existence of higher-order norms that enjoin us to punish violators of norms of a lower order. To repeat, this conception of a network of shared belief and common emotional reactions does not commit us to thinking of norms as supraindividual entities that somehow exist independently of their supports.

The contrast between norms and rationality need not generate a distinction between different kinds of actions. Both types of motivation may be among the determinants of a single action. Often, norms and rationality coexist in a parallelogram of forces that jointly determine behavior. When the norms require me to do X and rational self-interest to do Y, I may end up with a compromise. Or rationality may act as a constraint on norms: I do X provided that the costs—the direct costs of doing X and the opportunity costs of not doing Y—are not too high. Conversely, norms may constrain and limit the pursuit of rational self-interest.

III. THE BLOOD FEUD

Blood revenge can be obligatory in the sense described. When vengeance killing is motivated by social norms it invariably gives rise to counter-vengeance or feuds, because the act of revenge itself is an affront that must be avenged. Societies that have had norms regulating feuds or vendettas include medieval Iceland,[8] the Balkans[9] and other Mediterranean countries,[10] as well as South American tribes.[11] It is hard to believe that any of these societies could have been influenced by any of the others or by a common source. The feud is not an accidental or freakish institution, but one that seems to crop up with some regularity in premodern societies. I shall not attempt to offer sufficient conditions for the institution of feuding to emerge, but limit myself to looking at similarities and differences among the forms it has taken in the societies where it has emerged.

---

analysis of culture, although for my purposes I would give more emphasis to emotions and less to cognitive representations.

8. For my knowledge of the feud in Iceland, I draw heavily on W. Miller, *Bloodtaking and Peacemaking: Society and the Disputing Process in Medieval Iceland* (Chicago: University of Chicago Press, in press).

9. See, notably, M. Hasluck, *The Unwritten Law in Albania* (Cambridge: Cambridge University Press, 1954); C. Boehm, *Blood Revenge: The Anthropology of Feuding in Montenegro and Other Tribal Societies* (Lawrence: University of Kansas Press, 1984); and M. Djilas, *Land without Justice* (London: Methuen, 1958).

10. J. Busquet, *Le droit de vendetta et les paci corses* (Paris: Pedone, 1920); and J. Black-Michaud, *Cohesive Force: Feud in the Mediterranean and the Middle East* (New York: St. Martin's, 1975).

11. N. Chagnon, "Life Histories, Blood Revenge, and Warfare in a Tribal Population," *Science* 239 (1988): 985–92.

The following aspects of the feud are all regulated by norms. What constitutes an affront that must be avenged? Who are allowed or required to exact revenge? What means can legitimately be used in taking revenge? How soon is vengeance allowed or required to take place? Whose death shall expiate an affront? What fate is reserved for those who fail to take revenge when the norms require it? I shall consider all of these at some point or other in the subsequent discussion. First, however, I need to say something about the ideal of honor, which is central in all feuding societies and which generates or sustains the more specific norms of revenge.

Honor is an attribute of free, independent men, not of women, slaves, servants, or other "small men." (The latter can however, as we shall see, be very much concerned with honor.) It is achieved or maintained by victories over equals or superiors, where "victory" can mean anything from getting away with an insulting look to raping a man's wife or killing him. No honor can be gained from subduing slaves or servants, although it may be lost by not doing so.[12] Several writers emphasize that the game of honor in feuding societies is zero sum.[13] One achieves honor by humiliating others: what is lost by the one is gained by the other.

Others suggest that the game could be less than zero sum, for a variety of reasons. First, the norms of feuding do not always take the form of a *lex talionis*. Sometimes the rule is "two for one," not "one for one."[14] Second, as just observed, in conflictual relations between free men and their subordinates, honor can only be lost, not gained.[15] Lastly, the conception of honor itself may be such that it can never be acquired or increased, only lost. For women in Mediterranean societies, the analogue of honor is "shame" (sexual modesty), an attribute which "is negative, absolute (a woman either has it or does not—there are no degrees of shame), cannot be increased and can be demonstrated, as it were, only in the breach."[16] An analysis of feuding in Pakistan suggests that the same could be true of moral honor (*ghrairat*), as distinct from political honor (*aizzat*). "*Ghrairat* is perhaps best understood as personal worth or integrity. As Kohistanis explain, *ghrairat* is natural, a part of *imam*, and therefore a gift from God (in fact, God's most valuable gift). Every muslim

12. Miller, chap. 1.
13. Ibid. Black-Michaud, p. 179.
14. Boehm, p. 55. Later (p. 113) he also refers to the fact that "each clan tended to overperceive insults that it had received and to underperceive the insults that had been suffered by its enemy."
15. Miller avoids this conclusion by the following device. Assume that A loses honor by not killing an insubordinate servant B. The honor lost is not gained by B but spread among all A's equals. That argument, however, seems inconsistent with the universally affirmed idea that honor is increased only by personal achievements. To be sure, A's equals can achieve honor at his expense by calling him a coward (provided that he has not already lost so much honor as not to be worth insulting), but that would be a separate transaction.
16. Black-Michaud, p. 218.

is born with *ghrairat,* and although it can be polluted by the actions of others, as one's shoe is polluted by stepping in manure, it can only be lost by the failure of its owner to protect it."[17]

The zero-sum conception of honor fits the idea of honor as an inherently positional good. The less-than-zero-sum conception fits the idea of honor as personal worth—a good that can be destroyed but not transferred. Could honor relations be more than zero sum? If the preservation or increase of honor demands the actual death of the other party, they cannot. If honor demands only the willingness to expose oneself to risk, they could. Playing Russian roulette offers an example. Closer to the present topic, the European notion of honor as chivalry may be consistent with this idea. Duelists usually fire one shot only. If both survive, both go out of their duel with their honor enhanced. Similar phenomena occur in blood feuding. Writing about Albania, Margaret Hasluck observes that "in the early days of a feud the father or brother of the victim might in his furious rage kill the murderer and shoot a second time at the lifeless corpse. When the feud was older, it was not permitted to kill and shoot again. A murderer seldom looked at the corpse, a fact which gave men quick-witted enough to fake death a chance to escape."[18] By and large, however, blood vengeance seems to have required the actual death of the offender or one of his kinsmen. Having risked one's life to kill did not itself obliterate the insult.

These concepts of honor are not mutually exclusive. In actual societies, the search for honor takes on all of these aspects. Their common thread is that honor is an intensely interactive phenomenon, gained and lost only by direct, conflictual interaction. I shall have more to say about this aspect of honor toward the end of the article.

I now turn to some specific aspects of feuding, beginning with the initial cause of a feud, that is, the first event in what was potentially an interminable series of killings and reprisals. Here are some representative accounts:

> Protecting *ghrairat* depends on following a clearly defined code of conduct. One must provide wives and daughters with appropriate food and clothing to the degree one's wealth allows; one must never permit wives and daughters to speak to men not closely related; one must never eat or exchange friendly conversation with the enemy of a close agnate; and one must always be ready to strike out at those who sully one's *ghrairat*. If other men stare at a wife or daughter, reflect light from a snuff box mirror on a wife or daughter, propose intimacy with a wife or daughter, flee or attempt to flee the community with a wife or daughter, or have illicit sexual relations with a wife or daughter, the husband's or father's *ghrairat*

---

17. R. Lincoln-Keiser, "Death Enmity in Thull," *American Ethnologist* 13 (1986): 489–505, at 500.

18. Hasluck, pp. 228–29. Unfortunately, she does not say whether wounding the target under such circumstances counted as expiation.

is sullied. The murder of a close agnate, verbal abuse, theft, and assault also pollute *ghrairat* and demand vengeance.[19]

Most fights begin over sexual issues: infidelity and suspicion of infidelity, attempts to seduce another man's wife, sexual jealousy, forcible appropriation of women from visiting groups, failure to give a promised girl in marriage, and (rarely) rape.[20]

[The] causes for revenge lay in a complicated mixture of religious and fraternal feelings and also in the highly developed retaliatory responses that could be expected in a warrior society, all combined with a keen and compelling sense of honor. This last produced both a low personal tolerance for insults and a strong tendency to insult other people in the name of manly fearlessness. Most feuding began through such an insult to honor, which resulted in homicidal re-taliation. This could be initiated by a verbal, by a direct nonverbal communication that was insulting, or through some action that intentionally or inadvertently besmirched the honor of a household or of a clan. Prominently mentioned in the historical sources are abduction of a maiden to marry her, seductions of maidens, adultery, runaway wives, and breach of betrothal agreements, as well as disputes over pastures.[21]

I cannot produce any similarly succinct statements about the origins of feuds in medieval Iceland. From William Miller's account it would seem that the role of affronts to women was smaller and the importance of harm to servants and conflicts over property larger.

Important causes of feuds were acts undertaken with the knowledge that a feud might ensue, and undertaken only because a feud might ensue, although not for the purpose of causing a feud. These were acts of brinkmanship—insults carried to the point where there was a real risk that the offended party might retaliate. "The exchanging of insults, then, was a very delicate art that involved ultimate risk taking. Decisions as to what to say next were potentially matters of life and death, since simply to maintain one's honor one had to take at least some small risks of being killed."[22] Here the underlying notion of honor is zero sum: one party tries to capture or steal the honor of the other, by betting that the other's instinct for self-preservation will be stronger than his feeling of outraged honor. Other causes of feuds owed less to the possibility that a feud might ensue. As is clear from the summaries cited above, feuds frequently originated in affronts to women. Although it is sometimes hard to tell when offenses to women had their cause in primary sexual urges and when they derived from a wish to dishonor their menfolk,

19. Lincoln-Keiser, pp. 500–501.
20. Chagnon, p. 986.
21. Boehm, p. 103.
22. Ibid., p. 146.

many cases clearly belong to the former category. (In addition, a man's prior loss of honor might increase the likelihood of sexual aggression toward his women, by reducing the risk of retaliation.[23]

It was not always crystal clear whether an act required retaliation. Many triggering events deliberately left scope for interpretation. The insulting party usually took care to leave the door open for several interpretations because his goal was to humiliate the other party, not to provoke him to reply in kind. Some affronts, however, could not be overlooked without an intolerable loss of honor. The norms of revenge unambiguously required retaliation. Once the first killing had occurred, a process had been set in motion that in theory could go on forever. Even if a feud had been formally settled by payment of compensation, the resentment, which could not be made to go away, might flare up at the tiniest provocation.[24]

Ongoing feuds can be subject to very elaborate norms, richly documented in Margaret Hasluck's study of the unwritten law in Albania. Norms regulate the obligations and liabilities of third parties. If A kills B, there are norms stipulating which of B's kin are under an obligation to retaliate, subject to loss of honor if they do not. In addition, B's household might recruit some of their friends to join the feud on a voluntary basis. If one of these friends kills a member of A's household as part of a raid directed by a member of B's household, the friend need not fear that he will be singled out for retaliation. But "if he had been alone when he killed the man, he would have 'brought the feud home,' i.e. involved himself in a separate feud with the victim's family while leaving his friend's feud unaffected."[25] There are norms stipulating which of A's kin or tribe members are legitimate targets for retaliation. Special norms govern behavior during the period of "boiling blood" after a killing, usually set to twenty-four hours.[26] Only during this period could expiators for a crime be chosen outside the household of the killer. Similarly, "Montenegrins recognized 'boiling blood' as a very special and all-consuming psychological condition; and as a moral justification, boiling blood went far in exonerating a person if he broke a truce."[27]

It should be clear by now that feelings run high in the vendetta. Two main kinds of emotions are involved. First, there is the state of mind of the person seeking revenge, memorably described by Milovan Djilas in his memoirs:

> This land was never one to reward virtue, but it was always strong in taking revenge and punishing evil. Revenge is its greatest delight

23. Chagnon, pp. 986–87; Hasluck, pp. 231–32 (cited more fully below).

24. This notion of the "interminable feud" is controversial. For two different views on the Mediterranean case, see Black-Michaud; and Boehm.

25. Hasluck, p. 220.

26. Ibid., pp. 224–25. The ideal was "to take vengeance as soon as possible" (ibid., p. 231). The Icelandic practice, by contrast, conformed to the saying that "Vengeance is a dish that tastes best when eaten cold" (Miller, chap. 5).

27. Boehm, pp. 118–19.

and glory. Is it possible that the human heart can find peace and pleasure only in returning evil for evil? . . . Revenge is an overpowering and consuming fire. It flares up and burns away every other thought and emotion. It alone remains, over and above everything else. . . . Vengeance . . . was the glow in our eyes, the flame in our cheeks, the pounding in our temples, the word that had turned to stone on our throats on our hearing that our blood had been shed. . . . Vengeance is not hatred, but the wildest, sweetest kind of drunkenness, both for those who must wreak vengeance and for those who wish to be avenged.[28]

Next, we must consider the feelings of the person who is under an obligation to take revenge, yet fails to do so:

The life of the individual who is exposed every day to the *rimbecco* is hell. . . . "Whoever hesitates to revenge himself, said Gregorovius in 1854, is the target of the whisperings of his relatives and the insults of strangers, who reproach him publicly for his cowardice." . . ."In Corsica, the man who has not avenged his father, an assassinated relative or a deceived daughter *can no longer appear in public.* Nobody speaks to him; he has to remain silent. If he raises his voice to emit an opinion, people will say to him: avenge yourself first, and then you can state your point of view." The *rimbecco* can occur at any moment and under any guise. It does not even need to express itself in words: an ironical smile, a contemptuous turning away of the head, a certain condescending look—there are a thousand small insults which at all times of the day remind the unhappy victim of how much he has fallen in the esteem of his compatriots.[29]

A man slow to kill his enemy was thought "disgraced" and was described as "low-class" and "bad." Among the Highlanders he risked finding that other men had contemptuously come to sleep with his wife, his daughter could not marry into a "good" family and his son must marry a "bad" girl. As far south as Godolesh on the outskirts of Elbasan, he paid visits at his peril; his coffee cup was only half-filled, and before being handed to him it was passed under the host's left arm, or even under his left leg, to remind him of his disgrace. He was often mocked openly.[30]

These passages illustrate the two emotional mechanisms by which norms of revenge have an impact on behavior. On the one hand, they are internalized in a compulsive urge for vengeance, "the most terrible and sweet-tasting of passions."[31] This is not a spontaneous, presocial anger directed at another person (or, for that matter, a material object)

28. Djilas, pp. 86, 105, 106, 107.
29. Busquet, pp. 357–58. For a subtle discussion of the predicament of the man who fails to avenge an offense, see also P. Bourdieu, "The Sentiment of Honour in Kabyle Society," in *Honour and Shame: The Values of Mediterranean Society,* ed. J. G. Peristiany (Chicago: University of Chicago Press, 1969), pp. 191–214.
30. Hasluck, pp. 231–32.
31. Djilas, p. 36.

that has harmed or hurt us. The passion for revenge is embedded in a way of life that revolves around the notion of honor, and in which "boiling blood" is a socially recognized category. Spontaneous revenge is directed at the author of the affront, whereas norm-guided revenge casts its net much wider. The fact that the net is widest during the period of boiling blood shows better than anything the gap between the impulsive and the norm-guided—one might want to say compulsive— forms of revenge. Revenge is universal: norms of revenge are not. On the other hand, the norms are mediated by the devastating feeling of shame experienced by the man who fails to avenge an insult and who is constantly reminded that he is less than a man. The cited passages also illustrate the material deprivations suffered by the man who is perceived to be a coward, but these seem to matter much less than the loss of self-esteem. When others punish him by withholding opportunities for mutually beneficial transactions they are also punishing themselves, and it is this fact that shows him how much he has fallen in their esteem.

IV. THE RATIONALITY OF REVENGE

In this section I consider the individual rationality of revenge behavior. I restrict myself to arguments to the effect that revenge can be rational in terms of the selfish, material interests of the agent. If broader motivations—like the concern to uphold one's honor—are allowed, the task of proving the rationality of revenge becomes easier but also less interesting. Whenever a norm is invoked in explaining an action, one can turn the account into a rational-choice explanation by saying that the agent is concerned with upholding his self-image and reputation as a norm follower. While true enough, such statements are uninformative. In particular, they contain no guide to how the agent could rationally choose between alternative means to the stipulated end. Many of the means, in fact, will themselves be regulated by norms. It seems better, therefore, to make a clear break and stipulate that revenge, to be rational, must be so in terms of material ends.

The explanandum of a rational-choice account could be either actual revenge behavior or credible threats of revenge. Why would a rational person ever carry out an act of revenge? Why would anyone believe a rational person if he threatened to do so? The following answers have been proposed or could be proposed.[32] First, in societies with norms of revenge an individual may be worse off if he fails to avenge an affront, because of the external sanctions to which he thereby exposes himself. Second, a person who demonstrates that he cares about getting revenge will often have an edge when dealing with people who do not. Last, revenge can be viewed as a tit-for-tat strategy in iterated games.

The first argument is very general and not restricted to norms of revenge. All norm-guided behavior, or so the argument goes, is kept in

---

32. I cannot cite written sources for any of these arguments. When discussing revenge with economists, however, I have met all of them.

line by the fear of external sanctions that make it individually rational for the agent to abide by the norm. There is no need to invoke internal variables like emotions to explain why people act against what appears to be their self-interest: it is sufficient to observe that the alternative is even worse. The tangible costs of violating norms exceed the tangible costs of adhering to them.

Now, the case of revenge is one in which this account is particularly implausible. If it were correct, revenge behavior would be singularly overdetermined, because the internal, emotional forces also seem to provide a sufficient explanation. The argument also fails more generally, for reasons that apply to all norm-guided behavior. We have seen that violators of a norm shared with other members of their society are indeed exposed to sanctions by these others. But then we have to ask what reason others could have for sanctioning the violators. What's in it for them? The obvious answer is that for any ordinary norm there is a meta-norm[33] that enjoins people to punish people who fail to punish violators of the first-order norm. A system of sanctions might, in theory, keep people in line even if nobody believed in the norm.[34] But this argument soon runs out of steam. Expressing disapproval is always costly, whatever the target behavior. At the very least it requires energy and attention that might have been used for other purposes. One may alienate or provoke the target individual, at some cost or risk to oneself. On the other hand, as one moves upward in the chain of actions, beginning with the original violation, the cost of receiving disapproval falls rapidly to zero. Empirically, it is not true that people frown upon others when they fail to sanction people who fail to sanction people who fail to sanction a norm violation. There do not appear to be fourth- or fifth-order norms.[35] Consequently, some sanctions must be performed for other motives than the fear of being sanctioned.

The second argument from the rationality of revenge behavior derives from Schelling[36] and amounts, in substance, to an argument for the rationality of appearing to be irrational. Consider for instance the game depicted in figure 1.

33. R. Axelrod, "An Evolutionary Approach to Norms," *American Political Science Review* 80 (1976): 599–617.

34. G. Akerlof ("The Economics of Caste and of the Rat Race and Other Woeful Tales," *Quarterly Journal of Economics* 90 [1976]: 599–617, at p. 610) argues that expectations about sanctions "can lead to an equilibrium in which all expectations are met and economic incentives favor obedience to the caste code—even in the extreme case where tastes are totally neutral regarding the observance of caste customs." A theoretical argument to the same effect is found in D. Abreu, "On the Theory of Infinitely Repeated Games with Discounting," *Econometrica* 56 (1988): 383–96.

35. Akerlof asserts that "those who fail to follow, *or even to enforce* the caste customs do not gain the profits of the successful arbitrageur but instead suffer the stigma of the outcaste" (p. 610; my italics). I am denying that this statement is true at any number of removes from the original violation.

36. T. C. Schelling, *The Strategy of Conflict* (Cambridge, Mass.: Harvard University Press, 1960), chap. 5.

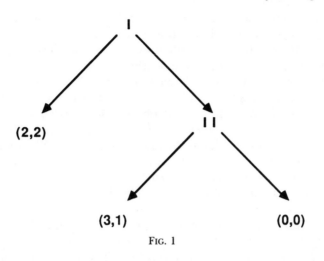

FIG. 1

Assume first that both players are fully rational and not moved by backward-looking considerations. Player I then knows that, if he goes right, II's self-interest will induce her to go left, thus ensuring the best outcome for I. Consequently, I will move right.

Assume next that II is believed to be truly irrational, because in the past she has consistently refused to let bygones be bygones. Player I knows that if he goes right, she will resent it sufficiently to go right herself, effectively cutting off her nose to spite her face. Being rational, I will go left. It would be a pointless play on words to say that II, when behaving irrationally, is in fact being rational. Her irrationality is useful to her, but it is none the less irrational.[37]

Assume now, however, that II is fully rational but deliberately engages in acts of vengeance to create an impression that she is irrational. If I is rational, he will not take these acts at face value. He will know that there is some probability that II is in fact irrational and also some probability that she is just faking irrational behavior to build up a reputation for toughness. Depending on the equilibrium probabilities and on what is

37. This argument does not establish a case for the unconditional usefulness of obeying a norm of revenge. It establishes at most that one could benefit from obeying the norm when dealing with other people who do not. If everyone abides by the norm, an individual might well do better not abiding by it. This argument has to be stated carefully. I do not mean that, in actual feuding societies, unilateral cowardice is rational. Social ostracism by third parties might well make that option unacceptable. What I claim is that if the only cost of cowardice were the loss incurred in conflictual encounters, an isolated coward might do better for himself than the average norm-follower. Followers of the norm of revenge would tend to meet other followers. If they have a substantial chance of being killed in each encounter, because neither side will back down, their life expectancy will be poor. The coward who yields up a contested resource without protesting might do better for himself. I return to these issues in Sec. VI.

at stake, he might well decide to abstain from provoking her. By this mechanism, it could indeed be rational to engage in acts of revenge.[38]

Note, however, that this mechanism is parasitic on the existence of some genuinely irrational persons in the population. What drives the argument is the common knowledge that society has some rational and some irrational members, but that they do not bear their rationality or lack of it on their face. In a population of individuals known by each other to be fully rational nobody would ever exact revenge. This remark parallels a comment I made on the first argument for the rationality of revenge. There, I said that sanctions cannot sustain a norm of revenge unless some of the sanctioners are genuinely moved by the norms. Here, I am saying that faking adherence to the norm cannot be a rational strategy unless some people genuinely adhere to it. Neither mechanism, therefore, can fully explain revenge practices as rational behavior. A third variation on this theme is offered in Section VI below.

The third argument for the rationality of revenge does not rest on the presence of some irrational believers in the norm.[39] Rather, it asserts that threats of vengeance can be part of a cooperative equilibrium because the knowledge that defectors will be punished keeps everybody in line. It is well known that if punishments (including punishments for failures to punish, etc.) are allowed to be arbitrarily severe, any outcome that gives no player less than his maximin payoff can be sustained by such threats.[40] Here, the purpose of punishment is simply to deter. The threat would fail if it had to be carried out. Actual revenge would occur only if someone acted irrationally, but then it is not clear that revenge would be a rational response to that act. A person who by defecting has shown himself to be irrational might not be moved by revenge. By this argument the rationality of the revenge threat itself is called into question.[41]

Leaving this question aside, the third argument fails on several counts. For one thing, it cannot explain actual revenge behavior. For another, it cannot explain why people would go out of their way to initiate conflict by the kind of brinkmanship behavior described earlier. More generally,

---

38. A formal model of a mechanism of this kind is presented in D. M. Kreps and R. Wilson, "Reputation and Imperfect Information," *Journal of Economic Theory* 27 (1982): 253–79. The problem of revenge can be seen as an analogue to their chain-store game, in which one vendetta corresponds to the game between the chain store and one local branch.

39. In its most elaborate version the third argument is very similar to the first argument, since both assert that the prescribed behavior can be maintained by a hierarchical system of sanctions. Simpler versions of the third argument, however, do not rely on punishments of those who fail to punish violators of the norm. The standard iterated Prisoner's Dilemma argument illustrates this case.

40. For a survey, see D. Fudenberg and E. Maskin, "The Folk Theorem in Repeated Games with Discounting and Incomplete Information," *Econometrica* 54 (1986): 533–54.

41. For a discussion of this conundrum, see K. Binmore, "Modeling Rational Players," *Economics and Philosophy* 3 (1987): 179–214.

I do not believe rational-choice arguments can capture the phenomenon of honor, which figures so prominently in all accounts of revenge.

V. THE FUNCTIONS OF REVENGE

Even if revenge behavior cannot be shown to be individually rational, it might be socially beneficial. Cooperative behavior might offer an analogy. Although choice of the cooperative behavior in collective action situations is usually not individually rational, it offers clear social advantages. The analogy also offers a problem, however. The social benefits from cooperation are obvious, but how could a society benefit from aggressive, destructive behavior? I shall survey some answers that have been offered to this question and also ask whether the alleged benefits of revenge could enter into an explanation of the behavior.

Feuding occurs mainly (although not exclusively) in societies without a strong centralized state. This fact suggests that feuding may serve the role of a legal enforcement system—a code of violence that serves the function of reducing the level of violence below what it would otherwise have been. In his analysis of blood feuds in Montenegro, Christopher Boehm writes that "feuding served as a kind of sanction, because it suppressed certain immoral behaviors that people knew were likely to start feuds. They also knew that feuds were dangerous, stressful, economically costly, and generally inconvenient from a practical standpoint. We must assume, therefore, that excessive quarreling and giving of insults, in addition to other provocative acts such as breach of contract, property disputes, and 'fooling around' with the women of other clans, tended to be avoided because of the perceived threat of starting a feud."[42]

This cannot be quite correct. Boehm himself shows how the possibility of a feud was an incentive to the giving of insults rather than a deterrent: the prospect that the insult might trigger a feud was what made it a source of honor. Later, he repeats the functional argument with a significant addition: "I believe that the effects of feuding as a social sanction were highly significant for this very aggressive people, who deliberately chose to live their lives with the near absence of any coercive authority in human form. What I am suggesting is that feuding served as a substitute for such authority, in that the probability of lethal retaliation and then a costly feud sharply curtailed certain socially disruptive behaviors. *The question remains, however, whether feuds created more disruption than they controlled*" (my emphasis).[43]

The phrase that I have italicized fits in with the observation just made, that the institution of the feud served as an incentive to violence. To decide whether the feud served the function of reducing the overall level of violence, some unanswerable questions would have to be answered. What were the feasible alternatives? This question is unanswerable because

42. Boehm, p. 88.
43. Ibid., p. 183.

there are no ground rules for how far back in history we are allowed to go to create counterfactual alternatives. The Montenegrins as they existed in the nineteenth century would probably not have accepted other means of conflict resolution. If we go far enough back in their history we could no doubt tell a story in which alternative institutions, ranging from a council of elders to a full-fledged legal system, could have emerged. But I do not see a nonarbitrary answer to the question of how far back we can go. And even if there was an answer, I do not see how the comparative calculus of violence could be carried out.

One might argue that the comparison should not be with alternative institutions, but with the absence of institutions, that is, with the state of nature. To be functional, a system of conflict resolution need not be optimal. It suffices that it allows for a more civilized life than in the state of nature. If we define this state by (i) the absence of coercive institutions and (ii) rational selfish motivations, two differences might be expected. On the one hand, there would be less violence because people would not harm others just to get even. On the other hand, there would be more violence, because people would not fear that others might retaliate just to get even. The net effect is anybody's guess.

The reduction of violence is not, however, the main function that Boehm ascribed to the feuding system. He also argues, inconsistently, that feuding benefits the Montenegrins mainly by raising the level of violence. Feuding acts as an "adaptive mechanism"[44] of a classical Malthusian kind:

> [Where] a particular tribe badly needed additional pastures in order to survive, it was likely to encroach on the territory of neighbors. This, in turn, could lead to quarrels over pastures, which could easily turn into feuds. Once the two tribes were feuding, this would increase the likelihood that the hungrier tribe, or else the larger tribe, might try by force to appropriate the other tribe's pastures. If stiff resistance were met, such a move could result in active warfare between tribes, replete with headhunting. . . . One consequence of such protracted feud and of this very rare intertribal warfare was that some of the surplus male population, which had created the problem, would be killed off. This would reduce population for a time. Similarly, when overpopulation would cause intensified raiding, then the Turks might eventually become aroused to the point of attacking the unruly tribe. If the Montenegrins lost, this could result not only in population losses but also in reduced nutrition because of Turkish taxes. For the overall tribal system, the beauty of these mechanisms was that clans and tribes that were overpopulated were most likely to begin feuds or to incur the wrath of the Turks. This meant that the increase in death rate was targeted where it would do "the most good" for the balance between natural resources and territorial groups.[45]

44. Ibid., p. 177.
45. Ibid., p. 178.

Later, Boehm introduces an additional complication. In their perpetual state of conflict with the Turkish rulers, it was not in the interest of the Montenegrins to wax too strong. A man may not mind a fly buzzing in his room, but he will try to get rid of a wasp. In this perspective, "feuding helped to keep the Montenegrin tribes divided among themselves so that they never posed enough of a threat to be more than a nuisance to a large empire. . . . To summarize, feuding was a well-integrated part of the very effective adjustment that the Montenegrins made both to their mountains and to their external enemies."[46]

Phrases like "adaptive mechanism" and "adjustment" suggest that these observations are offered as an explanation of feuding. This is not a plausible argument. It is unclear whether the ecological benefits or the military benefits provide separate sufficient explanations, so that, once again, the institution of feuding would be overdetermined. More important, merely pointing out that group behavior provides benefits for the group does not provide an explanation of the behavior, since we also need to know the mechanism whereby the benefits sustain the behavior.[47] Boehm observes that "there is no ethnohistorical evidence that [the Montenegrins] resisted having their feuds pacified because they feared that the resulting stronger confederation would antagonize the Turks."[48] This is not merely an unfortunate gap in the historical record, since the implied intentional explanation of feuding is absurd. The Montenegrin feuded when and because honor required it, not because they perceived that acting for the sake of honor might ensure an optimal degree of internal division. The existence of some causal feedback mechanism is not much more plausible.

Jacob Black-Michaud's analysis of feud in the Mediterranean and the Middle East also relies on functional argument, embedded in which is a suggestion that feuding can be individually rational. Following Simmel and Coser, he draws a distinction between realistic conflicts over material resources and nonrealistic conflicts over honor. Feuds, clearly, belong to the latter category. Given the norms of society, feuding is more legitimate than realistic conflicts. Hence individuals will try to manipulate the norms of revenge, by presenting what is in reality a material conflict as a matter of honor. If "one or both the parties to a dispute concerning property or access to natural resources believe that they will not obtain satisfaction from the [customary] canon, the whole tenor of conflict is changed by introducing the motive of honor."[49] The main piece of evidence for this interpretation is the following passage from Hasluck's work on Albania:

> While two families were quarreling about a piece of land, the wife of Grimes one day voiced her opinions so volubly in Gjelosh's house

46. Ibid., p. 185.
47. See chap. 2 of my *Explaining Technical Change* (Cambridge: Cambridge University Press, 1983).
48. Boehm, p. 186.
49. Black-Michaud, p. 142.

that he lost his temper and pushed her out. She fell down some steps by the door and bruised her hip. She showed the bruise to the gendarmerie, who were sympathetic enough to arrest Gjelosh and to imprison him for three months. The woman, who cared more for the violation of her honor by the push than for the bruise, was not satisfied and instigated her son, a boy of twelve or thirteen, to vindicate her honour by killing Gjelosh's son, who was of the same age. Since the boys habitually herded their goats together, her son found the opportunity of pushing the other boy over a rock and as he lay there helpless he stoned him till he died. Then Gjelosh, still in prison, paid a man to kill the little murderer. Grimes retorted by killing Gjelosh's remaining son and dooming Gjelosh's family to extinction.[50]

Black-Michaud is not justified in taking the fact that the quarrel started over a piece of land as evidence that the ensuing feud was "really" about material goods. It would be absurd to suggest that Grimes and his household were willing to risk the death of their son for a piece of land, yet as far as I understand it this is what Black-Michaud's claim amounts to. The straightforward explanation in terms of honor seems much more plausible.

Nor is he justified in using the story as evidence that "individuals manipulate to their own ends the ambiguities and lack of precision inherent in the concept of honour."[51] It is true, and important, that codes of honor and norms of revenge often do not uniquely dictate and predict individual behavior, leaving scope for choice and interpretation. Icelandic feuds, for instance, were based on a professed norm of "one for one." Yet, William Miller writes, "the notion of balance was innately ambiguous, since it was not mathematical, but socially contingent on a host of shifting variables, some of which were subject to conscious manipulation by the parties. . . . The practical process of feud . . . was less a matter of models than of manipulation. . . . So much of taking revenge was simply the ideological gloss of taking pure and simple."[52]

Miller goes on to say, however, that the scope for manipulation was limited. "The range of possible actions was not infinite. Disputants had to 'sell' their choices of actions to others. And to do so the choices had to accord with people's sense of right and propriety. . . . This social fact did not elevate the norms of disputing into rules that governed outcomes and predicted rules, but it made them into something more than mere ways of speaking. They had practical consequences."[53] And indeed it is hard to see how it could have been otherwise. The cynical view of norms, if taken to extremes, is self-defeating. "Unless rules were considered important and were taken seriously and followed, it would make no sense

50. Hasluck, pp. 236–37, cited in Black-Michaud, pp. 142–43, 177–78.
51. Black-Michaud, p. 143.
52. Miller, chap. 5.
53. Ibid.

to manipulate them for personal benefit. If many people did not believe that rules were legitimate and compelling, how could anyone use these rules for personal advantage?"[54] Once again, for the third time, we must conclude that rational-choice reductions of norms collapse if we try to extend them to all norm-governed behavior.

Black-Michaud's argument from manipulation is embedded in a wider functionalist scheme:

> A conflict in which the stated goal is the defence or acquisition of honour may well be and usually is related to some material cause of friction—such as the disputed possession of a field—between the parties. The end result of such a conflict for honour may even be the illegitimate acquisition of the field, as well as honour, by one of the parties if they succeed in exterminating each other. The Albanian episode I referred to earlier is a case in point. But *in the eyes of the community* the material realistic prize will be a mere concomitant of the non-realistic prize and no one will feel obliged to jeopardise the unity of the community by proceeding to collective sanctions against the victors, who, it will be said, were after all only acting in defence of their reputation even if they did obtain the field at the same time. . . . Finally, the fact that conflicts over honour are strictly the concern of those whose honour is at stake inhibits their spreading to involve other members of the community. Unlike conflicts for realistic goals which may be interpreted by those not directly implicated as a menace to their own future security, conflicts purportedly over honour make it possible for hostile groups to expend their aggressive energies upon each other without drawing in the society as a whole. Honour in this case, where customary legislation and public opinion forbid territorial encroachment, serves four different purposes simultaneously. It is (1) a licit means of achieving an "illegal" material end; (2) an affirmation of aptitude for leadership; (3) a medium for the escalation of conflict for material ends beyond a level at which hostilities of this type are no longer normally tolerated by the society at large and would in principle (were the pretext of honour not invoked) be liable to legal sanctions; (4) a means of ensuring the non-proliferation of such conflicts throughout the social structure.[55]

The argument suffers from a number of flaws. It is implausible to assume that while nobody cares about their own honor, everybody believes that others care about theirs. Also, the tell-tale use of the word "means" both in the individual context (honor is a means for the individual to get material goods) and in the social context (it is a means for society to contain conflict) suggest that Black-Michaud conceives of society as an

54. R. Edgerton, *Rules, Exceptions and the Social Order* (Berkeley: University of California Press, 1985), p. 3.
55. Black-Michaud, pp. 193–94.

organic entity that protects "itself" and assures "its" cohesion by the use of force. The title of his book, *Cohesive Force*, points in the same direction.

VI. REVENGE OF THE GENES

In his work on feuding among the Yanomamö (a tribe of South American Indians), Napoleon Chagnon argues that the tendency to seek revenge might enhance reproductive fitness (and be explained by its enhancement of reproductive fitness) in two ways:

> First, kinship groups that retaliate swiftly and demonstrate their resolve to avenge deaths acquire reputations for ferocity that deter the violent designs of their neighbors. The Yanomamö explain that a group with a reputation for swift retaliation is attacked less frequently and thus suffers a lower rate of mortality. They also note that other forms of predation, such as the abduction of women, are thwarted by adopting an aggressive stance. Aggressive groups coerce nubile females from less aggressive groups whenever the opportunity arises. Many appear to calculate the costs and benefits of forcibly appropriating or coercing females from groups that are perceived to be weak. Second, men who demonstrate their willingness to act violently and to exact revenge for the deaths of kin may have higher marital and reproductive success.[56]

Chagnon does not make it clear which of the following two sociobiological models of revenge he has in mind. On the one hand evolution could develop "vengeance genes" that predispose individuals to seek revenge when their material interests are harmed, even if the retaliation involves some cost or risk to the avenger in excess of the extent, if any, to which the original damage is undone. On the other hand, evolution could produce a tendency to learn from others and acquire the patterns of behaviour that make for reproductive success. If revenge is seen simply as a form of behavior, on a par with foraging or tool using, either model could work. If revenge is perceived, more realistically, as a set of behaviors together with a set of characteristic emotions, only the first model is plausible. One can imitate behavior, but not acquire emotions, by imitating others.

Several recent studies have argued that emotions like anger or vindictiveness can yield a strategic advantage to their bearers.[57] The basic reasoning is the same as that explained in connection with figure 1: if a person is perceived as irrationally bent on punishing others if he does not get his way, others will let him have his way, if they are rational. In a population of rational individuals, who engage in aggressive behavior only when it pays to do so, an irrational person may have a reproductive

56. Chagnon, p. 986.
57. R. Frank, *Passions within Reason* (New York: Norton, 1988); J. Hirschleifer, "On the Emotions as Guarantors of Threats and Promises," in *The Latest on the Best*, ed. J. Dupré (Cambridge, Mass.: MIT Press, 1987), pp. 307–26.

edge. After a while, the proportion of irrational people in the population will increase. This change will also lead to a reduction in the payoff for mindless aggressiveness, however. When two irrational individuals meet each other, as they increasingly will when the number of such people go up, neither will yield, and one or both may be killed. In equilibrium the population will have a mix of both genotypes, with equal expected reproductive success.[58]

Chagnon's empirical findings seem to confirm this idea, although he is far from explicit about it. He cites evidence to the effect that *unokais,* that is, people who have shot an arrow into an enemy during a raid on the enemy village, have more wives and more offspring than others. He mentions and dismisses the objection that surviving *unokais* might be a biased sample of the group, and that the higher rates of fertility of surviving *unokais* might be offset by lower survival chances. His counterarguments are weak, however. Moreover, he later implicitly admits the justice of the objection when he says that "among the Yanomamö, non-*unokais* might be willing to concede more reproductive opportunities to *unokais* in exchange for a life with fewer mortal risks and fewer reproductive advantages."[59] This is consistent with the idea that the two groups have the same expected fitness.

The emergence and propagation of socially shared norms of revenge could also be explained by a genetic model or, less pretentiously, story. As I shall tell the story it has two stages, which in actual cases would develop simultaneously. Assume that a polymorphic equilibrium has emerged, with some individuals having a propensity for taking revenge and others for behaving rationally. The former will clearly be the dominant social group. Even if they do not have more offspring, their role as warriors will ensure that they have more prestige and enable them to impose their values on others. These values then become the social norms. This will change the payoffs for cowardly (i.e., rational) behavior. In addition to losses suffered in conflictual encounters with the revenge takers, rational individuals will suffer losses in their interactions with third parties. If A yields to B, A may lose his property to B. In addition, C may not give his daughter in marriage to A. The equilibrium will be upset, because the expected fitness of those who take revenge now exceeds that of those who do not. In the new equilibrium that is eventually reached, there may still be some who act rationally, but it is also possible that all are revenge takers. Although individual-level selection for reproductive fitness is what causes the move to the new equilibrium, average fitness will fall. On this account, norms of revenge are not functional for society.

---

58. For an exposition of this basic Hawk-Dove game, see J. Maynard-Smith, *Evolution and the Theory of Games* (Cambridge: Cambridge University Press, 1982).

59. Chagnon, p. 990. The language of concession is, however, incompatible with the genetic model sketched above.

A problem for this explanation is that it cannot account for the fact that many societies have no codes of honor or norms of revenge. As I said, spontaneous revenge behavior is universal: norms of revenge are not. In many societies there would, if anything, seem to be a norm against seeking revenge and, correlatively, injunctions to turn the other cheek.[60] There is a spontaneous tendency to seek revenge which must enter into any explanation of revenge behavior and of norms of revenge. Being universal, that tendency must have an evolutionary explanation. The explanation might be something like the frequency-dependent model sketched above or it might take one of the more complex forms sketched toward the end of the concluding section. Yet whatever the explanation of the tendency, it cannot by itself account for the facts about revenge behavior and norms of revenge. In the concluding section I offer some speculations about how that tendency might interact with other psychological propensities to produce norms of revenge.

VII. CONCLUSION

So far the tenor of this article has been largely negative. A number of explanations of revenge behavior have been tried and found wanting. The most promising is perhaps the idea that revenge behavior could be part of a stable genetic polymorphism, but even that proposal is at best incomplete. I am not, in this section, going to offer an alternative explanation. What I shall try to do is better described as pointing toward the direction in which an explanation might be found.

I believe the phenomenon of honor to be the key to understanding revenge. Asserting one's honor, like enjoying other people's envy of one's assets, is an aspect of a deep-rooted urge to show oneself to be superior to others. It is, however, a more interactive phenomenon than envy and its companions, envy provocation and envy enjoyment.[61] Envy can arise simply through comparisons of material possessions, without any interaction with the envied person. It is, in that sense, an external relation.[62] The provocation and enjoyment of envy can, similarly, occur without interaction. I can flaunt my assets before other people to provoke their envy without actively challenging them. Honor, by contrast, arises in internal relations. It depends on actions, not on assets.[63] The paradigm of envy enjoyment is conspicuous consumption. The paradigm of the

---

60. I am indebted to Lawrence Becker for this point. Commenting on an earlier draft of this article he wrote that "any adequate explanation or justification of norms *of* revenge should also be capable of accounting for equally powerful and pervasive norms *against* revenge."

61. For a more extensive discussion of envy, see my *The Cement of Society,* pp. 252–53.

62. For this notion, see my *Logic and Society* (Chichester, N.Y.: Wiley, 1978), pp. 20–25.

63. A similar distinction between action-independent and action-dependent emotions (e.g., between malevolence and anger) is made in Hirschleifer.

strive for honor is Hegel's master-slave dialectic. Far from resting his claim to superiority on a larger amount of material possessions, the master derives it from his willingness to risk his life and thus to ignore the purely material aspects of existence.[64] Although Hegel notes that the acquisition of honor leads to more consumption, honor is not (*pace* Black-Michaud) acquired for the sake of consumption. Its aim is sheer self-assertion and self-esteem.[65]

Hegel's analysis is not fully applicable, however. He asserts that the search for honor through the domination and humiliation of another is self-contradictory. The self-esteem of the master derives from the esteem accorded him by the slave. But esteem is worthless unless reciprocated: to ask for esteem from a slave is like a nation asking diplomatic recognition from one of its own colonies.[66] The contradiction disappears once we recognize that honor is a triadic rather than a dyadic relation. A gains honor by humiliating B in the presence of C. Hence the insistence in feuding societies that killings be publicly recognized: "It was everywhere 'held dishonourable' to kill and not to tell. It was also thought unfair for reasons that varied with the locality. In Mirditë the victim's relatives might go mad if they did not know the identity of the murderer; in North Albania the murderer's kinsmen would not know to hide while the avenger's blood was boiling; in South Albania the crime might be laid at the wrong door. Besides, the normal murder was a matter of boasting; committed only to avenge some wrong or insult, it showed that the murderer was spirited enough to resent ill-treatment."[67]

I believe the urge for honor, like the enjoyment of other people's envy, are universal phenomena. They can be controlled but not fully suppressed. They arise in the mind spontaneously but need not have any further effect if we can recognize them and avoid acting on them. Needless to say, they can also have a massively important impact on behavior. Feuding societies embody the quest for honor in a particularly striking form. In these societies, the urge to prove oneself superior to others fuses with the spontaneous urge to seek revenge, to produce norms of revenge. In other societies that emphasize honor, revenge is less important. I have in mind here the Asian societies in which "face" is a major consideration. In still other societies, the urge for superiority takes the form of provoking other people's envy.

64. Hegel, *The Phenomenology of Mind* (Oxford: Oxford University Press, 1982), pp. 112–16.

65. In *A Theory of Justice* (Cambridge, Mass.: Harvard University Press, 1971), John Rawls argues for a subtler link between self-esteem and (among other things) consumption. Self-esteem is the most important primary good, without which consumption yields no satisfaction. Yet Rawls does not suggest, nor do I think the argument could be made, that people seek self-esteem as a prerequisite for deriving pleasure from a given amount of consumption goods, any more than they seek it to increase the amount of consumption goods available to them.

66. For an elaboration of this argument, see my *Logic and Society*, pp. 70–77.

67. Hasluck, p. 228.

In these remarks, innate psychological tendencies and urges bear the main explanatory burden. In addition to the obviously speculative and conjectural nature of this explanation sketch, it is clearly incomplete. Why do people have these urges? It seems clear that an evolutionary sociobiological explanation is needed, but we have to be careful as to the form this account would take. Evolutionary explanations do not take the narrow form "Feature X exists because it maximizes the genetic fitness of the organism." Rather, their general form is "X exists because it is part of a package solution that at some time maximized the genetic fitness of the organism." The latter form allows for two facts that the former excludes. First, there is the omnipresent phenomenon of pleiotropy. A tendency to search for honor might detract from genetic fitness and yet be retained by natural selection if it is the by-product of a gene (or a set of genes) whose main product is highly beneficial. Second, the general form allows for time lags. A social norm may be maladaptive today and yet have been adaptive at a stage in history when the human genome evolved and, for practical purposes, became fixed. I do not believe current knowledge enables us to say which of these explanatory types would enable us to account for the existence of norms of revenge.

Vulgarity*

M. W. Barnes

There is a sense in which I am obligated not to buy and display a pink china poodle. Doing so would be vulgar. Other examples of vulgarity, according to an informal poll, are boasting of one's wealth, shopping in an undershirt, "beautiful music" stations, public spitting, loud arguments, and most of what goes on on television. The first thing that strikes one about this list is its variety. What could all these things have in common? It is more helpful than it would seem to say that they are all relatively harmless, and indeed in many cases have so little practical significance that they can scarcely fail to be harmless. And yet they are taken seriously. Allowing for a little literary exaggeration, Wilde's remark to the effect that "as long as war is regarded as wicked, it will always have its fascination. When it is looked upon as vulgar, it will cease to be popular,"[1] represents a genuine attitude. Some people, at least, would rather be thought immoral than vulgar. Another peculiarity of the category of vulgarity is that it creates a strange set of obligations. My obligation not to be vulgar is not peculiarly mine; it is possible for me to accuse another person of vulgarity and to achieve agreement with others as to what actions are vulgar. Nevertheless, the obligation is not general. There are actions that would be vulgar if I performed them but not if others did. There are even, in many cases, ways for me to do the same action without vulgarity, and I can sometimes get away with saying "I think it is really vulgar, but I like it" —but not if I say it too often.

Clearly one distinction that must be made is between vulgar persons on the one hand and vulgar things and actions on the other. It is strictly a historical question whether one of the two senses is prior in time, but from the standpoint of obligation the issue of priority is clear enough. Nobody, including the civilized person who seeks to avoid vulgarity, is

* An earlier version of this paper was presented to a joint colloquium of the Philosophy Departments of the University of Hartford and Trinity College. Thanks are due to the members of both departments and to Kathleen Buck for many helpful criticisms and suggestions.

1. Oscar Wilde, "The Critic as Artist (Second Part)," *Intentions* (New York: Boni & Liveright, n.d.), p. 204.

This essay originally appeared in *Ethics*, vol. 91, no. 1, October 1980.

under an obligation to avoid particular vulgar things or actions. In addition to the fact, mentioned above, that occasional exceptions are generally permitted, there is the fact that publicity is frequently involved. There are innumerable things that can be done in private that would be vulgar if done in public. There can be no objection to a woman's putting her hair in curlers if she cares to do so, but we rather wish she would not wear them to the supermarket. What we ought to avoid is being a vulgar *person*.

Because our basic concern is with the concept of the vulgar person, we need not worry about the obvious relativity: the specific actions and things that count as vulgar vary with place and time. But if vulgarity, in the personal sense, is an attitude, the variations in content are not particularly important. In this respect the idea of the vulgar person can be usefully compared with the rather old-fashioned conception of the "scofflaw." As the name suggests, the scofflaw is a person who breaks the law casually, because he follows his convenience without concern for whether his actions are legal or not. Unlike the criminal, the scofflaw usually restricts himself to minor violations: after all, being punished is an inconvenience. More importantly, the scofflaw differs from the criminal in that the latter has no particular feeling about the law: he breaks it for profit or some other need, whereas the scofflaw breaks it casually. As the foregoing indicates, it is perfectly possible to discuss what a "scofflaw" is without referring to particular actions. If I habitually make right turns on red in some states I am a scofflaw, but not if I do it where it is legal. I presume, in addition, that a scofflaw would make right turns on red anywhere, so that he could act as a scofflaw even though what he was doing was legal. Similarly, vulgarians (and the scofflaw may well be among their number) are not so because of particular acts but because of a casual attitude toward what they do.

The discussion so far indicates that vulgarity is an attitude, although, of course, one that must be exemplified in action, and further reasons can be offered for this conclusion. If I acquire a pink china poodle and display it for the purpose of shocking my friends, I am not being vulgar. A joke can be vulgar, of course, but one can defend oneself against a charge of vulgarity by claiming that he was joking. Hamlet's "they do but jest, poison in jest—no offense i' the world" (3.2) is ironic because, while one can certainly poison in jest, the *act* is an "offense," and thus the fact that it is done in jest is irrelevant. We would probably all agree that there are actions so vulgar that even doing them in jest is vulgar. Nevertheless, even in those cases we take joking to be an inadequate defense, not an irrelevant one. Innocence is also a defense. A young girl might keep a pink china poodle without our thinking she is vulgar; we might even find it charming, as something fitting for a child. We expect barbarians to be barbaric, and even actions that we could not perform, even in jest, without vulgarity, might be accepted in a "primitive" if carried off with what we usually describe as "naturalness." The defense of innocence again points to the fact that vulgarity is an attitude. When the attitude is not present, no blame is attributed.[2]

Another odd feature of the category of vulgarity is relevant here. Rather than use an ostentatiously ugly vase, I might choose to put flowers in a mayonnaise jar. Nobody would say that the jar was beautiful or even tasteful, but I have avoided vulgarity as surely as if I had used some exquisite product of the ancient Orient. In fact, using the Oriental vase could be vulgar—for example, if I were using it to flaunt my wealth—but it is difficult to see how using the jar could be. There is much that is mysterious in this situation, but once again it indicates that an attitude is involved. Overt[3] actions normally have only two modes when looked at from a value standpoint, namely, done or refrained from. We may think of exceptions like lying, telling the truth, or keeping silent, but there refraining from acting is valued differently from either overt action.

Vulgarity, then, when attributed to persons, is an attitude, vulgar actions and things being symptomatic of that attitude. What attitude is it? Our examples have been primarily esthetic, but we should not be misled by them, or by the fact that vulgarity is sometimes called "bad taste," into thinking that it is a matter of lack of esthetic taste. I may conceivably be wrong in preferring Mozart to Verdi; my taste may be faulty, but my preference is vulgar only in case it derives from something esthetically irrelevant like a desire to seem upper class or intellectual. Alternatively, some instances of vulgarity, such as boasting of one's wealth, can hardly be objected to on esthetic grounds. In any case, it is clear that ignorance, as such, cannot constitute vulgarity, whether that ignorance is esthetic, moral, or factual.

Even a cursory reflection on examples suffices to show that vulgarity is not a moral category. Some actions, such as commenting loudly on a woman's figure as she passes, are both morally wrong and vulgar, but the two ranges do not coincide. Some actions that are both morally wrong and vulgar are so for different reasons. It is probably significant that a large number of the cases where the vulgar and the morally wrong coincide involve the degradation of a person. The previous example, commenting on a women's figure, is typical. An interesting difference appears, however. To treat a person as just so much flesh is morally wrong, but it can be done with varying degrees of vulgarity. "Dig the jugs on that chick" is considerably more vulgar than "That young lady is very well endowed." It would seem that the moral offense is somehow

2. Because of this fact, any subsequent statement to the effect that something is or may be vulgar should be understood as containing an implicit restriction to whatever group of people we think should know better.

3. By "overt" actions I mean those, like poisoning, that (to use the phrase of Alfred Schutz) "gear into the world," and thus cannot be undone.

increased by the vulgarity, although from a strictly ethical standpoint treating a person as a thing should be unjustified no matter how it is done. Perhaps it is only that the vulgar utterance leaves no doubt of the moral offense, whereas the other might permit the act to be morally defended as an esthetic appreciation, a factual statement, or a misguided compliment.

The relation of the category of vulgarity to class prejudice is more difficult to understand. After all, etymologically speaking, being vulgar is to resemble the *vulgus*, the common people. But common in what sense? Surely being poor is not vulgar, nor is doing the things that are characteristic of being poor, such as living in slums, using food stamps, etc. We might even point out that among the things that are generally regarded as vulgar are things that the poor cannot do, such as flaunting one's wealth. Exhibiting class prejudice is also frequently regarded as vulgar. Nor could the class prejudice be thought of on occupational lines. Working with one's hands, for example, is not generally regarded as vulgar. The *vulgus* in this context is not defined on class lines at all but, as the Greek expression *hoi polloi*, "the many," suggests, on the basis of ordinariness. Being ordinary is lacking refinement. Until rather recently, the word "vulgar" was used in a more or less neutral way. The "vulgar tongue" was simply ordinary language that had not been Latinized or otherwise polished. Berkeley uses the word in that sense when, in a famous passage, he recommends that we continue to "speak with the vulgar." When the word appears in its nonneutral, pejorative sense, a curious change occurs. In this sense, the *vulgus* can do vulgar things but cannot be vulgar, for being vulgar amounts to person who can be expected to exhibit refinement behaving like one who cannot be. That is why not knowing any better is a defense against a charge of vulgarity.

After this long preamble, it is now possible to offer an account of the nature of vulgarity. Vulgarity is indifference to the distinction between better and worse. If I know, or should know, that one thing is better than another, but my actions are those of a person who has no such knowledge, I am being vulgar. We will have more to say later about the kind of knowing that is involved, but there is surely a sense in which one can be said to know orders of value, or at least to know that there are such orders. To act in indifference to that knowledge is vulgar. In view of the previous discussion and the diversity of examples, it need hardly be added that the orders of value involved are not restricted to any particular type, and that indifference to those orders is independent of the correctness of one's belief about their actual ordering. Mistakenly believing that one thing is better than another need not be the result of indifference, and need not be vulgar.

The one type of value that is difficult to fit into this account is the moral. Indifference to the distinction between better and worse in the moral realm is, it would seem, not vulgar but immoral. Indeed, it is one of the things that is most certainly immoral. However, moral indifference is wrong because of its relation to moral action, to orders of rightness; it is vulgar to be indifferent to orders of goodness. Thus doing anything that lowers the dignity of a person is wrong, but making it obvious that human dignity does not matter is vulgar.

Another way of expressing this is to say that vulgarity is lack of respect for excellence. The excellence involved can be esthetic, ethical, even intellectual, and the exact meaning of "excellence" will have to be deferred for a later and much longer discussion.[4] But to be aware, or to be in a position in which one should be aware, that something is more excellent than another, without adjusting one's behavior accordingly, is vulgar. The adjustment of one's behavior need not be an attempt to achieve excellence or that particular excellence. It is not humanly possible to achieve or even strive for all forms of excellence. The mayonnaise jar example given earlier may serve as an illustration. A respect for excellence is shown when one refuses to use something ugly in favor of something merely functional when the beautiful is not available. It also involves a serious attempt to become aware of possible orders of excellence not previously appreciated.

Given an order of relative excellence, vulgarity can consist in ignoring the order, or willfully inverting it. Thus, flaunting practically anything is likely to be vulgar. What is flaunted is claimed to be excellent—otherwise, why flaunt it? If it really is something excellent (e.g., knowledge or moral sensitivity), its use as an instrumentality for the relatively low value of being admired is vulgar. If it is not at a very high level of excellence (e.g., sexiness), flaunting it is ignoring the order. Since there appear to be many different orders of excellence, vulgarity might also result from casually confusing the orders, although clear examples do not come easily to mind (perhaps building a hamburger stand in the form of the Taj Mahal). The important word here in any case is "casually." One way of exhibiting respect for orders of excellence might be to suggest that our perception of some order is mistaken and to offer a revaluation of some kind. The respect that is needed is for the orders of excellence themselves and not for any item that may or may not have a place in some order.

One complication needs to be carefully examined. We all know people who cannot be said to be innocent, who in fact are extremely careful to avoid what they take to be vulgarity. However, their conception of what is vulgar is restricted to wearing "proper" clothing and avoiding the obvious social crudities. Their notion of vulgarity is narrow,

---

4. One thing should be made clear, however. The English word "excellence" generally implies competition, outdoing others. I am using the word in a sense in which it is unlikely but not impossible for everyone to be excellent. I will defend this departure from ordinary usage on the ground that the word is being used as an inadequate translation of the Greek *aretē*. In short, if it is not ordinary English, it is ordinary Greek.

and often simply wrong. Worse, there seems to be a tendency in such people to let "respectability" function as a substitute for ordinary human warmth and decency: if you wear a vest and do not belch in public, it does not matter to them if you are a racist. Sometimes, in fact, they approve of moral evils because they are practiced by the class they want to emulate. A peculiar feature of this is that a civilized person, encountering this phenomenon, is tempted to do something vulgar for shock value—to illustrate the shallowness of this misplaced fastidiousness.

The first thing we are inclined to say about this case is that it is the shadow without the substance. The person described above is not respecting orders of excellence. At most, he is imitating those who do—generally the imitation is second order, an imitation of imitators. Since the values here involved are primarily embodied in social interchange (rather than individual espousal) in a manner to be discussed later, it is quite possible to carry on the kind of imitation we have been describing. It is inherently vulgar because it reflects a lack of respect for excellence, especially by not trying to extend one's awareness of it. In addition, the imitation produces a new dimension of vulgarity. Anyone's sensitivity to orders of excellence is limited, and many of the limitations are embodied in the practice of some subgroup; for example, the bourgeoisie. To be bourgeois is not necessarily to be vulgar; but imitating the bourgeoisie is not being bourgeois, for it involves valuing their limitations, not just having them. Finally, in the case where respectability becomes a substitute for decency, there is both moral indifference and a failure to respect orders of goodness, thus both wrongness and vulgarity.

It may be asked: isn't it rather vulgar to be so concerned with the category of vulgarity? Does it have an importance that justifies this concern? Vulgarity is an example of a marginal value system. It does not belong to either of the great value ranges, the ethical and the esthetic. It is precisely for that reason that it, and others like it, are of interest to the theorist, for they are much simpler than the greater, and admittedly more important, ranges. As such, they provide a kind of laboratory in which important value considerations can be closely examined without the distractions of the more complex systems.

We have already seen one reason why vulgarity is worth our consideration: it has a bearing on the concept of excellence, which is central to many discussions of value. Ancient ethical theory in general, and Aristotelian ethics especially, is haunted by this concept. It is noteworthy, for example, that most of the bad characters so amusingly described by Theophrastus involve conduct that we would think of as vulgar rather than immoral or wrong. Committing a monstrous oversimplification, we can say that Aristotle's answer to the question "What ought I to do?" is "Whatever leads to excellence." Ethical theories centering on the concept of excellence suffer from an inability to define the concept in a way that is both defensible and precise enough to serve as a guide for action, especially after the diversity of conceptions of excellence became apparent to philosophers through the recognition of civilizations other than their own. Ethical theory depending on the concept of excellence survived for a while with the assistance of a theology that represented God as knowing what human excellence is and as giving us commandments for achieving it, thus solving both difficulties. That possibility died with the Medieval synthesis, and the moderns, by and large, had to try to do without the concept of excellence. To see how difficult that was, one only need refer to J. S. Mill's well-known problem about the "quality" of pleasure. Mill has to fall back on the idea that a person with the appropriate experience will recognize the superiority of one pleasure to another and prefer the higher. Our discussion of vulgarity shows that Mill was wrong, that people who should know better do not choose in favor of the higher; and in any case, the real question concerns the basis on which the choice is made. But Mill is right in thinking that, for whatever reason and on whatever basis, we recognize orders of excellence, have preferences that respect those orders, and despise those who should do the same but do not. Perhaps we should emphasize here that the concept of vulgarity may be a mistake: the fact that people take it seriously does not prove that there are or should be orders of excellence. That is, after all, the fallacy of intuitionism: the idea that because something is believed there must be a basis in reality for that belief. Nevertheless, the concept of excellence survies, if only by negation. We despair of knowing what excellence is, but we suspect we can know what it is not.

There are other theoretical concerns raised by the category of vulgarity. One is the light it throws on certain generalizing arguments that are common in ethical theory. A well-known example of this type of argument is found in chapter 4 of Mill's *Utilitarianism*: "No reason can be given why the general happiness is desirable, except that each person . . . desires his own happiness." The weakness of Mill's argumentation at this point is notorious and perhaps would best be passed over as one inexplicable aberration of a great man were it not for two facts. One is that any ethical theory, like that of Mill, that is rooted in actual preferences must ultimately make use of some such argument. It is needed in order to move from "I prefer *A* for myself" to "We ought to prefer *A* in general." The other reason for taking it seriously is that it has been used in varying forms in other ethical theories. William James uses it less explicitly in "The Moral Philosopher and the Moral Life" by claiming that "claim and obligation are, in fact, coextensive terms; they cover each other exactly."[5] Sartre uses a rather subtler form of it: " . . . Once a man has seen that values depend upon himself, in that state

5. William James, *The Will to Believe* (New York: Longmans, Green & Co., 1896), p. 194.

of foresakeness he can will only one thing, and that is freedom as the foundation of all values. That does not mean that he wills it in the abstract: it simply means that the actions of men of good faith have, as their ultimate significance, the quest of freedom itself as such."[6] What all of these arguments seem to conclude is that one's particular preferences or values have general features that must therefore be valued in general, not only as they are involved in one's own life, but in others' lives as well. Depending on the particular theory, the generalization requires the promotion of that value, respect for others' right to pursue it, or an obligation placed on others to pursue it. Now it seems clear enough that this is not universally true. If we reflect (for example) on the difference between feeling pleasure and thinking about it, we understand that the way something is involved in one's choices and preferences is different from the way it is in one's general obligations. In Whiteheadian language, the confusion is between propositions and eternal objects. The arguments are unsound, but there is a catch. There really is a connection between valuings and values, a connection these arguments are trying to exploit. We must try to discern what the connection might be.

While it is sometimes objected that one cannot be motivated by abstract principle, the obligation to avoid vulgarity seems to be an instance of just that. The preceding discussion concludes that the general principle is the respect for excellence, but even if that is incorrect, the almost total pragmatic insignificance of most vulgar actions indicates that we are responding to some abstract principle, and that it is one that can be only tenuously rooted in our vital desires and needs. The obligation cannot be the result of a generalization on them. Perhaps, however, it could be argued that the respect for excellence is derived from a striving for excellence. That is, because we desire to strive for excellence, we ought to respect it in all its forms. We might try to strengthen the argument by suggesting that, since we cannot strive for all forms of excellence, our avoidance of vulgarity is a kind of homage to those excellences we must otherwise neglect. The reference to a *desire* to strive for excellence is needed here. There may be people who are inherently mediocre, recognize the fact, and correctly conclude that they cannot strive for excellence at all. If they nevertheless are fastidious in avoiding vulgarity, it may be because they desire to be excellent, even though that desire is frustrated. It is far from clear that such people could really exist, but certainly there are some whose desire to strive for excellence would be frustrated by economic, social, or other circumstances. We would scarcely demand that they strive in vain.

There are, however, serious objections to this line of reasoning, most of them deriving from the difficulty of assigning a clear meaning to the idea of "desiring to strive for excellence." Surely one cannot be said to

6. Jean-Paul Sartre, *Existentialism and Humanism*, trans. P. Mairet (London: Methuen & Co., 1948), p. 51.

desire to strive for excellence in the same sense that one desires to eat, to escape danger, or even to experience pleasure. The "innate striving" so commonly referred to in vague, high-flown (and often vulgar) rhetoric is simply a fuzzy reference to the fact that humans are perennially dissatisfied. Whatever "excellence" means, it is not synonymous with "what people want." One way of illustrating the confusion might be to recognize that some of the worst vulgarities come from people who are seeking excellence in the preposterous belief that wealth, or the values associated with the wealthy, constitutes excellence. A person who genuinely strives for excellence does so *because of* a respect for it. The respect is not derived from the striving, but the striving from the respect. Ortega's characterization of the "select minority" is incorrect. It is not that they "make great demands on themselves, piling up difficulties and duties,"[7] but that they care *what* they demand of themselves. Any successful businessman makes "great demands" on himself for the sake of success; so, for that matter, does a flagpole sitter. The seekers of excellence, the true select minority, think it matters what they count as success. Perhaps we should say that they do not desire to strive for excellence but strive to desire what is excellent. In this context we ought to refer to two other generalizing arguments that are significantly different from the ones referred to earlier, those of Josiah Royce and Eliseo Vivas.[8] The difference is that neither philosopher assumes that the generalization is merely a matter of reasoning. Both emphasize that it takes not merely intelligence but a *moral* intelligence to generalize beyond one's own concerns. That is, the generalization is not the result of a desire to pursue one's own concerns but of a desire to pursue them rightly. For both Royce and Vivas, the concerns generalized on are already moral. Royce sees the generalization as being from a loyalty that gives significance to one's own life to a "loyalty to loyalty" that respects and furthers the loyalties of others. Similarly, for Vivas it is a person with a set of values already formed who can make the move to the "ethical," namely, to the espousal of the primacy of the person as central. Although Vivas represents the move as motivated by sympathy, neither he nor Royce suggests that mere de facto valuations can be generalized upon.

Thus, the respect for excellence places on those who have it no obligation to be excellent or to strive for excellence, although it might be a strong motive for doing so. One's respect for excellence also does not produce any general obligations with respect to others. If I believe something is vulgar, there are some people whose doing it I would

7. José Ortega y Gasset, *The Revolt of the Masses* (New York: W. W. Norton & Co., 1932), p. 15.
8. Josiah Royce, *The Philosophy of Loyalty* (New York: Macmillan Co., 1908), esp. chap. 3; Eliseo Vivas, *The Moral Life and the Ethical Life* (Chicago: University of Chicago Press, 1950), pt. 3.

disapprove of, others whom I might try to convince of its vulgarity, and still others whose innocence in that particular matter I would not tamper with. Similarly, since I do not regard everyone as obligated to follow my example, I also am not obligated to encourage all others to do so. Finally, while I am obligated to respect others' right to follow my example or to pursue their own vision of excellence, that is a moral obligation that exists whether I respect excellence or not. Since the generalizing argument does not work in this case, it cannot be said to be generally cogent without modifications of the sort that Royce and Vivas introduce.

Another issue the discussion of vulgarity may bear on is the status of value. There is less today than there once was of the loose talk about the "values of one's society," as though any society had a uniform and coherent system of values, but it would be useful to know how values are involved in societies. Now the concept of vulgarity illustrates that at least in this case the values involved cannot be the result of consensus. Vulgarity, as we usually understand it, assumes a lack of consensus, namely, a group of people who do not see the value of doing and avoiding what civilized people do and avoid. Given the meaning of "excellence" used here, the existence of an out-group is not an essential feature, but in practice we can and do assume there is one. Even among the group who can be expected to respect particular excellences, which contains the vulgar and the civilized but not the innocent, there can be no explicit consensus, for then vulgarity would be rare or impossible. Unlike moral error, vulgarity seldom has any strong motive: that is another consequence of the pragmatic insignificance of most vulgar actions. Additionally, inclination is accepted as an excuse for occasional vulgarity, presumably because it is tolerable when the respect for excellence is clear. Thus there is no good reason why a person who knew what was vulgar would ever do anything vulgar. Alternatively, those who do not know what is vulgar are excused from the charge of vulgarity on account of their innocence.

This looks like a variation on the *Meno* paradox. If we know what is vulgar we have no good reason to be so, and if we do not know, we cannot be. The paradox is stronger here because "implicit" knowledge, at least in most of its meanings, could not be acted on and thus would function merely as a form of ignorance. There is, however, one kind of implicit knowledge that may offer an escape. Lévi-Strauss claims to have found in social structures levels of significance that are not explicitly recognized by the members of the societies involved, but are nevertheless used.[9] A myth, a kinship system, even a system of cuisine can embody messages that are not, possibly cannot be, expressed in discur-

9. These concepts are so diffused through Lévi-Strauss's work that I despair of giving a clear reference. See, however, the following: Claude Lévi-Strauss, *Anthropologie structurale* (Paris: Plon, 1948), chaps. 11 and 12; *Le Cru et le cuit* (Paris: Plon, 1964), Ouverture; *L'Homme nu* (Paris: Plon, 1971), Finale.

sive language, in propositional form. These messages are not strictly implicit; they are so simply for us who identify explicitness with linguistic discursiveness. The messages are there, embodied in their respective systems, and by acting within the systems we encounter them, "read" them in the only way they can be read. Even if we do not agree with Lévi-Strauss's particular interpretations of these structures, we may very well suspect the messages are there. As it happens, his "readings"— which he insists are interpretations rather than "decodings"—would indicate that there is very frequently a strong normative component in those messages. I propose to call the values thus embodied in social usage "suspended" values because they are rather like particles suspended in a medium. They exist there the way the rules of grammar and syntax normally exist in a language, used but not discursively known. Undoubtedly some or all of them could be made explicit in our sense, namely, expressed in a discursive formula. That, however, is a theoretic transformation in which the relations of the values to one another and to the life world are also transformed and perhaps obscured. Civilized people generally regard this transformation as valuable, and so it is, since communication *about* values is facilitated by it. But explicitness in this sense cannot be thought of as a substitute for the *savoir faire* that characterizes the truly civilized, a "knowledge" that is really a full attentiveness to the suspended values of their culture. To insist on discursively expressed rules in the absence of that attentiveness is very often described as "vulgar moralizing."

The nature of suspended values and their relation to value theory is obviously too extensive a topic to go into here. We can see that suspended values would have to be a social product, not produced by individuals or even a consensus of individuals. Presumably many different types of values are involved, some perhaps reflecting the need of the particular society to cope with its special environment, others perhaps reflecting the general conditions of social life, still others the society's conception of itself, etc. It is clear that individuals would have varying awareness of the suspended values of their own society. Children, for example, would still be discovering them, and others might have experience so limited that part of the suspended value system never comes within their notice. It is also likely that individuals would exist, at least in complex societies, who fail to respect the features of the system that should be manifest to them. In that group, but not coextensive with it, we will find the vulgar.

It is reasonable, I believe, to conclude from the preceding that the examination of marginal values like vulgarity can actually give us some insight into value in general. We see that the ancient concept of excellence still survives, by negation at least. Perhaps it can be revived in some form that reflects the differences between the ancients' experience and our own. We also see that there is at least one case in which a value involved in one's own choices cannot be simply generalized upon so as to produce commitments beyond those choices. Finally, we have examined a sketch of a theory about the status of values in societies as a response to some paradoxes illuminated by the concept of vulgarity.

Wickedness*

S. I. Benn

EVILS IN NATURE AND EVILS IN PERSONS

When philosophers talk of the problem of evil, they generally mean a problem in theodicy. Anyone who believes in a morally perfect, omniscient, and omnipotent God needs to explain and justify the existence of evils in the world. Unbelievers have no such problem. Nevertheless there are still uses to which the concept of evil can be put. Diseases, deformities, earthquakes and floods that destroy crops and wreck cities—these are, for anyone, too intelligibly evils, instances of what I shall term "evils in nature." I do not confine that term, however, to what we commonly call "natural disasters" but use it to denote any object, property, or happening about which it is both intelligible and correct to say that it would be a better state of affairs if that object et cetera did not exist or occur.

I take evil in nature to be a simple fact. It is a feature of the world that animals and human beings alike suffer pain, that there is ugliness as well as beauty, that there are bereavements and grievous disappointments. These things simply happen and are no less natural evils for their happening to conscious and rational beings. I do not mean, of course, that consciousness of the evil is never a necessary constituent; clearly this must be so in the case of a bereavement or a disappointment, though it is more problematic in cases of evils of ugliness. But bereavements and disappointments, while evils for human beings, are not evils in human beings. I shall make no attempt to say why such things are accounted evil; on the contrary, evil in nature I take for present purposes to be unproblematic, so that I shall not consider that I am begging any questions if I use that concept in explicating evil in human beings.

One kind of evil in human beings is "wickedness"—a word that has fallen undeservedly on bad times with the secularization of moral discourse.

* An earlier version of this article was presented to a seminar in Sydney sponsored by the Australian Society for Legal Philosophy and the Department of Jurisprudence of the University of Sydney. I wish to acknowledge the help I received from John Kleinig, who commented on the paper, and from other members of the seminar, from Jerry Gaus, who made valuable suggestions for the analysis of malignity, from Sam Goldberg, and from Miriam Benn, whose criticism was, as always, penetrating, even though she found this topic rather lowering.

This essay originally appeared in *Ethics*, vol. 95, no. 4, July 1985.

Wickedness in human beings is still one kind of evil in nature, but one which raises special problems because, having in general a capacity for rational action and judgment, wicked people not merely are evil but also do evil, with evil intent. My purpose in this article is to inquire into forms of human wickedness, their relation with other evils in human beings, and their relation to freedom of choice and motivation to evil.

By "wickedness" I mean whatever it is about someone that warrants our calling him a wicked person. It is therefore a different notion from what makes an action an evil deed, for an evil deed may be done by someone who is not wicked but only weak or misguided. Neither is every wrongdoer evil, for one may do wrong with good intentions or even (some would say) because in some situations whatever one did would be wrong. And conversely, someone who was fully conscious and rational but also completely paralyzed and aphasic, who spent his life hating everyone about him, rejoicing in their misfortune, wishing them ill, and reveling in malignant fantasies, would be a wicked person who did no wrong at all. Indispensable, however, to the notion of a wicked person is a cognitive capacity, or at the least a capacity to envisage states of affairs in the imagination, conjoined with a set of attitudes toward such states of affairs. G. E. Moore, whose account of evil is in terms not of persons but of "states of things," nevertheless describes the "great positive evils" as "organic unities" constituted by "cognitions of some object, accompanied by some emotion," where "emotion" is roughly equivalent to what I mean by "attitude."[1]

Common, however, to both wickedness in action and wickedness in attitude is an evil maxim, in something like Kant's sense. A person perceives situations, real or imagined, under certain descriptions and has attitudes in respect of them in accordance with general maxims. If I recognize someone as virtuous and hate him just for being virtuous, I have the maxim, Virtuous people are to be hated. Vandals act on the maxim, Beautiful objects are to be destroyed, racists on the maxim, Blacks are to be despised or hurt, egoists on the maxim, No one's interests but my own are to count. In each case the gerundival form of the maxim specifies a kind of action or attitudinal response, in accordance with what that person takes as a rule of life.

A person may be wicked because the maxims that order his life are, by and large, evil maxims, that is, maxims that no one ought to act on at all. Sometimes this may be seen as a kind of mistake on his part; he may believe to be good what is really evil, and vice versa. And then we may need some way of distinguishing culpable and nonculpable mistakes. But in other instances there is no mistake: a person may act on an evil maxim, knowing it to be so. That is the nature of malignant or Satanic wickedness. These are both problematic issues to which I return.

---

1. G. E. Moore, *Principia Ethica* (Cambridge: Cambridge University Press, 1903), p. 208.

It is possible, however, for a person to be wicked not because the first-order maxims of his actions are inherently wicked but because they are regulated by some higher-order maxim which systematically excludes consideration of any good which might circumscribe his first-order maxims. An example of such a restrictive higher-order maxim might be, No maxim is to be entertained as a rule of conduct that would circumscribe the duty to obey the orders of superior officers. Selfish wickedness and conscientious wickedness, which I shall consider a little later, are restrictive in much the same way, for whether or not, in either case, the maxims of action are inherently evil, the regulating principle will be found to be excluding in the required sense. These forms of wickedness I shall term "wickednesses of exclusion."

By contrast with those who act on evil first-order maxims, or who so order their first-order maxims as to exclude what ought nevertheless to be taken account of, the merely weak willed and the morally indolent and the people who cannot control their passions are not wicked people, for the maxims they really do acknowledge and on which they would wish to act are good ones. Such people are morally defective, and therefore bad, precisely because their actions fall short of their good intentions. That very incoherence is a mitigating condition, though not, of course, an excusing one.

I shall outline, in most of the remainder of this article, a typology of wickedness, which will shed some light on difficult moral and philo-sophical questions of responsibility and culpability and on the possibility of evil actions knowingly performed. The primary distinctions are between self-centered, conscientious, and malignant forms of wickedness. In each case I shall ask how far ignorance, error, or incapacity is necessarily or possibly a feature of the actions and the maxims of action under discussion and what difference it could make to the judgment of wickedness.

SELF-CENTERED FORMS OF WICKEDNESS

The least problematic kind of self-centered wicked person is the selfish one, but the category includes as well any person whose maxims are regulated by a higher-order maxim restricting consideration to goods and evils respecting only subjects and groups defined by reference to the agent himself. So a person who devoted himself exclusively to promoting the interests of his family or of his firm or to the aggrandizement of his nation might be wicked in this way if he did so with a ruthless unconcern for whether other people might be entitled or required to act on cor-responding maxims of their own. The cruder kind of chauvinist or jin-goist—My country, right or wrong—acts on just such a self-centered principle, providing he does not universalize it for the citizens of others countries too.

The merely selfish person recognizes his own well-being as a good and acts for the sake of it. That is to say, in being selfish he does not embrace evil as such, under that description. Self-interest is not merely an intelligible motive but also one that many philosophers have thought to be a paradigm of a motive, the motive of self-love. Selfishness is wicked not on account of its end but for what it excludes, for it consists in closing one's eyes and one's heart to any good but a self-centered good. In Kant's view, this is the most characteristic form of human wickedness.

According to Kant, the moral law, as the law of reason, is not merely accessible to any rational being but also, for human beings at least, always one spring of action, necessarily motivating in some degree. So it is not that the selfishly wicked person is motivated by a perverse antagonism to the moral law. Rather, self-love, which is for any rational person a genuine spring, assumes an irrational precedence over the moral law. Accordingly, a wicked person is not one whom the law cannot motivate but rather someone who "reverses the moral order of the springs in adopting them into his maxims; he adopts, indeed, the moral law along with that of self-love; but . . . he makes the spring of self-love and its inclinations the condition of obedience to the moral law; whereas, on the contrary, the latter ought to be adopted . . . as the sole spring, being the *supreme condition* of the satisfaction of the former."[2]

The selfish person may, however, be mistaken in his belief that what he intends is really good, even from his own narrow perspective; it may in reality be damaging, even to himself. Someone altogether committed to increasing his own wealth or power—a miser or a megalomaniac— may be wrong to value such things, at any rate as ends instead of as means to other goods. That error is not, however, an excuse for his wickedness since his specific wickedness as a selfish person derives from what is excluded rather than from the end he actually seeks. That, of course, can add to his wickedness. Sadistic wickedness is more shocking, perhaps, than miserliness because the suffering of others, to which the miser or the vain person may be merely indifferent and inattentive, is for the sadist itself the source of the pleasure which makes it seem a good. In taking it to be so, however, the sadist may still be mistaken, even in his own terms, if, for instance, the pleasure is part of a self-destructive rake's progress of personal degradation. There would be no inconsistency, however, in deeming the sadist wicked on account both of the intrinsic evil and of the exclusiveness of his maxim while yet feeling compassion for someone who is destroying himself so worthlessly.

PSYCHOPATHY

In contrast to selfish wickedness, the form of self-centered evil in persons manifested in a psychopathic personality may not count as wickedness at all. This takes the form of a kind of moral imbecility. The psychopath, like the selfishly wicked person, acts from self-love. He is capable, at least

2. I. Kant, "Of the Indwelling of the Bad Principle along with the Good, or On the Radical Evil in Human Nature," in *Kant's Theory of Ethics*, trans. T. K. Abbot (London: Longman, Green & Co., 1927), p. 343.

within limits, of instrumental deliberation, though he may be prone to discount future satisfactions heavily in favor of immediate gratification. So he may be liable to do evil impulsively to satisfy a whim. But the more significant point is that he does not see it as evil, except, perhaps, in a conventional sense: This is something that I know most people do not like being done, so I had better conceal the body. But the kind of considerations that might justify and rationalize conventional disapproval can get no purchase on his understanding. To the extent that the psychopath has, and perceives in himself, the capacity to make decisions which can make a difference to the way things turn out—to the extent that he is capable of forming beliefs taking account of evidence and argument and of acting on those beliefs—he satisfies the minimal conditions for being a rational chooser or, one may say, a natural person.[3] Full rationality does not, however, consist only in the capacity to take account of relevant considerations advanced by others. It includes also the capacity to decenter: to conceive of ways of looking at the world, and at oneself, from someone else's standpoint or from no particular standpoint at all—from the standpoint of anyone. It is this capacity that the psychopath lacks. Whereas the selfish person understands well enough how the well-being of other persons can be a reason for someone's action or forbearance but disregards such reasons, the psychopath is simply unable to see how that could be a reason for him at all. To be asked to take account of such a reason would be, to him, like being asked to have regard to the sensibilities of a stone or, perhaps, to the relevance of the color of someone's hair when deciding whether to make off with his wallet. While it would be wrong to say that the psychopath has no view of good and evil (for he knows what he would enjoy and what he would prefer not to suffer), he is incapable of understanding that distinction in any but a self-centered way. So though his maxims never take account of others' interests, it is not because a higher-order maxim excludes them; it is that first-order maxims embodying them are simply unintelligible to him. Such a person does not act on an evil maxim, knowing it to be evil, nor does he act on a self-centered second-order maxim that excludes relevant first-order maxims since he can hardly be said to have any second-order maxims at all. Such a person cannot be wicked. Nevertheless, he may be both an evil in nature and an instance of evil in a person.

Moral imbecility may well fill us with horror; certainly it is frightening. As much might be said, however, of other evils in nature, such as cancers or leprosy. But there may be something besides to account for our special hostility toward the moral imbecile. It is hard to see him simply as an evil but amoral force, like a man-eating tiger in a Bengal village, for he is defective in a capacity without which people in society could not live

---

3. For a fuller statement of the theory of natural and moral personality on which this article relies, see S. I. Benn, "Freedom, Autonomy, and the Concept of a Person," *Aristotelian Society Proceedings (1975–76)* 76 (1976): 109–30.

together. He seems at once to claim consideration as a fellow person and to disqualify himself from that consideration. Because he satisfies the minimal conditions for a rational chooser, he qualifies for the respect due to a person and is a bearer of rights, but as a moral defective, he is incompetent to bear the corresponding obligations and responsibilities. In assessing his moral status, it is hard not to judge him by the standards appropriate to a person of normal capacities, of which he is a monstrously deformed travesty. Nevertheless, though qualified as a person, he is disqualified from counting as a wicked one. And precisely because he is a person, we are subject to moral constraints in dealing with this evil that do not apply to our dealings with man-eating tigers.

CONSCIENTIOUS WICKEDNESS

The conscientiously wicked person is distinguished from the self-centered one in that the maxims of his actions are seen by him as universally valid and applicable. Unlike the crude chauvinist's complete indifference to other nations' claims, the conscientiously wicked nationalist might hold that his nation's supremacy would be a universally valid and overriding good, perhaps because it would be good for all humanity, perhaps because it had some excellence which any rational being would have to recognize as generating an overriding claim. The higher-order maxim by which the conscientiously wicked person lives is not self-centered; rather, it rules that all considerations not directly validated by his primary ideal goal or principle are necessarily subordinate when they conflict with it. So a conscientious Nazi need not always be indifferent to the claims of humanity instantiated in the plight of Jews. Were they anywhere but in Germany, or perhaps anywhere but in Europe, and were they not (as the Nazis claimed) an international conspiracy against the German nation, there would be a case for not exterminating them, perhaps even for manifesting concern for their well-being; but any such considerations were necessarily and totally overridden by the Herrenvolk ideal, which thus, in a Nazi's view, legitimated the Final Solution. Of course, the conscientious Nazi was himself one of the Herrenvolk, but it was not for that self-centered reason that he maintained its exclusive moral priority.

As with self-centered wickedness, conscientious wickedness can arise when the putative ideal is genuinely a good but is pursued with a ruthlessness that excludes other goods which ought to be taken account of. But it is also possible that the putative ideal is itself a monstrous error. In both cases it is alike necessary to build into the analysis criteria of culpability for the misjudgment of values. Suppose, for instance, that Aztec priests truly believed that human sacrifice gave pleasure to the god and that to please the god was good not because that way the harvests would be good (an acceptably valuable if not always an acceptably overriding end) but just as a good in itself and, further, that individual human beings as such were of subordinate concern. But suppose, also, that there was nothing in their moral consciousness with which such beliefs would not cohere. It is hard to see how they could then be called wicked. It is that reservation, however, that their moral consciousness be coherent, that makes their case problematic, where the case of Adolf Hitler is not. We must deplore murderous behavior as evil since slaying human beings is evil in nature, and if it is the result of intentional action, it must count as an evil in persons that they could act like that. But for it to count as a wickedness in persons, they must have within their repertoire some humane principles that the Aztecs (at least the Aztecs of my hypothesis) did not have. That exoneration cannot be extended, however, to tyrants and fanatics nearer home—Adolf Hitler, for instance. The resources of the European moral tradition afforded him ample reasons for treating the sufferings of Jews as of some account even set against the objective of racial purity, itself an end which that tradition provided ample grounds for questioning.

Conscientious wickedness is rarely a case of pursuing an end unaware of attendant consequences as evils; it is more often a case of a single-minded pursuit of an objective which (unlike racial purity) can reasonably be seen as good, but at the cost of a callous insensitivity to evil done by the way. It is not that the person believes the incidental evil to be itself good but rather that, having reason to think it evil, he nevertheless systematically disregards it. It is not that one cannot honestly believe, with Robespierre and Saint-Just, that out of a Terror can emerge a Republic of Virtue or, with the IRA, that only through indiscriminate violence can a united Ireland arise but that to go through with it one must almost certainly stifle sensibility to the horrors through which one must wade to bring it about. That sensibility, too, is a part of one's moral consciousness, no less than the perceived ideal. For a person whose conception of the moral law has developed within a moral tradition that recognizes indiscriminate murder as evil, such single-mindedness may be possible only if he has a sense of mission so great or an arrogance so overwhelming that he can desensitize himself, school himself to a callous disregard for considerations to which he nevertheless can and ought to attend.

Doing evil that good may come of it, or a greater evil be avoided, is not, however, a sufficient condition for wickedness in a person. Everyone responsible for major political decisions is likely to have been confronted with such difficult and painful choices. The history of atomic warfare is a record of one such dilemma after another. The mark of the wicked person is that such choices are for him neither difficult nor painful since the considerations that would make them so are systematically neutralized. It may, indeed, be a causally necessary condition for making such choices that one make of oneself a wicked person in this sense; in an evil world, perhaps only the wicked are callous enough to do the evil that needs to be done. "Whoever wants to engage in politics at all," wrote Max Weber, ". . . must know that he is responsible for what may become of himself under the impact of these paradoxes. . . . He lets himself in for the diabolical forces lurking in all violence. . . . Everything that is striven for through political action operating with violent means and following an ethic of responsibility endangers the 'salvation of the soul.'"[4]

Conscientious wickedness is not so radically different, then, from selfish wickedness. In both cases it is the refusal to acknowledge the moral significance of evils which one nevertheless knows or could reasonably be expected to know as evils that constitutes the person's wickedness.

HETERONOMOUS WICKEDNESS

The kinds of wickedness identified so far are manifested in people whose responses to situations, whether active or merely contemplative, are their own; theirs is the judgment, theirs the act, theirs the wickedness. But if the Nuremberg defendants were arguably like that, Eichmann in Jerusalem pleaded that he simply obeyed orders and could not therefore be responsible for the evils in which he had participated. He had not, he said, felt any hatred of the Jews or any pleasure from their sufferings and destruction. He had committed himself conscientiously to a line of duty, but unlike Hitler and his leading henchmen, he could plausibly disclaim responsibility for having adopted the aims to which his official duties directed him. His defense amounted to the claim that what he did must be seen under the global description of doing his duty, not of pursuing evil, and the former is not itself a description of wickedness, not in any of the terms that I have set out so far. If, then, wickedness in a person requires that he adopt an evil maxim, how was Eichmann wicked? In a perceptive discussion of Hannah Arendt's report of the Eichmann Trial, Barry Clarke has created the category of "heteronomous evil" to cover such a case, and I shall follow him in this, though I shall call it "heteronomous wickedness."[5]

Clarke's argument depends on a distinction between acting spontaneously and acting autonomously. Eichmann not only relied utterly on his superiors for directions for acting in all relevant regards but in joining the Nazi Party and the bureaucracy also opted out of critical judgment in all matters affecting his official duties. He had chosen heteronomy, and the evil that he did followed from that decision.[6] Could he be said, then, to have possessed the capacity for free choice that is the mark of

4. Max Weber, "Politics as a Vocation," in *From Max Weber*, ed. H. H. Gerth and C. Wright Mills (London: Kegan Paul, Trench, Trubner & Co., 1948), pp. 125–26.

5. Barry Clarke, "Beyond 'The Banality of Evil,'" *British Journal of Political Science* 10 (1980): 417–39 (on Hannah Arendt, *Eichmann in Jerusalem: A Report on the Banality of Evil* [London: Faber & Faber, 1963]).

6. "Eichmann made two exceptions in his merciless anti-semitic programme, once when he helped a half-Jewish cousin, and another time when at his uncle's request he helped a Viennese Jewish couple: but his conscience bothered him so much afterwards that he 'confessed his sins' (Eichmann's phrase) to his superiors" (John Kleinig, "Always Let Your Conscience Be Your Guide?" *Interchange* 1 [1967]: 107, referring to the account in Arendt, p. 131).

a person, the condition for responsibility for oneself, and therefore a necessary condition for one's being a wicked person?

A correct perspective'on such an argument must distinguish between the ordinary practical capacity of a normal minimally rational chooser to make decisions (which I have elsewhere called "autarchy"—a self-directing condition) and the capacity to make autonomous judgments.[7] The salient conditions for autarchy were outlined above, in discussing the moral status of the psychopath, who in my view satisfies them while yet lacking moral responsibility. In some people, however, autarchy is impaired, in various degrees ranging from catatonia through autism to compulsions of various kinds. Under hypnosis, a person loses autarchy to a considerable degree; a person acting under posthypnotic suggestion less so. Such people are programmed—and by other people—and are therefore heterarchic. To the extent that one is autistic, compulsive, or heterarchic, one lacks the capacity to decide for oneself, which is the condition for free, responsible action, and to just that extent one lacks the capacity for wickedness. But Eichmann was heteronomous, not heterarchic, and heteronomy is not merely consistent with autarchy—it requires it.

By autonomy I understand a character trait amounting to a capacity to act on principles (i.e., in accordance with a *nomos*) that are one's own because one has made them so by a process of rational reflection on the complex of principles and values that one has assimilated from one's social environment. It is a process in which one confronts the incoherences and conflicts within that complex and works to resolve them into something like a coherent set of moral attitudes. We do not invent our morality ex nihilo; we make it our own by creatively testing it for consistency. Now Eichmann certainly did nothing like that. On the contrary, he handed over his conscience to the care of the party, the state, and the Fuehrer, thereby imposing on his power of autarchic decision (which remained all the same quite unimpaired) constraints which he thereafter would not look at critically. But, of course, nothing made it impossible for him to do so. He had, as Clarke puts it, elected for heteronomy, and though as time went on it no doubt became increasingly difficult, psychologically speaking, to challenge the system to which he had put himself in thrall, still he had made it so himself; he had willfully made himself the compliant and unreflecting tool of wickedness, which is a perversion of the moral nature of persons as choosers.

I do not mean that one may never accept moral leadership from others or commit oneself to a role in a movement or an organization, nor do I mean that in the performance of the duties of an office one must always do precisely what one would have chosen to do irrespective of the requirements of the office. Social practices and institutions would

---

7. See my analysis of autarchy and autonomy, heterarchy and heteronomy, set out at greater length in Benn.

lose their point if that were the case; they are, after all, ways of coordinating the acts of many people toward common goals and will work as such only if people can rely on one another to do what is expected of them. But this does not entail a duty to suspend all judgment. In accepting the guidance of an authority, we are responsible for satisfying ourselves that the principles for which it stands are ones which in general we can endorse; though its particular injunctions may sometimes puzzle us, we must be prepared to monitor its performance over all.

We have to distinguish, therefore, between a conditional and an absolute heteronomy. A person who chooses a conditional heteronomy may reasonably submit to the guidance of the party or the church, providing he does not surrender the power to judge whether it remains true to the principles that led him to choose just that one as the good one. We resign ourselves absolutely to heteronomy at the risk of becoming, like Eichmann, people of evil will, with a capacity in no way impaired to grasp the evil that we do in obeying wicked orders but willfully disregarding it as evil. As with the conscientiously and the selfishly wicked persons, the heteronomously wicked has become insensitive to certain morally significant states of affairs just because the maxim of his actions and attitudes leaves no place for them in his moral constitution.

WICKEDNESS AND MORAL LUCK

Of course, not every absolutely heteronomous person is necessarily wicked. Someone who submits in this total fashion to the guidance of a saint may be less than admirable as a person; but it would be both perverse and wildly censorious to call him wicked. For that one must be disposed to act, or respond, in accordance with evil maxims or in disregard of good ones. The saint's disciple will do neither. But a person who does evil by reason of having elected to put his moral judgment into the keeping of evil persons or institutions has taken a gamble that, as a morally responsible person, he is not entitled to take—and has lost.

This qualification suggests a more general and far-reaching one, affecting all the categories of wickedness discussed so far. Selfish people, people dedicated solely to their families or to the interests of their firms or their countries, and fanatics conscientiously pursuing a blinkered ideal all have it in them to be wicked people. But if the actions picked out for them by their restrictive second-order maxims happened never to be evil actions, it would be harsh to call such people wicked, even if their first-order maxims were always self-centered or narrowly principled. For, as I suggested earlier, such maxims are not always intrinsically bad. Imagine someone who acted single-mindedly on a maxim of self-interest but whose actions were, by social circumstances, under such close scrutiny that any action that damaged someone else, or any denial of help to someone in need, would invite the penalties of public censure. He would have reasons for taking account of appropriate other-regarding maxims, though they would be reasons encapsulated in a self-interested strategy. Such a person would be morally unworthy, but his social institutions would save him from actualizing the wickedness which was latent in him. The Puritan communities of the seventeenth century maintained strict moral surveillance over their members because they were more concerned with saving people from doing the wickedness of which they were capable than with moral worth, which, they believed, few, if any, people possessed, and then only by divine election. But we do not have to accept the doctrine of predestination to believe that what preserves many quite ordinary people from wickedness is the good fortune of their circumstances and that in a Belsen or an Auschwitz they might be capable not merely of the desperate meanness of so many of the inmates but also of the wickedness of very nearly all the guards.

MALIGNITY

In all the forms of wickedness treated so far, the regulative maxim has been directed to something understood by the agent, however perversely, as a good. For some philosophers, as we shall see, this has been held to be a necessary condition for any rational action at all. The kind of wickedness, however, which Coleridge saw instantiated in Iago as "motiveless malignity," and which Milton's Satan epitomizes in "Evil be thou my good," throws doubt on this supposition.

Iago and Satan are, of course, the paradigm instances in literature of the unalloyed wickedness of malignity, of pursuing evil under the aspect of evil. According to Kant, "In order to call a man bad, it should be possible to argue a priori from some actions, or from a single consciously bad action, to a bad maxim as its foundation, and from this to a general source in the actor of all particular morally bad maxims, this source again being itself a maxim."[8] But Kant denies that human beings can adopt as a fundamental maxim, informing all rational choices as a kind of perverse moral law, the maxim, Do evil for evil's sake. A "malignant reason," a "bad Rational Will," would require that "antagonism to the law would itself be made a spring of action . . . so that the subject would be made a *devilish* being."[9] Kant believes that human beings cannot be like this, yet it is not easy to see why since he believes that devils, who are presumably also rational, can be. Perhaps to be a devil is to be irrational in the special way that, while apprehending the moral law, one responds to it, like Satan, antagonistically, finding in it not a spring of action but a spring of counteraction. I shall consider in a moment whether it is logically possible to make evil one's end, but if it is not, then it must be impossible for devils too. And if the impossibility is not of this kind, I cannot see why human beings may not also be Satanic.

I suggested earlier that the attitudes and actions of a selfishly wicked person are governed by a conception of the good, albeit the good of the

8. Kant, p. 327.
9. Ibid., p. 342.

agent himself; his wickedness consists in his indifference to other values. A malignant person, by contrast, would take account of the suffering of someone else as a reason for action, irrespective of self-love, just as much as would a benevolent person. But unlike the latter, he would promote it. It is as evil that he rejoices in suffering and not because he sees it, in some partial or distorted way, as a good, even for himself. He does not think himself better off for it; he is no less disinterested in rejoicing in it than is a benevolent person who rejoices in someone else's good fortune. Just as the prospect of satisfying one's own sexual desire is pleasurable to contemplate, as a good, so, for the malignant person, someone else's suffering is a pleasure to contemplate, but as an evil, apprehended as such. Correspondingly, it is unalloyed wickedness to hate the good, apprehended as good, and because it is good, and to seek its destruction on that account.

The unalloyed wickedness of malignity presents a logical or a psychological problem, not a moral one. The difficulty is not to decide what attitude to adopt toward it; if it exists at all, it is to be totally abhorred. The problem is rather to understand its motivation or, indeed, to decide whether the very description of it is coherent. Is it perhaps that we perceive something as unalloyed wickedness only because we haven't fully understood it?

According to Socrates, a man who knows the good cannot choose to do evil; no one intentionally chooses evil knowing it to be so.[10] Since my account of unalloyed wickedness implicitly denies this claim, it is necessary to consider why Socrates may have made it. But more than that, what account can we give of motivation to evil if the one given by Socrates turns out not to be true?

Socrates' paradox can be made plausible given a certain view of the motives of action. If we suppose that all intentional or voluntary action is undertaken with some aim, it must be supposed that what is aimed at must be desired; and if someone desires it, he must see it as a good thing to bring it about.[11] Accordingly, for Socrates, whoever aims at evil does so in ignorance of its true nature, under the misapprehension of it as good.

The trouble with Socrates' story is that it distorts the nature of true malignity. I said earlier that a malignant person recognizes the suffering of someone else as an evil and rejoices in it just because it is evil and that he would not rejoice in it were it not that he saw it as such. Even

10. See Plato, *Protagoras* 352a–358d. In the *Laws,* Plato asserts: "No wrongdoer is so of deliberation. For no man will ever deliberately admit supreme evil, and least of all in his most precious possessions. But every man's most precious possession, as we said, is his soul; no man, then, we may be sure, will of set purpose receive the supreme evil into this most precious thing and live with it there all his life through" (731c).

11. Michael Stocker has examined the claim that it is not possible to desire the bad in "Desiring the Bad: An Essay in Moral Psychology," *Journal of Philosophy* 76 (1979): 738–53.

more perplexing, on Socrates' account, is the case of self-destructive action prompted by self-hatred. One must go a long and devious way round to find a good that such a person might believe that he was promoting in spiting himself. Clearly if one aims at an outcome then, in a rather weak sense, one must desire it; but it is not, even for the person desiring it, necessarily desirable on that account. For what is desirable is what it is appropriate to desire, and the malignant person desires things very often precisely because they are not appropriate. Consider the case of Claggart, the master-at-arms, in Herman Melville's story *Billy Budd.* Claggart conceives a hatred of "the Handsome Sailor," "who in Claggart's own phrase was 'the sweet and pleasant young fellow,'" and falsely charges him with sedition in order to destroy him.[12] Claggart has no reason to hate Billy if by "reason" we mean reason of interest. There is no apparent good that can come to him, or to anyone else, from the evil that will come about. So far from moving him to act for the sake of something he sees as a good, his hatred moves him to spite and to destroy it.[13]

Claggart's reason for hating Billy is precisely his goodness. He can appreciate it only as a reproach, as something that diminishes him, that he must therefore hate and destroy.[14] There is a passage in Schopenhauer that expresses this state of mind most eloquently: "Very bad men bear the stamp of inward suffering in the very expression of the countenance. . . . From this inward torment, which is absolutely and directly essential to them, there finally proceeds that delight in the suffering of others which does not spring from mere egoism, but is disinterested, and which constitutes wickedness proper, rising to the pitch of cruelty. For this the suffering of others is not a means for the attainment of the ends of its own will, but an end in itself."[15] Schopenhauer's explanation is that such wicked persons suffer "an intensity of will" that nothing could assuage. "Every privation" (every frustration of desire) "is infinitely increased by the enjoyment of others, and relieved by the knowledge that others suffer the same privation." Moreover, an "attained end never fulfils the promise of the desired object." From "a manifestation of will reaching the point of extraordinary wickedness, there necessarily springs an excessive inward misery, an eternal unrest, an incurable pain; he seeks indirectly the alleviation which directly is denied him,—seeks to mitigate his own suffering by the sight of the suffering of others, which at the same time he recognises as an expression of his power. The suffering of others now becomes for

12. Herman Melville, *Billy Budd and Other Tales* (New York: New American Library of World Literature, Inc., 1961), chap. 11, p. 35.

13. See Peter Kivy, "Melville's *Billy* and the Secular Problem of Evil: The Worm in the Bud," *Monist* 63 (1980): 480–93, for a stimulating discussion of the problem of malignity in general and Claggart in particular.

14. Compare Iago, of Cassio: "He hath a daily beauty in his life that makes me ugly" (*Othello*, 5.1.19–20).

15. A. Schopenhauer, *The World as Will and Idea,* in *The Philosophy of Schopenhauer,* ed. Irwin Edman (New York: Modern Library, 1928), p. 293.

him an end in itself, and is a spectacle in which he delights; and thus arises the phenomenon of pure cruelty, blood thirstiness, which history exhibits so often in the Neros and Domitians, in the African Deis, in Robespierre, and the like."[16]

Of course, one might say that Coleridge was mistaken and that the malignity of Iago and Claggart, with which Schopenhauer's story accords so well, was not "motiveless" but was motivated by envy or resentment. But these motives are not motives of interest, prompted by a good to be brought about by action. They explain the action only by filling out further the description of what is done by giving us a better grasp of the organic relation between the state of affairs, the beliefs of the agent, and the attitude that binds them together. Envious and resentful people are not aiming to bring about a good; nor does the good that they recognize appeal to them. On the contrary, it inflames and enrages them.

I have interpreted the Socratic position up to this point as a psychological theory about how an end must be perceived for it to be a motivating cause, and I have tried to rebut this theory by showing that one can grasp the motives of Iago and Claggart without having to convert them into perceived goods, whether goods for the agents themselves or goods that the agents themselves perceived as appropriately desired.[17] Suppose, however, that we take the Socratic claim to be logical rather than psychological. On this interpretation, seeing something as good is to acknowledge that there is the strongest possible practical reason for seeking it, however one may fail in practice through weakness of will. Conversely, to see something as evil would be to recognize that there is a reason not to seek it. So it would be incoherent to adopt Satan's policy of pursuing evil for its own sake since this would be to have as one's reason for action what was logically a reason against action.

Schopenhauer's account of malignity is too plausible, however, for the logical objection to clinch the matter. That objection depends on an assumed nexus between recognizing that there is a reason for action, having that reason as one's own, and being motivated to act on it. There

16. Ibid., p. 294.
17. Iago makes some pretense that his animosity toward Othello is prompted by a report that the latter had seduced his wife. Supposing him really to have believed that, it is interesting to see how that could change our judgment of Iago. It would still be the case that he knowingly wished an evil on Othello, but not now simply for evil's sake. Revenge, responding to an injury, represents a primitive kind of justice; the maxim of his action would then have been not to do evil for evil's sake but to exact just recompense. And this, presumably, is where a retributivist's defense of punishment must begin since he defends the inflicting of evil not, like the malignant, for evil's sake but in the name of justice. To satisfy one's claim to vengeance is thus not merely an intelligible motive but also one that in some measure redeems malignity, as envy does not. Resentment straddles these two possibilities. Like Claggart and Iago, one can resent being diminished by goodness, which is no injury. But one can also resent a real injury, and someone who wished another ill on that account, though falling short of charity, would be a wicked person only to the extent that his justified grievance made him insensitive to counterconsiderations.

seem to be two ways, though, in which one could recognize the good (or the desirable) and the evil (the undesirable). Paradigmatically, it is true, to see a state of affairs as desirable is to acknowledge that, by criteria of value and appropriateness that one can acknowledge as one's own, there is a reason for desiring things so. But we can envisage a person imagining very well what it would be like to have such a moral experience, to make the appraisals that most people make, and to see why, indeed, they found desirable the things that they did, given the kind of people that they were. And he could envy them for being as they are while being filled, like Claggart, with resentment and hate for them and the things they love and value just because he knows that there is no possibility that he could be like them, think like them, feel like them, or care like them. Precisely because the good that he sees cannot motivate him, he hates it for its very inaccessibility. He grasps the attraction of the good and knows its opposite as evil, but in an encapsulated way that prevents its being also—for him—a reason for action in the way that it is for them. His acknowledging it as good amounts to seeing that it is a reason, but it is not a reason that he can have or that could be his motive.

The way in which the malignant subject experiences such a rancorous motivation to evil may be set out schematically as follows:

1. Properties $C_1 \ldots C_n$ in a person are virtues (V).
2. Anyone is a good person (G) if and only if he has properties V.
3. For any G, X is a reason for action (e.g., the principle that one should turn the other cheek).
4. I value someone's being a G if and only if I believe I could myself succeed in being a G.
5. I value V if and only if I can be a G.
6. I do not believe I can have X as my reason for action.
7. Therefore I do not believe I could succeed in being a G.
8'. Any properties that I would value if I had them (P), but which I believe I cannot succeed in having, are to be despised (maxim 1).
8". Any person (S) who succeeds in having P is to be made to suffer for having them (maxim 2).
8'''. Any action that only an S would have a reason for doing is to be avoided, and the contrary action is to be done (maxim 3).
9. To despise virtue, to cause good people to suffer, and to do wrong, that is, to act on maxims 1, 2, and 3, is evil.
10. So evil is to be done (maxim 4).

It might be objected that anyone adopting maxims 1–4 would do so only in order to assuage a sense of his own inadequacy and that this amounts to embracing evil only for the sake of a perceived good. But, of course, if one knew that this was what one was doing—crying "sour grapes"—the strategy would be ineffective. The malignant could assuage a sense of inadequacy only if he was really unaware of this aspect of his motivation; otherwise he would know when he said that he detested virtue that he really admired it. The explanatory methods of depth psychology consist precisely in constructing scenarios such that the end of every action is an intelligible good or the relief of an intelligible unease. But the putative unconscious strategies are by no means always successful— the malignant's rancor is not assuaged, nor does he feel any the less inadequate when his rival is laid low; for if it is indeed his own moral failing in comparison with his rival's virtue that dismays him, acting viciously as a reprisal can only aggravate the sense of inferiority. The method of depth psychology must explain, therefore, why the good that is the imputed objective is so ineffectually pursued. Meanwhile, whatever the psychiatric explanation, there can be little doubt that the malignant subject really is hating good and delighting in evil under precisely these descriptions, without feeling that there is anything logically incoherent in doing so. And while the phenomenology of rancor may not apply in precisely the same way to every instance of malignancy, it is enough to suggest that the nexus between recognition of a reason, having it as one's own, and being motivated to act on it can be broken.

Moral Death: A Kantian Essay on Psychopathy*

Jeffrie G. Murphy

No man is entirely without moral feeling, for were he completely lacking in capacity for it he would be morally dead. And if . . . the moral life-force could no longer excite this feeling, then humanity would dissolve . . . into mere animality and be mixed irrevocably with the mass of other natural beings. [Immanuel Kant][1]

The psychopath . . . is incapable of kindness and consideration for the rights of others, and he is lacking in gratitude, affection, or compassion. . . . Whether judged in the light of his conduct, of his attitude, or of material elicited in psychiatric examination, he shows almost no sense of shame. . . . He does not . . . show the slightest evidence of major humiliation or regret. This is true of matters pertaining to his personal and selfish pride and to esthetic standards that he avows as well as to moral or humanitarian matters. If Santayana is correct in saying that "perhaps the true dignity of man is his ability to despise himself," the psychopath is without a means to acquire true dignity. [Hervey Cleckley][2]

INTRODUCTION

This paper is concerned with an examination of the rights and responsibilities of those individuals having what psychoanalysts, psychiatrists, and psychologists call *psychopathic, sociopathic,* or *antisocial* per-

* I should like to express my gratitude to the National Endowment for the Humanities and to the Graduate College of the University of Arizona for grants which made possible the free time used in researching and writing this paper.

1. Immanuel Kant, *The Doctrine of Virtue*, trans. Mary J. Gregor (New York, 1964), p. 60; p. 399 of the Berlin Academy edition of *Metaphysische Anfangsgründe der Tugendlehre* (vol. 4 of the *Gesammelte Schriften*).

2. Hervey Cleckley, *The Mask of Sanity*, 4th ed. (Saint Louis, 1964), pp. 306, 372. The first edition of this work, published in 1941, soon established itself as the best psychological and psychiatric study of psychopathy.

This essay originally appeared in *Ethics*, vol. 82, no. 4, July 1972.

sonalities.[3] But it is also what Wilfred Sellars has called a set of "variations on a Kantian theme." For in coming to terms with the concept of psychopathy, one is also forced to come to terms with the question of what it is to be a *person*—an individual having the value which Kant calls "dignity" (*Würde*) and thereby meriting that special kind of respect which is entailed by a moral commitment to justice rather than mere utility. I developed some thoughts on this in my book *Kant: The Philosophy of Right*,[4] and this paper represents further thinking on the issue and a substantial rejection of much that I said in the book. In the book I argued (against H. J. Paton, primarily) that it is *Willkür* (capacity to choose) and not *Wille* (moral autonomy) which confers dignity or worth upon persons. In thinking about the psychopath, however, and in trying to develop a rational defense for my intuition that any such individuals would lack dignity or worth as persons, I have come to think that Paton was right after all—that it is *Wille* or moral autonomy, and not merely the capacity to choose, which makes the moral difference. Paton, however, had never been successful in articulating a theoretical defense for his correct intuition; and filling this theoretical gap will be one of my primary tasks in what follows.

THE CONCEPT OF PSYCHOPATHY

A problem of growing concern, particularly in the criminal law, is the existence of psychopaths—a class which, according to some researchers, is on the increase in our highly fragmented and alienated society. Psychopaths constitute the class of so-called habitual criminals, and the law is becoming more and more concerned with what to do to, with, or for them. Should they, for example, be excused from criminal responsibility on the grounds that psychopathy is a mental disease? This single question poses serious problems of great difficulty. For unlike the psychotic, the psychopath seems to suffer from no obvious cognitive or volitional impairments. He knows what he is doing (he has no delusions); and, since he typically does just what he wants to do, it would be odd to call him compulsive or to claim that he acts on irresistible impulses. Thus, he is by no means clearly "insane" by currently accepted medical or legal standards. We seem simply left, then, with the fact of his continual wrong-

3. These names all pick out approximately the same syndrome and thus represent little more than differing fashions in medical taxonomy—the latter two serving at most to emphasize the fact that the syndrome typically manifests itself in socially undesirable actions. Since such differences in nomenclature have little to do with the inquiry of this paper, I shall henceforth simply refer to "psychopathy" and "the psychopath."

4. Jeffrie G. Murphy, *Kant: The Philosophy of Right* (London, 1970), esp. pp. 65–86 and 161. Though the psychopathic syndrome was not clinically noted until the nineteenth century, it can be very illuminating to read classical moral philosophers (particularly Kant and Aristotle) with such cases in mind. See particularly Vinit Haksar's "Aristotle and the Punishment of Psychopaths," in *Aristotle's Ethics*, ed. James J. Walsh and Henry L. Shapiro (Belmont, Calif., 1967), pp. 80–101.

doing; and yet surely we do not want to let acts of wrongdoing be their own excuse. Thus, some criteria for the identification of psychopathy, independent of wrongdoing itself, must be located before one can be in a position to assess the responsibility of the psychopath.

Now some writers on this topic, Baroness Wootton, for example,[5] argue that any criterion will ultimately be circular—will ultimately boil down simply to wrongdoing, which can hardly itself be an excuse for wrongdoing. What always happens, according to Wootton, is the following: A man is charged with a crime, and his lawyer argues that he should be excused from responsibility for the crime on the grounds that he is a psychopath or suffers from some related mental aberration. When one then wants to know what evidence there is that the individual charged does in fact so suffer, the "evidence" produced consists largely of his history of wrongdoing and perhaps even of a description of the very act he is at present charged with! The circle here is obvious; and, if psychiatrists could do no better in formulating criteria for the disorder, Wootton's skepticism would be quite in order.

Some psychiatrists, however, though they would agree with Wootton's description of what often goes on in the courtroom, would also argue that a better and therefore noncircular criterion for psychopathy can be formulated. For example, Cleckley[6] and the McCords[7] maintain that there are clinically identifiable criteria for psychopathy that are independent (both causally and logically) from criminal wrongdoing. Indeed, some prominent politicians and industrialists (even, I am sure, some academics), though not legally criminals, may satisfy these criteria.

What are the criteria? In general, these clinicians want to argue that the psychopath is to be identified as an individual who lacks what in the eighteenth century was generally called *moral feeling* or a *moral sense*, what Kant also called *respect for duty*, and what we all ordinarily call a *conscience*. It is significant and illuminating, I think, that the disorder, first noted clinically in the nineteenth century, was initially called "moral insanity." Though psychopaths know, in some sense, what it means to wrong people, to act immorally, this kind of judgment has for them no motivational component at all. They do not *care* about others or their duties to them, have no *concern* for others' rights and feelings, do not *accept responsibility*, and do not know what it is like to defer one's own gratifications out of *respect* for the dignity of another human being. Quite significantly, they feel no *guilt, regret, shame,* or *remorse* (though they may superficially fake these feelings) when they have engaged in harmful

5. Barbara Wootton, *Social Science and Social Pathology* (London, 1959) and *Crime and the Criminal Law* (London, 1963).

6. See n. 2 above.

7. William McCord and Joan McCord, *The Psychopath: An Essay on the Criminal Mind* (Princeton, N.J., 1964).

conduct. They are paradigms of individuals whom Kant would call "morally dead."

Now the notions of moral feeling and moral sense obviously stand in need of philosophical, not merely psychological, explication.[8] For example, can a man who feels no motivation to do *A* really be said to have made the judgment that *A* is morally right? Writers like R. M. Hare, who believe that moral judgments are to be analyzed as prescriptions entailing imperatives, would answer this question in the negative. Though I believe that Hare is wrong on this, it is not this aspect of the issue that I want to pursue in this paper.[9] Neither am I concerned to argue about the clinical criteria *as* clinical criteria—that is, I have no interest here in discussing any of the empirical issues concerning psychopathy (e.g., are there now adequate diagnostic techniques for clinically recognizing all psychopaths and distinguishing them from individuals suffering from psychotic and neurotic disorders?). What I am interested in is the following: Supposing there are such individuals as described above—individuals who are morally dead in that they lack care, concern, respect, guilt. How should we respond to them? Are they responsible? Do they have rights? In answering no to both of these questions, I hope to illuminate the ideas of responsibility and rights. Thus, my interest here is primarily philosophical rather than practical; and the ideas I shall develop, for reasons I shall note at the conclusion of the paper, may have very limited or no legitimate application in legal reform.

RIGHTS, OBLIGATIONS, AND RESPONSIBILITY

It has been common for moral philosophers to approach the issue of moral and legal responsibility in terms of the free will–determinism con-

8. Guilt, for example, cannot be identified as a feeling and distinguished from other feelings solely in terms of how, subjectively, it *feels*. There must also be public criteria in the language, criteria which will necessarily make reference to guilt as, for example, the feeling *appropriate* to the doing of moral injury.

9. R. M. Hare, *The Language of Morals* (Oxford, 1952) and *Freedom and Reason* (Oxford, 1963). Hare argues that a judgment of the form "*A* ought to be done," if having no motivational component for the man who utters it, is not really a moral judgment at all but is rather what he calls an "inverted commas" use of the word "ought." When ought judgments are used in an inverted-commas way, they are really nothing but reports on other people's moral beliefs and can be rewritten without loss of meaning in the following way: "*A* 'ought' to be done" means "People in a certain society believe that *A* ought to be done." Thus, Hare would have to say that the psychopath, like an anthropologist studying another society, must use his "moral" judgments simply to describe the practices of others. But I see no reason why this must necessarily be the case, for it is intelligible to imagine a psychopath arguing in the following way: "People in my society believe that *A* morally ought to be done; but I, having studied moral philosophy and having been persuaded of the truth of the Principle of Utility, believe that not-*A* should be done since *A* is disutilitarian—but I still don't really *care* and do not propose to base by life on the principle." Even if one agrees with Hare, however, my argument can be rewritten in his language—that is, the psychopath can be defined as one who never really makes moral judgments; and my later arguments will still hold for the psychopath so defined.

troversy. Some, however, have wanted to go via different routes; and it is with one such different route that I shall be concerned here. I want to explore and develop the theory of responsibility sketched in the early part of this century by the eminent French penologist and legal philosopher Gabriel de Tarde in his book *Penal Philosophy*.[10] De Tarde's conviction is that the free will–determinism controversy is a red herring in disputes about responsibility. Determinism, he maintains, is obviously and universally true. It is true, without exception, of the criminal, the saint, and of each one of us that there are sufficient antecedent causal conditions that explain the occurrence of any action any of these persons performs. Thus, if we want to draw a responsible-nonresponsible distinction, this will have to be drawn *within* the class of determined actions. For the class of metaphysically (or, as C. A. Campbell would say, "contra-causally")[11] free actions is empty.

How might such a distinction be drawn? How can a theory of excuses or responsibility be formulated consistent with determinism? (A theory of excuses must be able to draw a distinction between responsibility and nonresponsibility. And, as Clarence Darrow clearly saw, if one tries to build such a theory on any distinction between determinism and metaphysical freedom, the emptiness of the second class will dictate that the theory of excuses take the form so often used by Darrow in court: Determinism is true; therefore everyone should be excused for everything. But this—as Darrow clearly *failed* to see—is not a theory of excusing at all, for it necessarily fails to draw for us any of the relevant sorts of distinction that we would expect from such a theory.) Now de Tarde suggests that our criterion of responsibility should be based on two notions: *social similarity* and *personal identity*. What we really want to know about a man in judging his responsibility is (1) if he is sufficiently like his fellows in certain relevant respects and (2) if he has a sufficiently continuous conscious history to count as a person. I want here to ignore (2)— primarily relevant for the case of psychotics—and concentrate on (1).

What de Tarde is getting at, and this view would be at least partly shared by other compatibilists like Hume and H. L. A. Hart, is that a responsible man is one not whose behavior was uncaused but, rather, one whose behavior was caused by normal or typical causes of behavior (desires, volitions, beliefs, etc.) and not by abnormal or atypical causes (epileptic seizures, blows on the head, etc.). To punish men in the latter class would be like punishing strangers or foreigners to the community. This theory of responsibility, by the way, may help us make some sense of the

10. Gabriel de Tarde, *Penal Philosophy* (Boston, 1912). A brief excerpt from de Tarde's book may be found in *Freedom and Responsibility*, ed. Herbert Morris (Stanford, Calif., 1961).

11. C. A. Campbell, *On Selfhood and Godhood* (London, 1957), pt. 1.

title of Camus's famous novel *L'Etranger*—a novel about a criminal psychopath.)[12]

Why the emphasis on normality? De Tarde is inclined to let his theory rest upon an institutional fact—namely, that for all our talk about free will, it is really the notion of social similarity which operates in our actual practical judgments of excuse. Indeed, when a law court inquires into whether a confession, say, was freely signed, it is pretty clear that the inquiry is into the *kind of cause* (did the prisoner desire to sign it, was he coerced under threats, etc.) and *not*, surely, into whether it was signed as a result of the prisoner's "contra-causal freedom." Very well. This is, at least latently, our ordinary practice. But is our ordinary practice reasonable? This worry de Tarde leaves practically untouched.

Now I should like to suggest that no theory of responsibility can be developed in the abstract—in isolation from a theory of obligation. Thus, I shall here sketch a theory of obligation, a Kantian quasi-social-contract theory,[13] which in my judgment lends great plausibility to de Tarde's intuitions about responsibility and social similarity. I do not know (or at this point care) if it will work for all kinds of cases; but it does, I think, allow us to say something plausible about the psychopath.

Before passing to the theory of obligations, however, it is important to note at the outset that de Tarde's theory of responsibility has one grave defect which any acceptable development of the theory will have to patch up—namely, that social dissimilarity *simpliciter* will excuse not merely the psychopath, but the moral saint or hero as well. And this is surely an unacceptable consequence. For example, we surely do not want to regard principled civil disobedients like Gandhi and Martin Luther King, Jr., as nonresponsible for their actions simply because they differ from the rest of us in the makeup of their characters. I shall argue, however, that this defect in de Tarde's account is remediable. For what needs to be done is to develop the theory not just in terms of similarity or dissimilarity *simpliciter* but, rather, in terms of similarity or dissimilarity with regard to *certain specific characteristics*—for example, moral motivation, capacity to conform one's conduct to rules, and the like. If this is done, then we may be able to show that persons like Gandhi, though dissimilar from the general community in terms of the *courage* of their convictions, are not different (as is the psychopath) in terms of the relevant characteristic of having a *moral sense*. The difficulty, of course, is in showing just what characteristics are conceptually tied to obligation and responsibility (why

---

12. I am not suggesting that Camus himself intended that the novel be taken in this way.

13. This theory is more fully developed in my book *Kant: The Philosophy of Right*. See also John Rawls's "Legal Obligation and the Duty of Fair Play," in *Law and Philosophy*, ed. Sidney Hook (New York, 1964), pp. 3–18. Rawls's essay has been reprinted in my *Civil Disobedience and Violence* (Belmont, Calif., 1971).

moral sense is relevant, for example, and courage is not); and it is to this task that I shall now pass.

I should argue that talk about *obligation* (as opposed to talk merely about what we *ought* to do or what would be *good* to do on grounds of utility) is necessarily tied down to social practices or institutions.[14] Obligations are necessarily institutional in character, arising with respect to, and only with respect to, social practices—for example, legal systems, the promising "game," and the like. For example, I ought to be kind to any child, but I am *obligated* to be kind only to *my* child—because of the institution of parenthood. Also, I should argue that the notion of *a right* (though not, of course, the notion of what it *is right* to do) is similarly institutional in character.[15] I ought to be benevolent, it would be good for me to be benevolent, but no one (barring some special institutional arrangement like marriage) can demand my benevolence as a right. I am *obligated* to keep my promises, however, and others can legitimately demand this by *right*. Kant was, I think, working toward this point in his distinction between perfect duties (duties of respect) and imperfect duties (duties of love). Perfect duties, resting on rights, may be legitimately coerced. Not so with imperfect duties. To violate an imperfect duty is to do something wrong, but it is not to wrong anyone. For imperfect duties rest not upon rights, but primarily upon the goodness of satisfying desires.

To neglect mere duties of love is *lack of virtue*. But to neglect duty that proceeds from the *respect* due to every man as such is *vice*. For no one is wronged when we neglect duties of love; but if we fail in a duty of respect, then a man is deprived of his lawful claim. . . . Violation of a duty of respect is not only a want of moral embellishment; it even removes the value of the respect that would otherwise *stand* the subject *in good stead*, and is therefore vice. For this reason, too, duties to one's fellow-men which arise from the respect due them are expressed only negatively . . . by the prohibition of the opposite.[16]

Now what are the presuppositions of the intelligibility of the obligation-rights body of moral discourse? To put the question in a Kantian transcendental way: What is required to make obligation- and right-creating institutions possible? I should argue, with Kant and John Rawls,[17]

14. For further development of this and related ideas, see the following: A. I. Melden, *Rights and Right Conduct* (Oxford, 1959); H. L. A. Hart, "Legal and Moral Obligation," in *Essays in Moral Philosopy*, ed. A. I. Melden (Seattle, 1958), and "Are There Any Natural Rights?" in *Philosophical Review* 64 (1955): 175–91; and John Rawls, "Two Concepts of Rules," in *Philosophical Review* 64 (1955): 3–22.

15. Because I want to leave room for the possibility of *natural* rights, I am here speaking of rights and obligations as "related to institutions" and as "institutional in character" rather than as necessarily being *within* institutions. This point will be developed later in the paper.

16. *The Doctrine of Virtue* (n. 1 above), pp. 134–35 (p. 463 of the Academy edition).

17. See, in addition to other works by Rawls already cited, his "Justice as Fairness," *Philosophical Review* 67 (1958): 164–94, and particularly "The Sense of Justice," *Philosophical Review* 72 (1963): 281–305.

that one important condition is that of *reciprocity* or *fairness*. That is, the very possibility of institutions (as systems of rules) rests upon the general willingness of those persons involved in them to defer the gratification of their desires by recognizing and respecting the (at least prima facie) obligations that they have, to their fellows, to abide by the demands of the practice—*particularly* when these demands conflict with their desires. A practice which allowed the violation of its rules in all cases where the individuals bound *simply desired* such violation could not (*logically* could not) truly count as a practice or system of *rules* at all. Such reciprocity (self-restraint on the assumption that others will exercise comparable restraint in similar circumstances) is thus a presupposition for the very intelligibility of obligation-rights talk. Jones, in claiming a right (and thereby noting someone else's obligation) under a practice, speaks legitimately only insofar as he is prepared to recognize *and respect* his obligation to defer to others' rights in similar kinds of circumstances. Justice, to put it briefly, can apply only to those having a sense of justice.

We are now in a position to return to the psychopath. He is socially dissimilar from the majority of his fellows in his lack of moral feeling, by his failure to be motivated by a recognition of the rights of others and the obligations he has to them. *Thus, he is in no position to claim rights for himself.* He violates a condition for the possibility of reciprocity which is, I have argued, in turn a presupposition for the intelligibility of the whole obligation-rights language game. And this explains (in a way which should not please the psychopath) why he *may* (though not necessarily must) be excused from responsibility and punishment—namely, punishment may be regarded as a *right*, and he is in no position to claim rights.[18]

But who would want to claim such a painful right? This is an obvious question, but one susceptible to an obvious answer. The right to be punished and regarded as a responsible agent, though sometimes painful when honored, at least leaves one's status as a moral person intact. One here gets what he has a right to in the sense that he deserves it, having brought it on himself by his choices. Thus, practices of punishment and responsibility are compatible with a recognition of human dignity in that they place a premium upon the status of persons as choosing beings. One alternative to this is *therapy*. One here gets not what one deserves but, rather, what one (in some paternalistic sense) *needs*—perhaps a total restructuring of one's personality. (Two novels which would give the reader some idea of what this may amount to are Anthony Burgess's *A Clockwork Orange*

18. The notion of punishment as a right may be found in Kant, Hegel, and Hartmann. For a contemporary and very sophisticated elaboration of this view, see Herbert Morris's "Persons and Punishment," *Monist* 52 (1968): 475–501. The plausibility, in some circumstances, of claiming punishment as a right is illustrated by the central character in Friedrich Duerrenmatt's novel *Traps*.

and Ken Kesey's *One Flew over the Cuckoo's Nest*.)[19] When one sees that this is a possible alternative to responsibility and punishment, one might very well want to irtsist on one's right to be punished—one's right to be taken seriously as a person.

Now before developing further thoughts on the psychopath, I should like to pause in anticipation of one objection that the reader may want to raise against what I have said thus far. It might be thought that, by conceptually linking rights with social institutions or practices, I am ruling out the possibility of there being what some philosophers have called *natural* rights, rights that persons may have antecedent to their participation in any social institutions. But this thought is mistaken. Natural rights, I should agree, do differ from conventional (e.g., legal) rights in that they may not be recognized within some particular practice or institution. However, I should argue that they are still conceptually linked to the idea of institutions in the following way: that natural rights, whatever else they may be, are rights a person may claim only insofar as he possesses those characteristics (particularly a sense of justice) which would make his membership in some institution or other *possible*. A man does not lack natural rights simply in virtue of the fact that he *actually* fails to participate in a social institution that recognizes them, but he cannot be said to have natural rights if he is the sort of being who is constitutionally *incapable of real participation* in cooperative social institutions or practices of any kind. For such incapacity would surely be sufficient to block the primary kind of argument in which natural-rights talk is employed: "Jones has a *natural* right to P; therefore, we should modify our institutions in such a way that Jones can participate sufficiently to enjoy a *legal* right to P." Such an argument is in place in many cases (e.g., with respect to slaves and the right to liberty), but it is quite out of place when its potential beneficiary is a psychopath.

Indeed, the psychopath seems in a *worse* position with respect to claiming natural rights than he might be in claiming legal or conventional rights. We might continue to recognize the legal or conventional rights of a psychopath, of a man without a sense of justice, not because they are

19. Of course, institutions of punishment may *in fact* be administered in such a way as to be just as dehumanizing as institutions of therapy, and that is why I made my point in as weak a way as I did—namely, that institutions of punishment are *compatible* with human dignity. Since therapeutic institutions are, by definition, going to be paternalistic in that they exist to restructure a man's personality, they are not even compatible with a respect for the autonomy and integrity of persons. The limitations of punishing institutions are contingent; those of therapeutic institutions are necessary. This is not, of course, to say that therapy is always wrong. Of course, it is not. Indeed, as I am arguing in the paper, the status of the psychopath as a being without rights invites the appropriateness of a therapeutic response. But it is important to see what values are lost in such a response—something often not seen by the ideologists of social psychiatry. For more on this, see my "Criminal Punishment and Psychiatric Fallacies," *Law and Society Review* 4 (August 1969): 111–22, and my forthcoming collection of essays, *Punishment and the Rehabilitative Ideal* (Belmont, Calif., 1972).

owed to him or because he *deserves* them personally, but because we have loyalty to the institution or practice itself and want to preserve it—even at the expense of some pretense about a few of the individuals who benefit from the institution. That is, we might (for example) keep our promises even to psychopaths because we (i) value the institution of promising and (ii) believe that our opting out—even when we have judged that we are dealing with a psychopath—would damage the institution. In other words, Kant's first formulation of the Categorical Imperative ("Act only on that maxim which you could simultaneously will to be a universal law") may give us good prima facie grounds for keeping our promises even to psychopaths. For we may not be willing to universalize the maxim "I shall opt out of my promise whenever I judge that I am dealing with a psychopath." (The worry here, which I shall explore further in the final section of the paper, concerns the legitimacy of extending a liberty of *judgment* which would invite substantial abuse and self-deception on grounds of self-interest.) When we consider Kant's second formulation of the Categorical Imperative ("Act so as to treat humanity always as an end in itself and never as a means only"), however, it seems singularly inapplicable to the psychopath. For reasons already hinted at, and to be elaborated in the next section, it is difficult to make any sense of the notion of a psychopath as an end in himself, as a creature having the value Kant calls "dignity." If this is so, of course, then the psychopath cannot be wronged, can be done no moral injury.

This, then, completes the point about natural rights: Since with respect to natural rights there is (by definition) no practice or institution to be preserved, any argument based on an analogy with the promising game for treating the psychopath as if he had rights will misfire. Thus, the only possible argument for regarding the psychopath as having natural rights would have to be based upon his dignity or worth as a person. But this is just what he does not have! Indeed, as I shall later argue, he is more profitably pictured—from the moral point of view—as an *animal*.

Before exploring this tendentious point, I should like to note in passing that the machinery developed thus far in the paper is sufficient to show why any political theory that is Hobbesian in character is doomed to failure. The men he imagines in a natural state (motivated solely by the egoistic desire for personal satisfaction and the preservation of their own lives) are *all psychopaths*. Thus, lacking a sense of justice, they do not satisfy the necessary conditions for the possibility of social institutions; and thus on this basis no theory of political obligation (dictating the necessity of civil government and the moral obligation to obey the law) can be generated. This becomes immediately apparent when we notice (i) that Hobbes's third Law of Nature—*justice* or the *obligation to honor covenants*—is absolutely required to justify on social-contract theory the passage from a state of nature to civil society and (ii) that this third law cannot be generated from purely egoistic premises, the only kind of premises Hobbes's theory allows.[20] From purely egoistic premises, one can generate only the *prudential maxim* to "honor covenants only so long as it is in my interest to do so" and never the *moral obligation* to "honor my covenants, because justice demands it, even when so doing may interfere with my self-interest." A man (like the psychopath) who could never sincerely avow the latter principle is a man uniquely *un*qualified for membership in civil society, for he is a man in whose life obligation *cannot matter*.

PSYCHOPATHY AND MORAL PERSONALITY

Psychopaths, I have argued, are in no position to claim any rights on grounds of moral merit or desert. We can act wrongly with respect to them, but they cannot be wronged. They can be injured, but they can be done no moral injury. This indicates to me that, from the moral point of view, it is very implausible to regard them as *persons* at all.[21] For it seems to me that it is the possession of rights that morally distinguishes *persons* (objects of respect and dignity in Kant's sense) from *animals*.[22] Because animals are sentient creatures, there are things —on grounds of utility— that we ought not do to them. But it makes little sense to worry about the *rights* of animals, for they do not satisfy the presuppositions for the intelligibility of this kind of talk.[23] Thus, the psychopath, by his failure to

20. See chapters 14 and 15 of *Leviathan*.

21. I include the phrase "from a moral point of view" because it is not solely within a moral context that we find it worthwhile to draw a person-nonperson distinction. Intelligence or rationality, often cited as distinguishing marks of persons, may function in these other contexts; but they will hardly do the job in morality—not, at any rate, unless one seriously wants to entertain the possibility of someday having to accord computers greater moral respect than one accords one's fellow human beings. If any kind of rationality is to be the criterion of the dignity of persons, it will have to be what Kant calls *practical reason*. And that would be just another way of putting the point I am making in this paper.

22. This certainly seems to have been Kant's view, as the passage initially quoted (n. 1 above) from the *Tugendlehre* makes clear.

23. Professor Lewis Beck has pointed out to me in discussion that we sometimes do speak of the rights of animals and of obligations we have toward them. We might say, for example, that I have an obligation to take my cat (though not any other cat) to the vet when it is sick and that this obligation cannot be analyzed solely in terms of not causing unnecessary suffering to the cat as a sentient creature. Similarly, we might sometimes speak of a horse's right to spend its declining years in a pleasant pasture after years of faithful service. Now I believe that I can account for our practices here in a way compatible with my general thesis. For I should argue that this way of speaking is intelligible only insofar as we regard our animals as in some (perhaps metaphorical) sense *persons*, as beings capable of moral feeling. If we are not regarding them in this way, how could we make any sense of talk about their being faithful, feeling guilty for breaking rules, and the like? We may be utterly deluding ourselves in thinking of our pets in this way, but the fact that we do so is further evidence of the conceptual link between rights and obligations, on the one hand, and personality and moral feelings, on the other. When it is just obviously absurd to attribute any moral qualities to our animals, then we should hardly want to speak—even in a highly meta-

care about his own moral responsibilities, his failure to accept them even if he recognizes them,[24] becomes morally dead—an animal rather than a person. He has no rights to stand on when, for example, he wants to oppose a certain kind of medicinal treatment that may be prescribed for him. All he can legitimately demand is that, since he is a sentient animal, we ought not—at least prima facie—cause him suffering. The man who, when told that his conduct harms the rights of others, sincerely responds "Who cares?" is hardly in any position to demand that others recognize and respect any rights that he might want to claim.[25]

Now many of my readers are inclined to think, I am sure, that this position is too harsh—that it is indeed the harshest possible position one could hold. But it may be too weak; for there is, it would seem, an even stronger position:

If there *could* be an instance of *sheer* corruption the individual concerned would *not* retain the status of a moral being, with all the practical implications of that status. It would, of course, still be true that we ought not to speak of him as 'merely an animal': we should do better to call him a monster. And as a monster (it might be held) not only would he not require to be treated with more respect than a brute, but he would lose his title even to such consideration as the brutes deserve.[26]

My thesis, however, is more charitable and can now be summarized as follows: *If there are psychopaths as have been described above, they have no rights as persons* (because they fail to satisfy a necessary presup-

---

phorical sense—of their rights and our obligations. With dogs and cats and horses, things go pretty well. But would anyone feel comfortable in speaking of his obligation to take his goldfish to the vet; or of the right of his salamander to spend its declining years in comfort?

24. For a probing discussion of the acceptance of responsibility, with specific application to the psychopath, see Herbert Fingarette's "The Acceptance of Responsibility," in his *On Responsibility* (New York, 1967), pp. 17–45.

25. In their book *Sense and Delusion* (London, 1971), Ilham Dilman and D. Z. Phillips ponder the character of Ivan Ilych in Tolstoy's story *The Death of Ivan Ilych*. Ivan Ilych, by Tolstoy's standards and by Ivan's own deathbed standards, is judged to have lead a *meaningless* life because it was an utterly selfish life, devoid of any care and concern for persons or his moral responsibilities to them. All he had cared about was obedience to conventional expectations as a vehicle for the increase of his own position and power. The question worrying Dilman and Phillips is the following: Is the judgment of meaninglessness here purely emotive, reflecting merely a subjective attitude toward Ivan's life, or can the judgment in some sense be said to be objective? The thesis I have developed in this paper provides, I think, a *start* toward securing its objectivity. For Ivan, by living a life with at least a strongly psychopathic tendency, can be said to have cut himself off from what it means fully to be a person, to be human.

26. W. G. Maclagan, "How Important Is Moral Goodness," in *Ethics*, ed. Judith J. Thomson and Gerald Dworkin (New York, 1968), p. 521; the essay originally appeared in *Mind* 64 (1955): 213–25. By speaking of "corruption" and "monsters," Maclagan would seem to be morally *condemning* individuals like the psychopath, saying that they are morally *evil* in some fundamental way. My thesis, however, is that such individuals stand totally outside the domain of moral discourse employing concepts like *desert, responsibility, blameworthiness,* and the like.

position of such rights), we have no moral obligations to them, and thus our moral response to them is to be on a par with our moral response to animals. We shall not hold them morally responsible; but neither shall we accord them moral respect.

It is worth noting that I have been able to deal with the rights and responsibilities of psychopaths without ever once considering the question of whether psychopathy is a "mental disease" or symptomatic of "insanity." And this seems to me a virtue of my account. For I submit that whether it is labeled "insanity" or not is irrelevant to moral responsibility and should be irrelevant to legal responsibility. What matters are the factors present in the syndrome itself and whether or not these factors come into conflict with the presuppositions of morality. Whether such factors *also* call for the name "insane" or "mentally ill" is, so far as I can tell, solely a matter of useful and economical medical taxonomy and therefore can have no important bearing on issues of rights and responsibilities. Indeed, I am inclined to suspect that the judgment that an individual lacks responsibility and is a defective person leads to the judgment that he is insane—not the other way around.

PSYCHOPATHY AND THE LAW

The practical implications of my argument thus far might seem to consist of something like the following principle: When an individual has been diagnosed a psychopath, his "rights" may be suspended and he may be subjected to involuntary indefinite preventive detention and therapy and perhaps even (if his case is hopeless) to painless extermination. There are, however, very grave objections to the adoption of any such practical principle; and I should like to conclude the paper by briefly elaborating these objections.

1. It may be impossible to diagnose, on impeccable clinical grounds freed from ideology, any clear cases of psychopathy as herein defined. We all have our psychopathic tendencies, and so all the actual cases may be neither black nor white but various shades of gray. And surely, considering the gravity of denying an individual the status of a person, the burden of proof must lie on those who seek this denial. One grave temptation, one inviting substantial self-deception, is the tendency to regard a man who simply morally disagrees with us (or who does not share our political ideology) as lacking a moral sense.

2. There are obvious and grave dangers, calling to mind Nazi Germany, in creating any political or legal authority to decide who is and who is not a person or to count as a person. This is not because, as may be supposed, that judgments of this sort are never true or reasonable. It is, rather, that political authorities could hardly be trusted to confine their actions to cases where they were true or reasonable. For this sort of political power immediately invites abuse and corruption of the very worst

sort. I am sure, for example, that even in the United States Justice Department there are those who would be delighted if they could have all longhairs, SDS members, and Black Panthers diagnosed as psychopaths and treated accordingly.[27]

3. There is the important problem of shared or collective social guilt. In many ways we may all be responsible, at least by omission, for allowing the kind of society to develop which produces psychopaths. Every time we vote for "law and order" over social justice and the elimination of poverty, for example, we may be voting unintentionally for an increase of the number of psychopaths in our society. For psychopathy may be bred in impoverished and malnourished conditions. As John Stuart Mill wrote, "If society lets any considerable number of its members grow up mere children, incapable of being acted on by rational considerations of distant motives, society has only itself to blame for the consequences."[28] Since, as in paragraph 1 above, the possibilities for self-deception here are enormous, any hasty self-righteousness about how psychopaths should be treated is quite out of order—another theme of Camus's *L'Etranger*.

4. Finally, and perhaps most important, psychopaths may be like infants or the senile—not now persons, but potential or former persons. And thus they may deserve some respect on these grounds alone, respect for what they were or what they might be able to become.

I am not saying that psychopaths should never, in practice, be treated in line with the thesis of this paper. But I am saying that, given the four points noted above, such cases may be so rare as to be without legal or practical importance.[29] Though a philosopher hates to admit it, the in-

27. For a fuller development of these worries, see my "Criminal Punishment and Psychiatric Fallacies" (n. 19 above) and my "Preventive Detention and Psychiatry," *Dissent* (September–October 1970), pp. 448–60. In both articles I explore the actual and potential dangers of social psychiatry.

28. *On Liberty*, chap. 4. The following kind of case, though no doubt too simple to be true, illustrates the worry here: Suppose it were discovered that there was a high correlation between psychopathy and a chemical deficiency in the brain related to very low protein diets—the kind of diets forced by economic necessity upon a substantial portion of the population. Who would be responsible for the social consequences of psychopathy then? By introducing these kinds of consideration, it may seem that the free will–determinism issue is creeping back into the discussion. But this is all right. The fact that certain kinds of causal discoveries provide an *additional* reason for excusing the psychopath does not show that psychopathy by itself is not also sufficient.

29. I do submit that, in thankfully extreme and rare cases, we may in fact respond justifiably to certain individuals as animals. Suppose we are living in a society where psychopaths are in control and where there are thus, as in the state of nature, no institutions of integrity that we have to worry about preserving. Karl Jaspers, living in Nazi Germany, lived in such a society; and he responded, quite rightly in my judgment, to the psychopaths running his society as though they were animals: "To me there seemed nothing left beyond at least being at all times clear about what I was doing and intending to do, and to act accordingly. What we had to do was to act naïvely, to pretend no interest in the affairs of the world, to preserve a natural dignity . . . , and if need be to lie *without scruples*. For beasts in possession of an absolute power to destroy must be treated with cunning and not as men and rational beings" (Karl Jaspers,

tegrity of social and legal institutions may depend upon the maintenance of certain fictions—particularly fictions about the characters of the individuals involved in these institutions. For once we begin to entertain practical proposals which involve considering individuals as less than persons, we help to perpetuate a way of thinking about man and society which, via social engineering and management, approaches—at best—*Brave New World* and—at worst—*1984*.

---

epilogue to *Philosophy of Existence*, trans. Richard F. Grabau [Philadelphia, 1971], p. 97. I have italicized the phrase "without scruples" to stress Jaspers's realization that his situation was not one where the normal obligation to tell the truth is overridden by even more important moral requirements but, rather, one where he was dealing with beings of a nature that precluded their imposing any moral requirements on him at all.) I am grateful to my colleague, Prof. Charles F. Wallraff, for calling this passage in Jaspers to my attention.

Forgiveness*

Norvin Richards

What is it to forgive someone? What would be a good reason to do so? Could the reason be so good that one would be wrong not to forgive, or is forgiveness a gift one is always free to withhold?

The first section of this paper criticizes the standard definition of forgiveness and offers a replacement. The second sets out an approach to the moral questions. The third considers the place this approach finds for the usual reasons to forgive—repentance, old times' sake, and so on—and for some less usual reasons as well. A final section offers an overview and replies to two objections.

I

In the following passage, Jeffrie Murphy opts for the account of forgiveness favored by most writers on the topic: "I shall . . . argue (following Bishop Butler) that forgiveness is the foreswearing of *resentment*—where resentment is a negative feeling (anger, hatred) directed toward another who has done one moral injury."[1] This conception ably distinguishes forgiving someone from merely forgetting what he did. And, since it makes forgiving a matter of controlling powerful emotions, it also explains why this can be a lengthy, effortful process, imperfectly successful or entirely beyond one's powers. Even so, I want to argue against it.

Notice, first, that it precludes forgiving anyone you do not first resent. Suppose that someone's especially treacherous behavior made you not resentful but contemptuous of her. Contempt is an abiding attitude, no less than resentment, but quite a different one: contempt is

* I am greatly indebted to Scott Hestevold for many helpful discussions of this topic. This work was supported by University of Alabama research grant 1328.

1. Jeffrie Murphy, "Forgiveness and Resentment," *Midwest Studies in Philosophy*, vol. 7, ed. Peter French, Theodore Uehling, and Howard Wettstein (Minneapolis: University of Minnesota Press, 1982), p. 504. See also R. J. O'Shaughnessy, "Forgiveness," *Philosophy* 42 (1967): 344; H. J. N. Horsbrugh, "Forgiveness," *Canadian Journal of Philosophy* 4 (1974): 271; Aurel Kolnai, "Forgiveness," *Proceedings of the Aristotelian Society* 74 (1973–74): 93 ff. (but see also p. 104, where forgiveness is defined as "re-acceptance"); Elizabeth Beardsley, "Understanding and Forgiveness," in *The Philosophy of Brand Blanshard*, ed. P. A. Schilpp (LaSalle, Ill.: Open Court, 1981), pp. 249–50, 252; Martin P. Golding, "Forgiveness and Regret," *Philosophical Forum* 16 (1984–85): 134.

This essay originally appeared in *Ethics*, vol. 99, no. 1, October 1988.

dismissive, in a way anger and hatred are not.[2] Since contempt is not resentment, if forgiving is *foreswearing* resentment it is impossible for you to forgive such a person. Of course, she might entreat you to view her differently, speaking perhaps of how sorry she was to have acted as she did, and her plea might move you. But it could not be forgiveness to which it moved you, according to the definition.

Similarly, it is possible for mistreatment to make one not angry or contemptuous but just very sad, if it is mistreatment at the hands of a loved one. Imagine, for example, that your grown son had badly let you down. This might make you angry, of course, but it might also make you feel deeply disappointed in him, instead. You are hurt that he should act in this way, not angry, not moved to hatred. Accordingly, if you were to abandon these feelings you would not be forgiving your son, on the definition in question, no matter how natural you and he might find it to say that you were, since you would not be abandoning an attitude of the specified kind. Again, the limitation seems arbitrary. It should also count as forgiveness to abandon negative feelings of these other kinds.

Finally, imagine a woman whose husband frequently belittles her in public. Most recently, he has done this in the company of some new acquaintances whose opinion was especially important to her. The episode has made her furious, and the anger has stayed with her. She seethes at the sight of her husband, entertains thoughts of violent revenge, and so on. However, such feelings and thoughts themselves distress her, for she believes we should always forgive those who wrong us, lest the Lord not forgive us our own misdeeds. So, she does her best to forgive her husband, and she does manage a certain shift in her emotions: she no longer wants to hit the man or to wring his neck. However, she can't seem to get any further than this. Now, the thought of him makes her laugh scornfully—and, sometimes, a little ruefully at herself as well, for putting up with such treatment all these years. "What a contemptible pair!" she says to herself, and resolves to leave the man as a first act of self-respect.

Is this woman *forgiving* her husband? She does qualify under the definition, since she has foresworn hatred and anger, abandoning resentment through an act of will. But I doubt he would think he was being forgiven, as she ridiculed his urgings that things should return to "normal" and went on packing her bags. And I doubt that *she* should consider that she had forgiven him, either. After all, her efforts to do so were founded in the hope that God would later do for her as she did for her husband. Surely she does not hope the Lord will merely move from hating her to holding her in icy contempt? She wants an embrace, not a different kind of rejection.

2. Certainly Murphy himself would accept the distinction. See, in particular, his agreement with Nietzsche that having contempt for someone is incompatible with resenting him (Murphy, "Forgiveness and Resentment," p. 505).

Evidently, then, abandoning resentment does not constitute forgiving, because a person can stop resenting and still have a hostile attitude of another kind: here, the dismissive one of contempt. The earlier examples suggested that neither must it be resentment that one is foreswearing: it should also count as forgiveness to abandon contempt for someone or disappointment in him. Taken together, these suggest that to forgive someone for having wronged one is to abandon all negative feelings toward this person, of whatever kind, insofar as such feelings are based on the episode in question.

One might have other reasons to take a dim view of him, of course. To forgive him for having done X is not to forgive him for everything he has done. So, we are not here equating forgiving with "re-accepting," as Kolnai is sometimes inclined to do.[3]

A broader difficulty with seeing forgiveness as reacceptance is that some wrongdoers were not "accepted" to begin with: there is no relationship to reestablish. Consider the stranger whose car drenches you with mud. Having seen this in her mirror, she stops to apologize, insists on paying your cleaning bill, and so on. Surely it is possible to forgive this woman, just as it would be if she were an equally repentant friend. But to call this "reaccepting" her or "reestablishing our relationship" is rather strained: there was no relationship, and there is none after she drives away.

This is not to deny that when, say, a husband wants his wife to forgive him he wants their relationship restored, wants things to be as if he had never misbehaved, and doesn't feel forgiven if they are not. Since there was a warm relationship prior to the misdeed, there will be many reasons for his wife to treat him with affection. If she is cool and distant instead, this will show that she has not forgiven him. For, if there really were no vestiges of the hard feelings founded on his one misstep, her behavior would be more affectionate. This is not because forgiveness is reacceptance, though, but because it amounts to abandoning all hard feelings founded on the incident, and her coolness shows she has not done that.

Thus far, we have widened the range of negative attitudes one can banish in an act of forgiveness but have put no restrictions on one's reasons for changing one's attitude. Regardless of why I change my attitude toward you, it will count as forgiving you. This is not quite right. Suppose that I do so as an act of mental hygiene. I am sick and tired of being so angry that my sleep is restless and my stomach upset. I resolve not to endure another day of it, and I manage, with professional help, to end this disruptive state of mind. Am I extending forgiveness to you in this instance?

It seems not, precisely because the process is so entirely self-absorbed. When we forgive we are concerned with other people, or with a more appropriate response to what they did. So we forgive them because they

3. Kolnai, p. 104.

are genuinely sorry, or because we realize they were not malicious but only careless, or for the sake of the children, and so on. To change one's attitude entirely out of self-interest might be (sensibly) to forget what someone did, but it is not to forgive him for having done it.[4]

II

What about the moral questions concerning this banishing of hard feelings? When should one do this? When should one not? And, how strong are these "shoulds"?

My answers turn on viewing acts of forgiveness and refusals to forgive as displays of character. I follow the lead of ordinary practice here, as when we think a person hard for refusing to forgive a particular supplicant, or weak for continuing to forgive someone who continues quite relentlessly to mistreat him. My idea is to take this apparently natural approach much further.

It will turn out that some acts of forgiveness (and, some failures to forgive) do enact flaws of character, just as we think. That is important, since it is always at least prima facie wrong to enact a flaw of character, whether the flaw is cowardice, or arrogance, or something with no simple name. This is not the only thing that can be wrong with an action, of course, nor is it always the worst thing.[5] Still, that behavior is, for instance, *arrogant* is a serious mark against it, and in lieu of unusual circumstances it is simply wrong to act arrogantly. In the same way, it is wrong to refuse to forgive when that enacts arrogance or some other flaw of character. And it is wrong to extend forgiveness when *that* does so.

On other occasions forgiving someone expresses a highly admirable trait of character, not a defect. Obviously, forgiving is not then wrong in the way described. But, neither would it be wrong *not* to forgive on such an occasion, just as it would not be wrong to fail to perform a rescue which demanded a true hero, for example. There are good reasons to do such deeds, and a person of a certain disposition will find them compelling, but no one is obliged to do them, no one acts wrongly in failing to do them. In the same way as the heroism is beyond duty, when forgiving requires a positive virtue it is admirable to do but not wrong to omit.

What determines whether forgiving (or failing to forgive) would enact a virtue or a defect of character? As we have seen, to forgive someone for something is to abandon all the hard feelings one bases on this particular episode. Were this positive effort not made, the feelings

4. This may be Jeffrie Murphy's point in following a similar example with this stipulation: "Forgiveness is not the overcoming of resentment *simpliciter;* it is rather this: to foreswear resentment on moral grounds" ("Forgiveness and Resentment," p. 506). I am grateful to Gary Watson for convincing me of the need for some such restriction.

5. A model for combining an action's several moral credentials is offered in Norvin Richards, "Moral Symptoms," *Mind* 89 (1980): 49–66.

would continue. Their presence, and their precise tendency to continue, is itself an expression of one's character. It is because of the sort of person you are that you are *this* angry with me for having done *that* to you.

Now, to forgive is to overrule this part of your character. The overruling expresses a different part of one's character: you are not only a person who will be this angry with me for having done that, you are also a person who will abandon such feelings in light of certain considerations (or, a person who will not). This second-level, self-regulatory part of one's character is what is in play in acts of forgiveness and refusals to forgive. When forgiving enacts a (self-regulatory) flaw of character, it is wrong to forgive; when it does not, it is not wrong to forgive. Similarly, a refusal to forgive is wrong if it enacts a flaw at this second, self-regulatory level, *not* wrong if it enacts a virtue or a neutral trait.

These matters will turn on what sort of character one would be overruling (or failing to overrule). There appear to be three possibilities.

1. It might be that in forgiving, you would overrule a flaw in your character. For example, perhaps your still hating me for the careless remark I made years ago expresses an intolerance for weakness in others, or a deep suspicion that people secretly dislike you, or some other trait without which your life would be a far happier one. The countertendency to overrule that unfortunate trait would at least diminish its impact, if not lead to your eventual reform. Thus the countertendency, expressed in forgiving, is itself a good trait. So, it would not be wrong to forgive on such an occasion—that is, to forgive would not enact a flaw of character.

What about refusing to forgive in such a case? This would amount to a disinclination to check what is (by hypothesis) a flaw in your character, either failing to see it as a flaw or being quite content to remain flawed in this particular way. That is itself a defect of character at a second level, it seems to me, at least where the first-level flaw is a relatively serious one. For one thing, it perpetuates the first-level flaw, increasing thereby its negative contributions to one's life. For another, to be blind to your serious flaws (or, content with them) adds an extra offensiveness of its own: an arrogance, a self-centeredness which is hard to swallow. In short, to refuse to overrule a (relatively serious) flaw is to enact a second flaw. That makes the refusal wrong: it is wrong not to forgive, when forgiving would abandon feelings which themselves express a (relatively serious) defect of character.

2. Alternatively, forgiving could overrule not a defect in one's character but something perfectly in order. Perhaps, for example, there is nothing at all wrong with taking remarks of the kind I once made as seriously as you do: we are not dealing with intolerance or paranoia on your part, but with a perfectly acceptable level of self-respect. If you were to have no tendency to overrule such feelings, that would hardly be a flaw in your character. It would serve to perpetuate, not a defect, but something perfectly acceptable. In short, to refuse to forgive would not be wrong in a case of this kind.

On the other hand, although it is not a flaw to be content with an acceptable feature of one's character, neither must it be a flaw to be dissatisfied with such a feature. Perhaps you aspire to be more than merely acceptably kind, or more generous than a person need be to rise above the miserly. Such aspirations need not collapse into narcissism or involve ignoring traits in a greater need of attention. Thus, the inclination to overrule an acceptable feature of character need not be a flaw. It needn't be wrong to forgive, then, when this overrules feelings it is perfectly acceptable to have. Nor, as noted earlier, is it wrong to decline to forgive, under those circumstances.

3. Finally, suppose that forgiveness would overrule a trait which is not merely acceptable but is essential to decent character: something it would be a defect to be without. Perhaps, for example, to feel no anger toward someone who had just swindled your aged mother out of her life's savings is like this. It is not merely "perfectly acceptable" to be angry at the swindler, that is: there is something wrong with you if you are not.

The inclination to banish feelings without which one would not be a decent human being can hardly be a virtue. It fosters bad character, no less than being satisfied with bad traits one already has. Enacting such an inclination is enacting a flaw in one's character. In short, it is wrong to forgive, when doing so overrules a trait which it would be bad character to lack.

I believe that each of these categories has instances, and thus that it is sometimes wrong to forgive, sometimes wrong not to forgive, and sometimes admirable to forgive but acceptable not to do so. There is a powerful tradition which denies this, however, teaching that one is never wrong to forgive, and, indeed, always wrong not to do so. I will close this section by explaining why I do not find that view compelling.

The point in dispute is not whether people of good character should be repelled by immoral behavior: both sides will agree that they should. Moral wrongs themselves are rather evanescent, however; they cease to exist once they are done. Hard feelings toward the wrongdoer serve to express one's feelings about the (now completed) wrong. In my view, there is nothing inappropriate about this. On the opposing view, there is: one should always hate the sin, but never the sinner.

Why not? Well, such feelings do have costs. They can be distressing, they can preclude certain close relationships, and they can dominate a person's life. However, it would be a mistake to conclude that they *must* be costly on balance. For one thing, there simply are people against whom it is better to be on one's guard, and there are pairs of people who seem to bring out the worst in each other if they attempt a close relationship. For another, it is a considerable exaggeration to think that unless we forgive we must burn with resentment, our lives consumed by bitter feelings and angry schemes. Resentment is a disposition which varies considerably in its intensity and in the length of its natural tenure. And, as Bishop Butler pointed out, some levels of resentment are perfectly compatible with a general good will toward the wrongdoer.[6] (Think here of the parent who is angry at a child for disobeying, but is certainly not transformed into a spiteful, single-minded avenger unless moved to forgiveness.)

Notice too that when we do hate the sinner, as well as the sin, we are not indulging some isolated quirk but are implementing a broad feature of human psychology. If you had been assaulted, you would feel differently not only about the person who assaulted you but also about the place in which the assault occurred and, perhaps, about a particular instrument your assailant used. The park where you loved to ramble would become a place you dreaded. Similarly, suppose you had been attacked in your own home, with your own kitchen knife. You would scarcely return it to the drawer with the others as just the thing for carving this year's turkey. Instead, the very sight of it would distress you, and the idea of using it would be repugnant. Are we only wrong to change our feelings toward wrongdoers, on the view that we must always forgive, or are we also wrong to feel differently about places and instruments? Neither answer seems particularly attractive.

Instead, how strongly you are repelled by the places, instruments, and agents of a harm is one measure of how bad a thing it was for you. How long such feelings last is another. There is a basis here for speaking of such feelings as in keeping with what happened, or as out of proportion to it. That would provide a way of speaking about your character, of judging that you take deeds of the kind in question as a person of good character would, or, that you do not. Such judgments make important points about us, it seems to me: points that are lost in thinking that good character simply requires immediate forgiveness on every occasion.

III

What place have the various standard reasons for forgiving, if we take the approach I have suggested? The pleas commonly offered are strikingly different. Some invoke special features of the misbehavior: it wasn't meant to turn out as it did; or, the wrongdoer had no idea it would mean so much to you; or, it was intentional but really only a rather minor misdeed; and so on. Other reasons ask that the deed be taken in a certain context: it was bad behavior, but she's your oldest friend; or, you've treated her this way yourself, quite often; and so on. Still others emphasize new developments: the wrongdoer is now very distressed over the way she acted, despises herself for it, and hopes you'll forgive her.

Often, the person seeking forgiveness is able to offer several of these reasons at once. Certain of them go together in a way, strengthening

6. Joseph Butler, "Upon Forgiveness of Injuries," in *The Works of the Right Reverend Father in God, Joseph Butler, D.C.L., Late Bishop of Durham*, ed. Samuel Halifax (New York: Carter, 1846), pp. 106–7. See also William R. Neblett, "Forgiveness and Ideals," *Mind* 73 (1974): 270.

each other: *since* she's an old friend she probably is *genuinely* sorry for what she's done ... But the more basic question is why each is itself a reason to forgive. So, it will be better to consider each in turn, as if it were the only consideration put forward.

A. *Excuses and Good Intentions*

In his sermon, "Upon Forgiveness of Injuries," Bishop Butler maintains that we very seldom injure each other out of malice. Nearly, always, says he, the harm is not done purposely but through ignorance or inadvertence.[7] Perhaps he is right about this. What is of current interest, though, is that he regards these excuses as reasons to forgive: he thinks the fact that you were wronged inadvertently or through a misunderstanding ought to change your feelings about the wrongdoer.

It might be replied that although such discoveries could call for a change in one's feelings, they could not call for forgiveness. The argument would run as follows. Excuses fall into two categories. Some are so good as to mean the 'wrongdoer' was not at all responsible for what befell the victim. In that case, there is nothing for the 'victim' to forgive this particular person. Such excuses are not reasons to forgive, exactly, but reasons to stop acting as if one had been wronged.

Jeffrie Murphy writes as if all excuses were of this kind: "To excuse is to say this: What was done was morally wrong; but, because of certain factors about the agent (e.g., insanity), it would be unfair to hold the wrongdoer responsible or blame him for the wrong action ... we may forgive only that which it is initally proper to resent; and, if a person ... was not responsible for what he did, there is *nothing to resent* (though perhaps much to be sad about)."[8] But, although the insanity excuse perhaps does erase all responsibility, not every excuse is so powerful. Commonly, excuses do not exonerate but only mitigate by showing that one acted less badly than it appears. Since they do leave one having acted somewhat badly, could they perhaps be the reasons to forgive which Butler thought they were?

Again, it might be argued that they could not. To forgive someone for having wronged one is not merely to reduce the intensity of one's hard feelings but to abandon such feelings altogether (insofar as they are based on the incident in question). As we just noted, the excuse leaves it the case that the agent did wrong the person. But if so, the argument continues, hard feelings of *some* intensity are called for: to abandon them would be both a poor defense against repetitions and a display of inadequate aversion to what was done. In short, only someone of bad character fails to resent a wrongdoer, and a wrongdoer with the common sort of excuse is still a wrongdoer. So, the argument concludes, the common sort of

7. Butler, p. 111.
8. Murphy, "Forgiveness and Resentment," p. 506.

excuse cannot be a reason to forgive, any more than the exonerating excuse could be.

The flaw in this argument, I believe, is the premise that only someone of bad character fails to resent a wrongdoer. That is certainly a contention Murphy would advance, and it seems to appeal to R. S. Downie as well.[9] However, although perhaps it is tautological that one should be averse to any wrong, no matter how minor, it does not follow that this aversion should always find expression in sustained hard feelings toward the source of the wrong. Compare here the man who dislikes the beach because that is where he dropped his ice cream cone in the sand. There is certainly nothing wrong with his regretting having lost his cone, but these feelings about the beach could show that he takes its loss too seriously. Certainly, there is no appeal whatever in the idea that unless he continues to hate the beach, he does not take the loss of the cone as seriously as he should.

Similarly, suppose our man dropped his cone not because a bully viciously twisted his arm but because he was jostled by a careless teenager. The jostling is mistreatment, and one should be averse to being mistreated. But it does not follow that our man will exhibit bad character unless he continues to harbor bad feelings toward the teenager—unless he refuses to forgive him, that is.

The idea is that even if, as Murphy and Downie would urge, good character does require being averse to all forms of mistreatment, it might not require sustained hard feelings toward the sources of the minor kinds. Conceivably, an excuse could show that a misdeed was a very minor one. It would thereby provide a reason to abandon those unwarranted hard feelings without contradicting the intuition that one should always be averse to mistreatment.

We can add to this Bishop Butler's own ideas concerning why excuses are reasons to forgive. Mistake, inadvertence, and so forth "we ought all to be disposed to excuse in others, *from experiencing so much of them in ourselves.*"[10] Tu quoque: but, why should this be a reason to forgive when the deed is done to me? Well, either I am also hard on myself for this same behavior, or I am not. To be hard on myself (as well as on others) over even minor mistakes and inadvertencies amounts to a broad intolerance of human limitations. No one can meet my expectations, since I expect perfection, and this must make me a very impatient, frustrated, and generally objectionable fellow.

Alternatively, suppose I am not hard on myself for minor bungles, but only on others. This suggests that I am not actually averse to the wrong as such but to my being wronged (however slightly) myself. Here I am flawed in a different way. I take myself too seriously, and I draw in my own favor a distinction without a relevant difference.

9. Ibid., p. 505; R. S. Downie, "Forgiveness," *Philosophical Quarterly*, vol. 15 (1965).
10. Butler, p. 111 (emphasis added).

In short, not to forgive minor misbehavior to which one is oneself prone exhibits either a general intolerance of human frailty or an unwarranted exaltation of oneself. It is wrong to enact either trait, for both are flaws of character. Thus, it is wrong not to forgive a person whose excuse makes the misdeed a minor one of a kind to which one is prone oneself.

Let me note that although this argument makes use of Bishop Butler's thinking concerning excuses, it does not reach as sweeping a conclusion as he did. He believed we should always forgive those who had excuses for wronging us (which, in his view, covered virtually everyone who did so). However, not all excuses do reduce the wrong done to a minor misstep of a kind to which one is prone oneself. Some only reduce murder to manslaughter, for example. Unlike Bishop Butler, then, my argument takes only some excuses to be reasons to forgive.

The fact that the wrongdoer had your best interest at heart appears to function in the same way. His good intentions can reduce the behavior to something trivial and familiar, and then they are a reason to forgive. But they can also fail to effect such a reduction, and then they provide no reason to forgive. Murphy, in contrast, sharply distinguishes excuses (which he believes cannot be reasons to forgive) from paternalistic motives (which he believes can be). His discussion of paternalistic motives, however, supports the idea that they are reasons to forgive only insofar as they effect the reduction I have described:

> A person who interferes with my liberty for what he thinks is my own good is, in my judgment, acting wrongly. . . . His grounds for interfering, however, are well-meaning (i.e., he seeks to do me good) even if his actions are misguided and morally insensitive. . . . It is hard to view the friend who locks up my liquor cabinet because he knows I drink too much as on the same moral level as the person who embezzles my funds for his own benefit; and thus the case for forgiving the former may have some merit.[11]

Again, just as not all excuses make misbehavior sufficiently minor that it ought to be forgiven, neither do all realizations that the behavior was only "misguided and morally insensitive" paternalism. Some acts of paternalism remain sufficiently serious mistreatments that it is certainly not bad character to take them sufficiently seriously to hold them against their perpetrators. So, it will not always be wrong not to be moved to forgiveness by the news that a certain person meant to be acting in your own best interest.

On the other hand, neither must it be bad character to accept another's effort to look after one. A fierce independence is hardly the only alternative to spinelessness. So, it can also reflect perfectly acceptable character to forgive someone who (after all) only meant to help.

---

11. Murphy, "Forgiveness and Resentment," p. 509.

B. Repentance

So far, we have been focusing on pleas that one's behavior was not really bad enough to merit the victim's attitude. It is a different move altogether to agree that the behavior was very bad and ask to be forgiven because one now *repents*. Repentance is perhaps the most familiar of the grounds for forgiveness. The question is, why should it work? What is it about the wrongdoer's repenting that justifies (or even mandates) forgiving him?

Actually, I think, repentance can present appeals of two distinct kinds. At least some forms of repentance involve a change in the wrongdoer from someone who saw nothing wrong with mistreating you in a certain way to someone who joins you in condemning that behavior. This alone might seem to make hard feelings against him rather pointless and forgiveness the only reasonable course.

Murphy and Kolnai both testify to the attractiveness of this line of thinking, though neither accepts it in the end.[12] There are two good reasons not to. First, repentance does not guarantee that there will be no future misbehavior. It is always possible that the wrongdoer will revert to his earlier views, or be vulnerable to temptations to violate his new ones. There might also be forms of behavior which his new view does not condemn but against which a general vigilance would provide a defense. (Think here of someone who now agrees that it was wrong to lie to you as he did but still has nothing against a very broad range of deceptive practices.) Since repentance thus does not obviate the need for defensive postures, it does not mandate forgiveness.

Second, the question whether to forgive does not turn entirely on whether defenses against repetition are needed. If it did, one would always be wrong not to forgive a villain who had passed out of one's life: the rapist who was killed while escaping, for example, or the embezzler using your funds to dwell happily in Brazil. Such people are no future threat to you. But, the fact remains that they have done you wrong, and that issues its own call for hard feelings against them.

Wouldn't the same be true of the wrongdoer who was very much at hand, but now repentant? Just like the rapist and the embezzler, even if such a person poses no future threat, he remains someone who did you wrong. That is a second reason to resent him, which is not erased by his repentance. Thus the change undergone in repenting does not render hard feelings pointless after all and does not mandate forgiveness.

It does accomplish something less dramatic, however. It provides a reason to forgive repenters who have changed in the way described. It makes forgiving them an option appealing to persons with one sort of good character: it makes forgiveness morally permissible. How it does this requires a bit of explanation.

---

12. Ibid., p. 511; Kolnai, pp. 101–2.

First, to repent in the way I have been discussing it is not merely to have newly negative feelings about what one has done, but to have these feelings as part of a change in one's moral views. To know all along that one is misbehaving and only have misgivings about it the next day does not qualify. Rather, we are speaking here of the person who has "seen the light," who has come to disapprove of a kind of behavior which she had thought of as perfectly permissible. A new moral principle is acquired, or there is a new realization that her old principles are inconsistent and that her behavior violated the more important of them.

Now, in such a case, the wrongdoer's permissive former principles are one reason why she acted as she did: she did it, in part, because she did not think it wrong to do. So, a change in her views would be a change in something which was partly responsible for the wrong. Her repentance is thus like repairing that part of a house which contributed to an accident. The child took a nasty fall right here, in part because the steps were uneven, but now I have fixed them; I shouted at the secretary in part because I did not think there was anything wrong with shouting at secretaries, but now I realize that there is.

Despite the change, this is still the house where the child fell and I am still the person who shouted at the secretary. So, there is still a question whether the victims ought not to have hard feelings in both cases. However, there has been a change in them qua source of suffering; there has been a replacement of (part of) what was responsible for the suffering with something which promises to be harmless. Accordingly, there would be nothing amiss in the association being broken—in the child feeling good about the house again, or in the secretary dropping her resentment of me now that I am (clearly) more respectful of her. Forgiveness has become a permissible option with appeal to persons of perfectly good character, rather than something which shows a failure to take the episode as seriously as one should, because the wrongdoer has changed something about himself which contributed to the wrong.

On the other hand, neither would there be anything amiss in the hard feelings continuing, despite the repairs to the stairs and to the wrongdoer's moral views. For one thing, it might not be so clear that the flaw has been repaired, particularly where this consists in reforming one's moral views. (Hence the significance of the allegedly repentant person's apologies, efforts to "make up for it," to be on especially good behavior, and so on.) For another, it might be that the harm was too serious for the change to relieve one's other associations between this person (that face, those hands, that smirk) and what she did to you, despite those features having not even partly caused the harm. So, there needn't be a flaw of character in being unmoved by the change in the repentant person, any more than there must be one in being so moved. On the view I am offering, it is permissible either to forgive or not to do so.

That brings us to the second way in which someone's repentance might provide a good reason to extend forgiveness: a way which applies not only to those who have undergone moral reformation but also to those who knew all along they were misbehaving, and whose repentance consists in their later feeling very sorry. Part of both scenes is emotional: remorse over what was done before the change occurred. In the classic description the repentant wrongdoer is contrite, or "bruised in the heart."

Exactly why the victim's forgiveness should relieve the pain of remorse is somewhat curious, especially if one takes the view that wrongdoing is an offense not just against its most obvious victim but against an abstract moral order and/or against all who refrain from the misbehavior.[13] Perhaps what bothers us about having done wrong is not the abstract fact that we have done it, but the fact that a particular person has suffered a wrong at our hands.

At any rate, the fact is that repentant wrongdoers are pained by their victims' hard feelings toward them. They are unhappy, sometimes deeply so, in a way which the victim could relieve by extending forgiveness. That is a reason to grant the forgiveness: an appeal to the victim's compassion for someone he can rescue from unhappiness. Of course, sometimes the rescue is enormously difficult, because the offense was deeply aversive to the victim and occurred quite recently. Moreover, sometimes the forgiveness seems unlikely to do the wrongdoer all that much good. Perhaps his unhappiness over the misdeed is genuine but not terribly deep, and seems likely to pass of its own accord before too long; and, perhaps it would do him good to suffer over this a bit longer. So there are surely times when there would be nothing wrong with being unmoved by the appeal the repentant person makes to one's compassion.

By the same token, however, generally speaking there are also times when there *is* something wrong with being unmoved by an appeal to one's compassion. Imagine that it would be quite easy to relieve considerable suffering, as when a single word from you would save the postman from a vicious dog. Wouldn't you be very wrong not to say the word? Shall we say that you would also be wrong not to forgive whenever a single word from you would rescue the wrongdoer from agonies of remorse?

I think not. The postman is simply an object of compassion. The wrongdoer is something more: a wrongdoer. The postman's troubles befell him through no fault of his. The wrongdoer is suffering because

13. See, e.g., J. Finnis, "The Restoration of Retribution," *Analysis* 32 (1972): 131–35 (Finnis attributes the view to Thomas Aquinas, as well as advancing it himself); Herbert Morris, "Persons and Punishment," reprinted in *Punishment and Rehabilitation,* ed. Jeffrie Murphy (Belmont, Calif.: Wadsworth, 1973), esp. pp. 43 ff.; Herbert Morris, *Guilt and Innocence* (Berkeley: University of California Press, 1976), esp. pp. 33–34; M. P. Golding, *Philosophy of Law* (Englewood Cliffs, N.J.: Prentice-Hall, 1975), p. 92; Jeffrie Murphy, "Three Mistakes about Retributivism," reprinted in his *Retribution, Justice, and Therapy* (Dordrecht: Reidel, 1979).

he did you wrong. You have thereby a reason not to be compassionate toward him, which you do not have regarding the poor postman.

That is enough, I think, to justify rejecting the idea that it is simply heartless to withhold forgiveness from anyone who is genuinely repentant. The reply is that it is not heartless to resist their appeal to one's compassion because they are not simply objects of compassion. However, it is worth considering more closely why their past behavior does make them so different and why compassion should not simply overrule this further consideration.

There is one (ultimately mistaken) account of this with considerable initial appeal. According to it, the key difference between the postman and the wrongdoer is that the latter deserves his current unhappiness. To leave him to stew in his own juice will not be simply uncompassionate but will be an exercise of your sense of justice. As Butler urged, it is absolutely vital that we have a firm sense of justice to supplement our tender feelings of compassion.[14]

However, there is a certain awkwardness in thinking of hard feelings as penalties one imposes in the interests of justice, on the same order as fines and imprisonments. They seem instead to be natural consequences of the misbehavior. The victim's resentment is rather like the sore muscles and occasional scratches which a mugger might find to be occupational hazards. Certainly we feel no sympathy for the thug who gets sore or scratched in the process of mugging, and we might express that by saying he "had it coming," or that it was "no worse than he deserved," just as we say such things about the victim's hating him. There's even something satisfying about his having come by these aches and pains in the process of his wrongdoing. But, this is not to say such things are part of what a person deserves for mugging. We are not in the least inclined to have scratches and soreness imposed on muggers who do not suffer these in plying their trade, or to reduce the sentences of óther muggers on the ground that (after all) they are scratched and sore. Rather, we treat these as extra misfortunes which we are not sorry the mugger suffers. It is just so, I am suggesting, with any regrets he suffers over his victim's hard feelings for him.

If we do stop thinking of the hard feelings as deserved penalties, however, how will we explain why the wrongdoer's having wronged us matters? How will we explain, that is, why his misbehavior distinguishes him from the simple object of compassion, such as the mailman whom it would be wrong not to save from the vicious dog?

The explanation I want to develop begins from the premise that we are right to be averse to what happens to us when we are wronged and, when the wrong is not trivial, to express this aversion in hard feelings

14. Butler, "Upon Resentment," in *The Works of the Right Reverend Father in God*, pp. 99–100.

toward its source. The fact is that there is a degree of incompatibility between having hard feelings toward someone and being moved by that person's suffering to go to his or her aid. If I hate a certain man, the news that he is having some minor misfortune does not make me unhappy and might even provide a certain satisfaction. I need not be proud of this—I might wish to be kinder or more generous. Still, part of hating him is wanting him not to flourish, just as part of liking someone is wanting that person to fare well. One measure of the strength of my hatred is the point at which I begin to sympathize instead. Another is the point at which my sympathies are sufficiently strong that I will exert myself to relieve this person's plight, despite disliking him.

Now, suppose that my hard feelings are not merely present, but are called for by his having wronged me, and that my imperviousness to his plight expresses those hard feelings. Then, that imperviousness is also not just present, but called for. His having wronged me is a reason not to go to his aid—it makes him not simply an object of compassion, like the postman under attack from the dog.

Of course, this does not collapse into saying that his having wronged me means I should never be moved by his troubles, no matter how grave they are or what form his mistreatment of me took. The claim is only that to be victimized by someone creates a perfectly proper obstacle to compassion toward that person. How substantial an obstacle it *should* create would largely depend on how grave the mistreatment was. (I think it would also depend, to some extent, on how recently the wrong was committed: at least some feelings should lessen in intensity as time passes.) How substantial an obstacle it *would* create would depend instead on how aversive the event was for the victim, which is quite another thing. It is obviously possible to take something more seriously than one should, and thus to be impervious to suffering that should move one.

I have argued that even though a repentant wrongdoer does make an appeal to compassion, it is not necessarily a flaw of character to be unmoved to forgiveness, even if it would be easy for you to forgive and a great relief to him. Depending on how badly he acted and how recently, it might be a flaw of character if you *were* moved. Thus, there are times when it would be wrong to forgive such people, but this is not because even repentant wrongdoers deserve to suffer one's wrath. It is because even repentant wrongdoers are wrongdoers, hard feelings are called for toward wrongdoers as sources of wrong, and hard feelings are incompatible with a certain degree of compassion.

Although it is thus sometimes wrong to respond sympathetically to the repentant wrongdoer, by the same reasoning it is also sometimes wrong not to. Suppose the wrong was done long ago and was not extremely serious, and it is quite plain by now that the wrongdoer has undergone a change of character and that your forgiveness would be a considerable relief to him. As Murphy urges, it is possible to take too lightly oneself and the wrong done to one; but, it seems to me, it must also be possible to take these too seriously. I have just sketched what would be involved in doing so.

Between these extremes lies the broad range of cases in which the wrong was neither dreadful nor trivial and happened neither a few minutes nor a few years ago, and over which the (apparently) repentant wrongdoer is remorseful but not devastated. Within this range it is neither wrong to forgive nor wrong not to do so. As Kolnai so nicely puts it, here forgiveness is "a venture of trust"—a venture not always equal in its risks.

C. Old Times' Sake

> I will forgive the person who has willfully wronged me because . . . of old time's sake (e.g., "He has been a good and loyal friend to me in the past").[15]
>
> *Old Time's Sake.* As with repentance we have here a clear case of divorce of act from agent. When you are repentant, I forgive you for what you *now are.* When I forgive you for old time's sake, I forgive you for what you *once were.* Much of our forgiveness of old friends and parents, for example, is of this sort.[16]

Although Murphy says here that we can properly forgive people for old times' sake, for what they once were to us, he does virtually nothing to explain why. Why should your having "been a good and loyal friend to me in the past" be a reason to forgive you for wronging me, rather than something which deepens the hurt? Does it matter whether you had been my friend at least until this episode, or are only someone to whom I was once close, long ago? What, if anything, is it about past or present friendly relationships that provides a reason to forgive?

Suppose we begin with the current friend. Such a person is entitled to have her actions interpreted with a certain generosity, it seems to me. It isn't only that one should not be positively suspicious of one's friends, expecting the worst of them. More than that, they should have the benefit of the doubt. Even when it does appear they have mistreated you, your inclination should be to disbelieve the appearances. To regard someone as a friend is to trust that this person wishes you well and thus would not have acted as it seems. To be incapable of such trust, of regarding people as friends, is a serious failing.

In my view, this means it is sometimes morally wrong not to disbelieve the evidence that a certain person has mistreated you. That is not a point about forgiving friends, however, but one about assuming that there is nothing to forgive. Your friend is entitled to the assumption that she has not wronged you—but that differs from her being entitled to your forgiveness when, in fact, you know that she has wronged you.

Perhaps we can bring the two together in the following fashion. Part of someone's being your friend is her wishing you well. Part of that is

15. Murphy, "Forgiveness and Resentment," p. 508.
16. Ibid., p. 510.

being especially averse to doing you ill. If such a person has wronged you, it is safe to assume there must have been some powerful reason for it, or that she did not fully understand what she was doing. And, it is also safe to assume that she is now quite unhappy over what she has done, in a way you could relieve by extending your forgiveness.

In short, her being a friend is a reason to suppose that you have one of the *other* reasons to forgive her. That is not the same as "old times' sake" being a reason in itself, of course. And, it is less compelling for the merely former friend than for the current one. Still, evidently someone's being your friend can be indirectly a reason to extend forgiveness, and that is at least a role for old times to play.

Consider next this stronger argument. Throughout, I have contended that a person ought to be averse not only to wrongs but to the sources of (nontrivial) wrongs. It seems equally plausible to hold that one should have positive feelings toward morally good actions and toward the sources of such actions, at least insofar as the actions are beyond minimally good behavior. Friendships involve many such actions—the doing of favors, small and sometimes large sacrifices of self-interest, and so on. Hence, one ought to have good will toward a friend, by virtue of the events constituting the friendship, just as one ought to have hard feelings toward a villain, as an expression of one's aversion to what the villain has done to one.

Earlier, it was suggested that hard feelings are incompatible with being easily moved to sympathy. By the same token, wouldn't warm feelings be incompatible with being easily moved to hostility? If so, a part of the good will which a past friendly relationship should have engendered would call for not taking offense at a certain range of wrongs. You simply would not be resentful over such matters if your friends meant what they should to you.

On finding that you *were* resentful, your proper course would be to strive to banish such feelings straightaway—to extend forgiveness, that is. Anyone who did not do this would show an inability to appreciate friends for their kindness and affection—an inability which would surely impoverish life in many ways. In other words, it would be bad character not to forgive a friend a certain range of small wrongs, just because he or she was your friend.

This is certainly not an argument that one should forgive a friend everything. The idea is that friendship is incompatible with being easily provoked to hostility, which suggests that the deeper the friendship, the more tolerant one should be. That does not deny that there is behavior so egregious that one's warm feelings should be overcome.

IV

I want to close with a review of the main elements of the position I have set out and a reply to two objections.

Perhaps the most fundamental idea is that hard feelings toward those who mistreat us are not only natural but are called for, as expressions of aversion to the mistreatment. Such feelings vary in intensity. That they do is one expression of the character of the person who has them.

To forgive is to abandon such feelings before they run their course. It thus amounts to overruling an aspect of one's character. Sometimes, it overrules a flaw, an inclination to take the wrong more seriously than one should. It would be wrong not to check oneself in this way, I've suggested—wrong not to forgive, in other words.

On other occasions, in forgiving one overrides not a flaw but something perfectly acceptable. Now, a person is certainly free to be dissatisfied with perfectly acceptable traits, to want to be more generous (even though not exactly stingy as it is), or kinder (though not now cruel), and so on. However, although there is nothing wrong with such aspirations, neither is there anything wrong with being content with a perfectly acceptable feature of one's character. That is, a person is also free *not* to aspire to a particular improvement, and thus not to be inclined to override a perfectly acceptable aversion. Where the hard feelings do express an aversion of this kind, it is neither wrong to forgive nor wrong to be unmoved to forgive.

Finally, there are also aversions which are not merely acceptable but essential to decent character: aversions it would be a flaw to be without. To stifle an aversion of this order would be to move toward developing a vice. The inclination to do so is itself a flaw, a defect in one's self-regulatory impulses. That self-regulatory flaw would be enacted in extending forgiveness: it would be wrong to do so.

All of this is awfully abstract, however. What determines which sort of aversion one would overrule, if one were to forgive? A basic variable is the seriousness of the wrong which occasioned the hard feelings. The worse it was, the stronger should be the aversion to it and to its source. The stronger the aversion should be, the less plausible the claim that it is too strong, that is, that there is bad character in not abandoning the hard feelings which express it. The weaker the aversion should be, the better the basis for saying that a person of good character would now see a reason to *end* this expression of it by extending forgiveness, or even that it would be bad character to be unwilling or unable to do so.

A second basic variable is the recency of the mistreatment. The longer your negative feelings persist, the more averse the event which provoked them must have been for you. Something you get over quickly is minor, in your personal scheme of things; something that stays with you is not. Whatever your personal system of aversions happens to be, you ought to be more averse to serious wrongs than to trivial ones, other things being equal. So, we can see that you take a certain thing harder than you should, by the fact that you still harbor resentment. Earlier, it might have been perfectly appropriate to dislike Brown for teasing you, but to *still* resent him is to take it more seriously than you should.

The various classic reasons to forgive fit into this framework in different ways. Excuses, when they do not completely exonerate, serve to reduce the seriousness of the wrong: conceivably, to a triviality which it is excessive to resent, or to something which one ought at least by now to have ceased resenting. As Butler suggests, this might be partly a matter of the less serious misdeeds being rather common, and thus deeds of a sort the victim will have often committed himself. For, if so, the victim's continued hard feelings will be part of either a general intolerance of human frailty or an unwarranted exaltation of the dear self.

Unlike an excuse, a wrongdoer's later repentance does nothing to lessen the seriousness of what was done. On the one hand, often repentance is a change in the views which permitted the wrongdoer to do the wrong. It is then a change in the respect in which he or she was dangerous and that can legitimize a change in one's feelings toward this person as a source of wrong. Here the seriousness of the wrong enters in a different way: the worse it was, the more difficult it should be to abandon such feelings despite the change.

The same holds for the other respect in which repentance provides a reason to forgive: its appeal to the victim's compassion. The worse the wrong, the less compelling that appeal should be, because the stronger one's hard feelings toward its source should be. In sum, although the fact of repentance can certainly make forgiveness acceptable where otherwise it would not be, and might even make it wrong to withhold forgiveness, the seriousness of the offense bears importantly on whether it does either. So, I think, does its recency: it is one thing to forgive the repentant person for what he did a good while ago, and another to forgive him for what he did moments earlier.

The seriousness of the offense imposes a similar check on forgiveness for old times' sake. Old times should provide a reservoir of good will, not easily replaced with resentment, but not bottomless either. Thus the failure to forgive old friends for some wrongs shows a defect of character, but the refusal to forgive them for others does not. Indeed, the willingness to forgive whatever an old friend does, however despicable, can be so far beyond the good will the friendship should have engendered as to be rather pathetic. Thus, it can be wrong to forgive for old times' sake, and the seriousness of the wrong (together with the depth of the friendship) is central to its being so.

Excuses, repentance, old times' sake, the fact that one acts in this same way oneself, the seriousness of the misdeed and its relative recency—in my opinion, there are several combinations of these under which a refusal or an inability to forgive would show a flaw in one's character. It would be wrong not to forgive on such occasions, just as it would be wrong to enact other flaws, such as cowardice and dishonesty.

This will seem to some to misalign forgiveness, in a certain sense. After all, we seek, ask, beg to be forgiven—we do not *demand* that we be. But if it really can be wrong not to forgive, surely a demand should be appropriate on those occasions. For, it seems to be a perfectly general truth that we can demand not to be treated wrongly, rather than merely seeking, asking, or begging not to be. The fact that, instead, a demand for forgiveness is always incongruous seems to show my contention to be mistaken.

In reply, I want to suggest that the incongruity has a different source. It is not due to our never being wronged when forgiveness is withheld, but to the fact that forgiveness is a change, for the better, in the other person's attitude toward one. First, demands are by nature rather unendearing. Since the object is to return to someone's good graces, demanding to do so is often simply bad strategy. Second, there are obviously special difficulties for the other party in abandoning hard feelings "on demand," as it were: anger, contempt, and the like are not so easily controlled. Third, even given time to meet the demand, the best it could effect might be a disappointment. What you really want is for the forgiveness to flow effortlessly from a reserve of affection for you, once the other person understands your version of events, how devastated you are by what you have done, and so on. That is not what you would get by demanding to be forgiven.

These considerations might make it awkward to demand forgiveness even when there are the strongest possible reasons why one should be forgiven: even when, as I want to say, withholding it wrongs the original wrongdoer. But just imagine "an abjectly repentant person who has done me only a little wrong,"[17] whom I nevertheless refuse to forgive. Might not my behavior justify this person in "breaking things off," ending our relationship? Perhaps her leaving me would have been morally dubious, before this, for any number of reasons. By behaving in this petty and vindictive way, however, wouldn't I have provided her a reason of considerable weight? She might not be obliged to stay for any more such treatment—to stay for further *mis*treatment, it seems plausible to say. Rather, I have wronged her by refusing to forgive her, and she is entitled to demand that I come down off my high horse and do so. Even if making such a demand would be futile for the reasons mentioned earlier, and her only genuine options are to leave me or to knuckle under, my behavior does seem to have transformed her into someone who has herself been aggrieved.

A final objection takes a different tack. The complaint is that (despite appearances, I hope) an account for forgiveness of the kind I've offered cannot be illuminating. My account says that some behavior is wrong because it enacts a flaw of character. But, a flaw of character is nothing but a tendency to behave badly. If so, in essence my account claims that some behavior is bad because it enacts a tendency to behave badly—a tendency, that is, to behave in ways like the present behavior. Surely this is too small a circle to be of any interest?

Two lines of reply are available. Suppose, first, that one believes traits of character to have intrinsic value and disvalue, in addition to

17. Ibid., p. 516.

whatever value they derive from the actions connected with them. On this view, dishonesty, for example, would be a flaw in itself, regardless of the extent to which it also meant one acted dishonestly. On this view, it is a very bad thing to be intrinsically rotten in one's person, even if this results in very little actual mischief because, say, one is extremely timid as well as dishonest. The badness of being dishonest does not derive from bad results in one's behavior. Accordingly, to observe that an action showed bad character is not merely to comment that it showed a tendency to act like this, as the objection has it. Instead, the point is that it shows the agent to be a human being with certain intrinsically bad features.

Alternatively, suppose that one held the value of a trait to be entirely a matter of the differences it made in one's conduct. A trait would be a flaw, on this view, just insofar as one acted substantially worse for having it than one would have acted without it. Of course, that would not mean one acted badly every time the flaw was in play. For example, a utilitarian could count dishonesty as generally contrary to utility, and thus a flaw of character, even though there would be occasions when a person's dishonesty meant the happier course was taken.

Even on those occasions, the utilitarian would be entitled to observe that the behavior was a display of bad character. The point would not be merely that it exhibited a tendency to act in ways "like this"—that is, dishonestly, or producing however much utility it did. The point would be that the behavior exhibited a tendency which was regrettable in the balance of its working.

Regretting the action on that ground would be analogous to regretting a bodily condition as a symptom of disease. One does not regret the coated tongue or rash solely because of its own power to cause harm, although that is certainly of interest: it might cause little or none, and still be regrettable as a symptom. Rather, one also regrets it because of what it means: because it means there will be trouble ahead unless the disease is cured. In the same way, it seems to me, a utilitarian should regret episodes of dishonesty not solely because of their own disutility but because, as symptoms of bad character, they mean the future will contain a particular pattern of actions contrary to utility unless the agent reforms.

These are matters requiring a fuller account than I can give here. Perhaps enough has been said to show that one can make a point of interest by observing that a bit of behavior shows bad character, whether one's views of character are deontological or utilitarian. I hope this paper has made such points concerning the behavior involved in forgiving and in failing to forgive.

Gratitude*

Fred R. Berger

Gratitude is not a subject much discussed in the philosophical literature, though hardly a book or article is published without some expression of gratitude by the author for the help of others. From the literature, one would have to conclude that gratitude plays a role in our moral life which, with only a few exceptions, philosophers have not seen fit to explore. Later I shall have a few suggestions as to why this is so. I cannot help but speculate now, however, that one source for this neglect has been the view that gratitude does not play an important role in morality and thus does not deserve extended treatment. I want to show in this essay that the study of gratitude is indeed fruitful, in that it reveals important aspects of our moral life. Gratitude may or may not itself be important to our morality; it is, however, intertwined with an aspect of our moral relations which I believe has been unjustly neglected and on which the analysis of gratitude sheds light.

The paper is divided into three sections. In the first, I shall explore important aspects of the duty to *show* gratitude: under what conditions that duty does or does not hold, precisely to what gratitude is a response, and ways in which this duty differs from other principles involving reciprocation. Using these results, I shall then, in the second section, turn to an analysis of the "internal" aspects of gratitude—that is, to an analysis of what it is that is shown or expressed in a demonstration of gratitude. In the concluding section, I shall attempt to show what the analysis reveals concerning the nature of morality. In particular, I shall hold that the analysis of gratitude shows that our feelings and attitudes (as well as our actions) play a role in our moral life which has been insufficiently acknowledged and stressed. Thus, I believe, we have not understood very well the morality of interpersonal relations.

*I should like to record some of my own acknowledgments of aid. I first discussed some of these matters a number of years ago with H. L. A. Hart, from whom I gained important insights; I also benefited greatly from discussion of these matters with Torstein Eckhoff, of the University of Oslo Law School.

This essay originally appeared in *Ethics*, vol. 85, no. 4, July 1975.

I

In this section I shall concentrate on the duty to show gratitude. I shall assume there is (at least in our culture) a general duty to show gratitude under certain conditions, though it is, to be sure, a somewhat unusual "duty." I shall not seek to elucidate the *sense* in which we recognize a duty to show gratitude; in a final section, though, I shall try to deal with some of the anomalies the notion of a duty to show gratitude presents.

The first point I want to make about the duty to show gratitude is that a show of gratitude is not simply a response to other persons having done things which benefit us. That this is so can be seen by exploring the questions of the conditions under which gratitude is due and what factors affect the issue of what is required in the way of specific performance.

Two such factors suggest themselves immediately: the value of the benefit to the recipient and the degree of sacrifice or concession made by the grantor. There are other important factors, however. Suppose someone does something involving a sacrifice on his part which benefits us, but he was forced by threats to do it. In such a case, gratitude is not due; the appropriate response may be to return the gift, if possible, or to make sufficient restitution or replacement of it. The voluntariness with which the benefits are produced for us is thus a factor in determining if gratitude is appropriate when others benefit us.

Suppose further that someone did something which benefited us, but he was utterly unaware of this fact. That we are benefited is a fortuitous and unforeseen consequence of something he has done without any intention on his part to help us. Where it is clear that such intention was lacking, gratitude is not due. Insofar as he did not choose to do something to give us benefits (which he could not do if he had no foresight of the consequences), he did not *grant* them to us. Similarly, if the person knew he was creating benefits for us, but engaged in the behavior only because it also brought him benefits, gratitude is not due; the benefits were a mere by-product of acts done for self-gain. We may be glad for the benefits, but no gratitude is owed. Of course, in actual cases, motivation may not be entirely clear, or singlefactored, and perhaps we owe one another the benefit of the doubt; but in the clear sense, gratitude is not involved.

These facets of our practice with respect to gratitude reveal something important. The kinds of considerations cited are indices that the act was or was not done *in order to help us*. If the act was done only because the actor chose the lesser of two evils or sacrifices to himself, or without any knowledge or thought that it would benefit us, or solely because it would bring him benefits, there is no debt of gratitude, because nothing was done in order to help us. Gratitude, then, does not consist in the requital of benefits but in a response to *benevolence*; it is a response to a grant of benefits (or the attempt to benefit us) which was motivated by a desire to help us.

This fact about gratitude can be used to decide difficult cases in ways which seem plausible. For example, we might want to know if we owe gratitude for benefits which are *owed* us, that is, in which those providing them are fulfilling their duties to us. The answer is complicated by cases which incline us toward divergent answers. We owe gratitude to our parents for the sacrifices involved in their caring for us and giving us a decent upbringing, though it is their duty to provide this to the best of their ability. On the other hand, with regard to most contractual transactions, we do not usually feel we owe gratitude to the other contracting party when he fulfills his part of the deal. Of course, we owe him the performance of our part of the bargain, but that is not, in itself, a show of gratitude. All this becomes easily dealt with once we see gratitude as the requital of benevolence. Though our parents are under a duty to give us a decent upbringing and to care for us, it is almost never solely for this reason that parents make the sacrifices requisite for proper care and rearing. These sacrifices are normally made because our parents care for us and love us and want us to have the benefits of a good upbringing. On the other hand, many a contemporary novel has made capital out of the justified lack of gratitude in situations in which parents have given children the outward manifestations of a good rearing in our society (e.g., clothes, good schools, etc.) but solely for selfish reasons such as keeping up the family name or social standing. Indeed, to the extent that a *really* good rearing cannot be given without love at its base, it is something which by its nature deserves gratitude. In contrast to this, contractual arrangements are usually thought to be means for advancing the interests of both parties and hence tend not to be cases of benefits granted in order to help another, and gratitude would be out of place. This is not to say, however, that one cannot enter into a contract to help another. People quite often accept unfavorable terms of a contract in order to help the other party. When this happens, we *do* think there is an obligation to show gratitude. These features of our moral practices are readily understood once we perceive gratitude as a response to benevolence.

Even more subtle features of the duty to show gratitude are explicable in these terms. While we have no hesitation in saying there is an obligation to show gratitude for help or for a gift, we do not feel at ease in saying it is something owed the grantor in the sense that he has a right to demand it.[1] Such a demand shows the help or gift to be something less than a show of benevolence; it appears to be something done in order to gain favor, and to the extent we feel this to be case, the duty to show gratitude is diminished.

The analysis of gratitude as a response to benevolence is also important because it forms part of the basis on which the duty to show gratitude is to be distinguished from other duties involving reciprocity. Consider a principle dubbed by H. L. A. Hart "mutuality of restrictions": "When a number of persons conduct any joint enterprises according to rules . . . those who have submitted to these restrictions when required have a right to a similar submission from those who have benefited by their submission."[2]

---

1. *Other* parties may rightly criticize the failure to discharge it, and even the person to whom it is owed may be entitled to complain of the *insult* such a failure represents.

2. H. L. A. Hart, "Are There Any Natural Rights?" *Philosophical Review* 64 (1955): 185. This principle should be compared with one called by John Rawls "the duty of fair play." He has

This principle, underlying cooperation, differs from gratitude in a crucial respect. Cooperation does not imply benevolence; it is compatible with complete, but enlightened, self-interest. Selfish motivation on the part of the participants in no way diminishes the obligation to reciprocate with the requisite behavior when one has enjoyed the benefits of the practice. The point of such an activity is to produce *mutual* benefits. One who has enjoyed the benefits of a cooperative scheme would not present an adequate justification for his refusal to cooperate if he merely pointed out that the others restricted their behavior in order to obtain the benefits of the practice. Unlike gratitude, such a fact is not a rebuttal to the claim that a duty of reciprocation is owed. In fact, it is part of the ground on which the duty to do one's share in the production of the benefits is based. The benefits were *not* a gift to him.

Thus we are led to our first major conclusion: showing gratitude is a response to the benevolence of others. I want now to turn to the question of what it is that is shown or expressed in gratitude.

II

Thus far we have dealt only with the external aspects of gratitude—the duty to show or express gratitude. What *is* it that we show or express? And why can we distinguish "sincere" from "insincere" expressions? Moreover, we speak of "feeling" grateful and of having "feelings" of gratitude. All this suggests that when we express gratitude we simply show or give vent to certain internal states. Even if this were correct, it would not go very far toward explaining why we regard gratitude as part of our moral relations—why ingratitude has been regarded by philosophers as a vice.[3] Nor would it explain why gratitude should be proportionate in the ways it is expressed, rather than in relation to the intensity of one's feelings. And it would not explain why sometimes mere *verbal* expression of one's feelings is not enough to constitute a sincere demonstration of gratitude. In what follows in this section, I want to attempt an account which goes some way toward dealing with these issues.

We should begin by noting that an act of benevolence evinces certain things about the actor. If I am the recipient of another's benevolence, his action indicates he cares about me, he values me, he respects me.[4] This is especially

---

discussed it in numerous places. See, for example, "Legal Obligation and the Duty of Fair Play," in *Law and Philosophy*, ed. Sidney Hook (New York: New York University Press, 1964), pp. 3–18. No doubt Hart's statement of his principle requires important qualifications to be acceptable.

3. See Immanuel Kant, *Lectures on Ethics*, ed. Lewis White Beck (New York: Harper & Row, 1963), p. 218, in which ingratitude is described as one of the three vices which "are the essence of vileness and wickedness."

4. There is an important ambiguity in this which I shall ignore in this paper. Benevolence can take a *general* and a *specific* form. Someone who cares about humanity (supposing this to be possible) may be motivated to act because he wishes to help people. *I* just happen to be the object of his largess by virtue of my humanity. On the other hand, it may be *me* he cares about, independently of any concern for humanity. In some contexts, this might be an important distinction. There is also some discussion of the issue by C. D. Broad in his treatment of Butler's ethics, as sometimes Butler seems to have supposed benevolence to be a concern for humanity

the case where any measure of sacrifice or concession or consideration is shown; he has been willing to incur a sacrifice of his own convenience or welfare to assist me. This shows that my welfare is valued by him in addition to his own.⁵ *I* am an object of his concern.

When we show gratitude, then, it is this display of the other's attitude toward us to which we are responding. Note that in each of the cases in the last section in which we said gratitude is *not* due, no such indication of concern or valuing of the recipient was involved. A sincere expression of gratitude thus involves at least the recognition of the other's having done something which indicates he values us. Clearly, more than just this is involved, however. It seems to me that all of the following are accomplished by sincere, adequate expressions of gratitude: (*a*) the recipient shows he recognizes the value of the donor's act—that is, that it was an act benefiting him and done *in order to* benefit him; (*b*) the recipient shows that he does not regard the *actor* as having value only as an instrument of his own welfare; and (*c*) a relationship of moral community is established, maintained, or recognized, consisting of mutual re-spect and regard. Reciprocation makes the relationship two-way.

If this account is right, then expressions of gratitude are demonstrations of a complex of beliefs, feelings, and attitudes. By showing gratitude for the benevolence of others, we express our beliefs that they acted with our interests in mind and that we benefited; we show that we are glad for the benefit and the others' concern—we appreciate what was done; we indicate that we also have an attitude of regard for them, at least in the respect that we do not look on them as objects in the world whose movements have happened to bring us benefits (for then no response would be necessary). And we show that we do not regard their sacrifices and concessions as mere instruments of our welfare. The donor has shown his valuing of the recipient; the donee shows the rela-tionship is mutual by some form of reciprocation, and each has demonstrated attitudes appropriate to members of a moral community.

It is important to note two features of our actual practice which this account is meant to tie in with. First, while some form of reciprocation is requisite, this need not be, and often *ought not to be*, the giving of the same or an equivalent benefit to the grantor. Not only is this not always possible, but sometimes it would destroy the force of the original gift. When someone grants us a benefit because of his concern for us, or because he wishes to make us happy, it can be an insult to return it or to show that we feel obligated to make a like return. The grant was made with no strings attached, with no desire to obligate us. To show that we feel we *are* obligated demonstrates that the gift misfired to a certain extent or, at worst, gives reason to think the donee misread

and at other times a concern for the well-being of particular persons. See C. D. Broad, *Five Types of Ethical Theory* (Paterson, N. J.: Littlefield, Adams & Co., 1959), pp. 70 ff. But also see the discussion of Butler in T. A. Robert's *The Concept of Benevolence* (London: Macmillan Co., 1973).

5. We sometimes distinguish ordinary men, great-hearted men, and saints according to how much they value the welfare of others in relation to their own. (Of course, we assume that they do not hate themselves.)

the intentions of the grantor. It is one thing to show that we think we owe a sign of appreciation; it is quite another thing to show we think we owe a gift in return. Sometimes the most adequate display of gratitude is a loving hug or a warm handshake, and anything more would be inappropriate in some degree.

On the other hand, there are times when a mere "thank you" or warm handshake will not do, when an adequate showing of gratitude requires putting ourselves out in some way, at least a little. The sort of continual sacrifice and caring involved in a decent upbringing is not reciprocated to parents by a warm handshake at the legal age of independence. While the notion of gratitude to one's parents can easily be overdone, it is clear enough that an adequate showing of gratitude to them cannot be made with mere verbal expressions.

The explanation of gratitude I have provided can give a partial explanation to these features of our practices. First of all, on the account given, a crucial aspect of the practices associated with gratitude is the showing of one's recognition of the value of the donor's act. But, if one scrupulously attends to reciprocating in kind, that may undercut this showing, since part of the value of the act is constituted by its being given with no objective of a return. Furthermore, it is not only a set of beliefs and feelings which are involved in gratitude but attitudes as well: appreciation for the gift and the actor's caring, along with mutual respect for him as a person of value in himself. But having an attitude or expressing an attitude is not merely a matter of saying some words. Attitudes are expressed through behavior also, and *certain* behaviors are the appropriate, concomitant expressions of attitudes. One does not take or have that attitude without some appropriate behavior. One cannot claim truly to care for someone and never act in certain appropriate ways. Indeed, gratitude is not so much the *expression* of our appreciation and respect as it is the *demonstration* of these attitudes. Sometimes we can demonstrate those attitudes by expressing them verbally; sometimes more is required for the demonstration to be adequate to the situation. Thus an adequate demonstration of our appreciation and concern for our parents could never be a mere handshake. A kiss on the cheek might suffice for a particular birthday present, but it is not an adequate demonstration of appreciation for years of care, inconvenience, and, perhaps, sacrifice. It is very hard to say just what is appropriate, and it may be that there can be no answer in the abstract, that it will depend on the nature of the particular family and the nature of the particular relationships within it. It is clear, however, that a handshake or kiss on the cheek normally will not do. The account of gratitude I have provided can explain, in part, why not.[6]

I have acknowledged that gratitude to one's parents can be overstressed,

6. The question of the "appropriateness" of a response is complicated by cases in which only *part* of the complex of beliefs, feelings, and attitudes involved in being grateful are present, e.g., when we resent the other's benevolence because we personally dislike him and do not wish to be indebted to him, or where we do not desire the benefit sufficiently to warrant the sacrifice made, or a commensurate response. Here, the duties to be sincere and to show gratitude are in conflict. My account can help to explain this, though, of course, it does not show how to resolve it.

and that one's response to others' benevolence can be overdone in various ways. These points indicate that the practices associated with gratitude may take what I shall call "pathological" forms. By considering some of these, I believe we can bring into sharper focus the features of gratitude and will be better able to see its role in our moral life.

The first kind of pathology I wish to pick out takes the form of the man who does favors for others in order to place them in his debt. Where it is clear that something is expected in return, of course, there need be nothing wrong. But the debt, then, will not be one of gratitude. On the other hand, the act may be one in which the actor plays on, and takes advantage of, the conventional practices associated with gratitude and the recipient's inclination to be grateful for favors and to demonstrate his gratitude. Such an act involves deception (at least with respect to motivation) and is pathological in that respect. But it is also pathological in the deeper sense that the practices involved in gratitude presuppose that the agents are manifesting their mutual valuing of one another as ends in themselves, whereas *this* act treats the recipient as an instrument of the donor's welfare and thus as having instrumental value only.

A second form of the pathological practice of gratitude involves the tendency to overemphasize it and to ritualize it, so that every act under the sun which benefits someone else is viewed as requiring gratitude, and the constant display of gratitude is insisted on. In its mildest form, this consists in reducing giftgiving and returning to the level of matters of etiquette of no greater moral importance than simple social amenities. There are, however, more trenchant forms. In Western cultures with a strong family life, it is a familiar story for young people to be in rebellion at the constant insistence that they behave in traditional ways, or assume certain roles, or take up certain religious practices, in order to show gratitude to their parents for the sacrifices made in bringing them up. Any act of disobedience is viewed by the parents as ingratitude, and everything done for the children is viewed as deserving gratitude. The combination of these two beliefs, of course, makes it impossible for the children ever to be properly grateful, unless they are willing to cater to every wish of the parents.[7] Such situations, when carried to extremes, are pathological in a number of respects. Even loving parents cannot claim that everything done for their children springs from their concern. Moreover, if truly done from love, these deeds would not be viewed as giving the right to make incessant demands on the children's life styles. The constant expectation of concessions as a sign of gratitude can be an oppression; and departure is a source of guilt, and the relations with the parents become clouded with feelings of resentment. All of this destroys love. In addition, this is a pathological misuse of the practices involved in gratitude, because it undercuts the moral relations presupposed by those practices (at least this is the case when the children have reached a certain age). To treat someone as a person in his own right entails granting him the right to work out the plan of his life as he sees fit. To use the fact of one's past

---

7. For a case history, see Philip Roth, *Portnoy's Complaint* (New York: Random House, 1969).

aid in order to control another's life is to deny him the independence befitting a moral agent. A set of practices which function to demonstrate mutual regard is employed by one party to impose behavior on another as the price of his past regard and to demand the signs of regard, irrespective of the party's own judgment as to the appropriateness of those particular expressions. If we really have a concern with the well-being of someone, there are some aspects of his life which we ought not to seek to control and which we cannot obligate him to let us control.

To summarize my main points briefly: (*a*) being grateful to someone involves having a set of beliefs, feelings, and attitudes which are manifested when we show gratitude; (*b*) but showing gratitude involves a *demonstration* of those beliefs and attitudes and, thus, may require forms of behavior in addition to verbal expression; (*c*) such a demonstration of gratitude is a response to another's (perceived) benevolence; (*d*) as such, it involves the mutual demonstration of respect and regard—the indication that neither treats the other, or the sacrifices of the other, as a mere means to his own welfare; (*e*) thus the practices associated with gratitude are a manifestation of, and serve to strengthen, the bonds of moral community—the sharing of a common moral life based on respect for each person as having value in himself.

Much more needs to be said about gratitude before we can be content that we have a very full understanding of it, even if the account I have given is correct. It would be important to know, for example, to what extent gratitude is conventional, whether there could be a community having a shared morality which did not incorporate gratitude in some recognizable form, the role of spontaneity in gratitude, the necessary and sufficient conditions of sincerity, etc. Without seeking to explore these issues further, I shall turn in the concluding section to speculate on the significance for moral philosophy of the points already made.

III

What I find most significant about gratitude, as I have analyzed it, is that it involves in a crucial way our feelings and attitudes toward people. Requisite behavior is involved primarily as a demonstration of those feelings and attitudes or as natural concomitants of them. This suggests the ancient view, held by Aristotle, that the moral life of a creature of a composite nature—having both rational and affective aspects—involves the right ordering of both elements. The moral virtues, then, involve not merely acting in certain ways but also having appropriate attitudes and feelings toward others.[8] Certain actions have value, then, *as* expressions of attitudes.

8. Aristotle stated his view in this way: "I mean moral virtue; for it is this that is concerned with passions and actions, and in these there is excess, defect, and the intermediate. For instance, both fear and confidence and appetite and anger and pity and in general pleasure and pain may be felt both too much and too little, and in both cases not well; but to feel them at the right times, with reference to the right objects, toward the right people, with the right motive, and in the right way, is what is both intermediate and best, and this is characteristic of virtue" (*Nicomachean Ethics* 1106^{b}25).

The recent history of moral philosophy shows great emphasis on such concepts as "right," "wrong," and "duty." These are notions applicable primarily to actions. Goodness tends to be treated either as something it is our duty to act to produce or as a property of actions themselves. Moreover, the notion of one's having a *duty* to have certain feelings and attitudes is problematical, at the least. There seems no room left for the affective life in our moral world; it is entirely ancillary or incidental, helping or hindering us from performing our duties, possibly the basis for excuses, but forming no essential part of the basic concepts of morality. Even in views which emphasize a good will or proper motivation as basic to morality, the subjective factor emphasized is that of intention, and it is the intention to *act* in particular ways which is involved. Missing almost completely in the literature is the idea of certain attitudes as underlying a common moral life and actions as being natural or conventional expressions and demonstrations of those attitudes.

It is for such reasons as these, as well as others, that gratitude is not much dealt with in the literature. Consider that we do not, generally, *punish* people for failing to show gratitude; there is rarely a *particular* act which *must* be done if we are to show gratitude; there are no acts which the benevolent person may *demand* as a grateful return for his largess; and, though we sometimes speak of an act as entailing a *debt* of gratitude, it is a debt which differs in important ways from others, and there seem to be no acts which it is our duty to perform in order to discharge the debt, even though a range of acts may be sufficient.

Far from showing that gratitude has nothing to do with morality, I think such facts show that the traditional ways of talking about morality, in which the concepts of "right," "wrong," "duty," "punishment," etc., are central, has led to an insufficient picture of what it is to have a morality. The sorts of feelings and attitudes involved in gratitude *do* play an important role in our moral life. Though we do not punish ingratitude, and though it *may* be logically impossible to make the having of certain feelings and attitudes (and thus their sincere display) a matter of duty, we nonetheless do not ignore gratitude in moral training. We teach that certain feelings and attitudes are appropriate and in *some* sense *ought* to be had in certain situations. Moreover, a statement like "You should be glad for his gift," while not a demand that one should be glad, *is* a criticism of moral character and does play a role in moral education. We do not blame people for character defects, but blame is not the only form of criticism and not the only impetus to reform; and we certainly do *praise* those who display exemplary character. We can, to be sure, encourage and develop in people certain feelings and attitudes and the sort of characters in which these are appropriately displayed. We do this through example, exhortation, being pleased when those feelings and attitudes spontaneously show through, etc. In any particular culture, many kinds of affective and attitudinal responses become appropriate in certain situations, and a well-developed moral personality is expected, as a matter of course, to display these. In Western cultures, worried concern is appropriate to the difficulties faced by friends and associates (would one *be* a friend if he did not have a concern for our tribulations?); distress is appropriate to the ill fare of loved ones, joy or gladness is appropriate to great gains made by those close to us, anger is appropriate to situations in which an individual does great harm to another.[9] Not only do we strive to develop the affective life in certain ways rather than others, expressing appropriate approval or disapproval at proper or improper displays of attitudes, but we regard the failure to have the requisite responses as a defect of character. Consider the judgment one would make of one who finds the pain of others humorous, or who is incapable of pitying the unfortunate, or who does not feel pride in the accomplishments of his offspring, or feels no genuine gratitude for the sacrifices made for him by others. There is something lacking in these cases in the relations held with others, and the attitudes of the individual are deficient. These lackings are not punishable *offenses* (nor, by themselves, do they seem grounds for saying the persons are *immoral*), but they are not mere personality defects, either, in the way that, say, being boring is merely a defect of personality. Ingratitude, in particular, may rightly prompt castigation and reproval—the marks of a moral defect.

In addition, gratitude shows the role of the affective life in morality in an especially cogent way. If my account is correct, among the feelings and attitudes expressed in gratitude are those of appreciation of the other person and one's attitude of respect for the other person as someone of value in himself, and not merely as the source of one's own welfare. Having this kind of regard, taking these attitudes toward others is essentially involved in having a morality. Those with whom we share moral relations are not merely creatures whose behavior exhibits certain patterns but whose behavior manifests attitudes of valuing, respect, and concern.

It may be that these points, though important in themselves, can readily enough be accounted for on traditional conceptions of morality, even that of the utilitarian tradition. For example, John Stuart Mill often emphasized the importance of the development of moral character, and that this involves the cultivation of appropriate feelings and desires. Indeed, he criticized Bentham and the utilitarian tradition for ignoring this aspect of morality.[10] Mill's reason for stressing the development of the affective aspects of man was that these have consequences for our actions.[11] We must get men to feel and desire properly in order to get them to act properly. Indeed, he advocated inculcating in people desires for things other than the general welfare, for the reason that by acting from such desires they will, in fact, produce the general welfare more perfectly than if they always and solely acted from the desire to maximize the general welfare.[12]

9. One writer who *has* stressed the idea that attitudes are appropriate to take and express to certain situations is J. N. Findlay. See his important article, "The Justification of Attitudes," *Mind* 63 (1954): 145–61.

10. John Stuart Mill, "Remarks on Bentham's Philosophy," in *Collected Works*, vol. 10, ed. J. M. Robson (Toronto: University of Toronto Press, 1969), pp. 7–8.

11. Ibid.

12. See "Utilitarianism," in *Collected Works*, 10:238–39. Also, the later editions of Mill's *A System of Logic* contain a passage at the very end which makes this point.

There is no question that the practices associated with gratitude and the feelings and attitudes which comprise it are useful in these ways. An amateur sociologist would have little trouble pointing out the ways in which such displays reinforce dispositions to giftgiving and enlarge the degree of concession and concern people show one another. This, however, seems to me an unsatisfactory account of why reflective people seek to maintain the conventions of gratitude. Quite without regard to any further consequences, we care how people feel toward us and how they regard us. It is not enough that our friend does the right things in our interrelationship; it is equally important that he does them (at least in part) because he *likes* and *cares* for us. We are not satisfied if a friend does a favor for us if we think he begrudges it to us for some reason. Gratitude plays a role in our interrelationships precisely because it involves the demonstration of our feelings toward another. Thus it has value quite without regard to any further contribution to the good of society, quite without regard to any further actions it tends to produce. Our conception of our status with respect to others involves our view of how they *feel* toward us, what their *attitudes* are toward us, how they *regard* us.[13] Our idea of how we are valued, how we are thought of by others, and, thus, our view of the basis of our moral relations with them, is bound up with these perceptions. We can put this point another way: having regard for someone as of value, as deserving respect and concern, involves having certain feelings and attitudes; thus when we display these, we exhibit what their moral status is in our eyes.

Still, it may seem, even these points can be accommodated within the utilitarian framework. It may be thought that what this shows is that our *happiness* requires that we perceive that others have certain feelings and attitudes toward us. Thus the practices involved in gratitude have value, since they produce an essential element of happiness directly. Mill, it seems to me, regarded our sense of our own dignity as human beings to be an essential element of human happiness, and so may well have found a view such as this acceptable.[14] I do not wish to speculate further as to whether happiness can be properly viewed this way, or whether some further aspect of gratitude resists utilitarian treatment or can be brought within the rubrics of traditional philosophical concepts. For my purposes, it will suffice to have shown that demonstrations of our feelings and attitudes and the proper ordering of our affective lives are

13. I would be remiss were I not to mention an important article by Peter Strawson, in which he stresses the great importance to us of others' attitudes and feelings toward us. And he interprets gratitude, as I have, in terms of what he calls "reactive attitudes" toward another's benevolence. Of "reactive attitudes," he writes: "What I have called the participant reactive attitudes are essentially natural human reactions to the good or ill will of others towards us, as displayed in *their* attitudes and actions" (P. F. Strawson, "Freedom and Resentment," in *Studies in the Philosophy of Thought and Action*, ed. P. F. Strawson [London: Oxford University Press, 1968], p. 80).

14. See especially "Utilitarianism," p. 212. I should note, however, that on this view it would appear that there is no moral difference between an insincere show of gratitude, in which the insincerity is completely concealed, and a sincere display.

importantly involved in morality, whether or not there is a way of dealing with these points in traditional terms.

I shall close by pointing out that, if the present analysis is correct, a number of similar topics bear serious philosophical treatment, as there are large patterns of our moral relations which involve elements of the kinds I have isolated in gratitude. Among such related topics are: friendship, trust, loyalty, fidelity, pity, charity, disgust, resentment, hatred, etc. These and other such notions are importantly involved in the morality of our interpersonal relationships, and some of them can be more important for us to understand in our daily lives than, say, the logic of promising or even the principles of justice.